Rebuilding Cities and Citizens

Rebuilding Cities and Citizens

Mass Housing in Red Vienna and Cold War Berlin

Margaret Haderer

Amsterdam University Press

Cover image: ullstein bild, media number: 00823500. Photographer: unknown, 30.06.1957.
© ullstein bild.

Cover design: Coördesign, Leiden
Lay-out: Crius Group, Hulshout
Printed and bound by CPI Group (UK) Ltd, Croydon, CR0 4YY

ISBN	978 94 6372 494 4
e-ISBN	978 90 4855 270 2 (pdf)
DOI	10.5117/9789463724944
NUR	648

Table of Contents

Für meinen Vater

'Flieg, Gedanke, auf goldenen Schwingen' (Nabucco)
... trotz allem und immer wieder.

List of Illustrations

Acknowledgements

This book has an unusually long history. Some seeds for it were sown in the winters of the late 1980s, when my parents took me cross-country skiing along the Iron Curtain and when I listened in to conversations about 'the West' and 'the East'. Other seeds were sown in Toronto, a city that became my second home in the late 2000s. As is often the case with people leaving their home, arriving at a new place triggers interest in the place left behind, in my case Vienna. These contingencies do, however, not yet account for writing an *academic* book. For this to happen, I had to come across the work by Margaret Kohn. Her books *Radical Space* (2003) and *Brave New Neighborhoods* (2004) pointed out a concrete way of how to connect the study of political ideas with the study of space, which motivated my PhD research at the University of Toronto. She skillfully advised and supported me throughout the PhD project. Thus, my first thanks go to her. Special thanks go also to Frank Cunningham, who is unfortunately no longer with us, and to Joseph Carens, whose academic advice was as dear to me as his personal advice. I would also like to thank numerous colleagues and friends from within and outside academia: Luise Stoisser, Özgur Gurel, Maya Eichler, Andrea Cassatella, Leah Soroko, Alex Livingstone, Kai Krüger, Inder Marwah, Martina Heuser, Igor Shoikhedbrod, Mihaela Mihai, Janna Lüttmann, Patricia Greve, Jörg Wittenbrink, Govind Rao, Adrian Atanasescu, Felix Butzlaff and Hauke Dannemann. In some cases, contact has been lost. This does, however, not change the fact that each of you mentioned here provided support with a view to this project in one way or the other. Thanks also to Ingolfur Blühdorn, one of my more recent academic teachers, for motivating me to bring this publication to completion despite being committed to other fields of research. Special thanks go to Simon Güntner and the Sociology Research Unit at TU Vienna, my new professional home base, for supporting this publication financially. At Amsterdam University Press, I'd like to thank Maryse Elliot, who walked me through the publication process with patience and skill. Thanks also to the reviewers of this book. Last but not least: I am grateful to my husband Philipp whose support was unwavering and to our children, Iliya and Philippa, who were keenly interested in the very undertaking of writing a book and also in when it is – finally – done. The book is dedicated to my father – a prime example of a highly accomplished person without any formal education. To him, school meant being at the mercy of fascist teachers. This made him an autodidact and everything he needed to know, he taught himself by doing it. He became a passionate farmer, carpenter and hobby opera singer and, as his daughter, I enjoyed waking up to the sounds of cows and arias by Mozart, Rossini or Verdi. This was beautiful. Thanks for this and so many other things. He was often proud of me because of my formal education – an admiration I'd like to hereby return and put into perspective.

Dieses Buch ist meinem Vater gewidmet – einem umfassend gebildeten Menschen ohne formale Bildung. Für ihn bedeutete Schule faschistischen Lehrern ausgeliefert zu sein. Das machte ihn zu einem Autodidakten. Alles was er wissen wollte, lehrte er sich selbst indem er es tat. Aus ihm wurde ein passionierter Bauer, Tischler und Hobby-Opernsänger. Als Tochter kam ich in den Genuss morgens zu den Geräuschen von Kühen und den Arien von Mozart, Rossini oder Verdi aufzuwachen. Das war schön. Danke dafür und für vieles mehr. Er war oft stolz auf mich wegen meiner formalen Bildung – eine Bewunderung die ich hiermit erwidern und in Perspektive setzen möchte.

1 Introduction: The Making and Remaking of Ideologies through Space

Abstract
In the twentieth century, the housing question served as a prominent battleground on which more was decided than simply the provision of shelter. It implied fundamental negotiations of how to 'rebuild' cities, citizens, and societies. This was the case in Vienna after WWI no less than in Berlin after WWII, where newly empowered political elites sought to anchor their respective visions of society in and through residential and urban space. This chapter makes the case for studying ideologies through space. This undertaking implies leaving behind the 'great books of great thinkers' approach, which is prominent in political theory, and delving into the 'trialectical' production of space: an interplay between grand visions of society and its spaces, existing spatial practices, and appropriations by inhabitants.

Keywords: political ideologies, the production of space, cities, mass housing, socialism, liberalism

'Every society produces its own space' (Lefebvre 1991, p. 31). Indeed, *any* society or 'social existence' that aspires to be real and to be reckoned with *needs* to produce its own space. Otherwise, it would constitute 'a strange entity, a very peculiar kind of abstraction', prone to 'disappear altogether' (ibid., p. 53). One way in which modern societies and 'social existences' (ibid.) such as political movements, parties, and states have sought to produce their own space and specific everyday realities has been the provision and regulation of mass housing. This was the case in Vienna after WWI no less than in Berlin after WWII. In both cities, the newly empowered political elites addressed the housing question head on. They did so because there was a dire need for housing. Yet they also did so because the provision of housing constituted a promising lever with which to anchor their

Haderer, M., *Rebuilding Cities and Citizens: Mass Housing in Red Vienna and Cold War Berlin*. Amsterdam: Amsterdam University Press 2023
DOI: 10.5117/9789463724944_CH01

respective visions of the society to come: socialism in Red Vienna and East Germany, and liberalism in West Germany. By rebuilding housing, Red Vienna's Austro-Marxists – no less than East Germany's socialists and West Germany's Christian Democrats – sought to create 'new men' [*Neue Menschen*]. The respective capital cities served as both laboratories and stages for the pursued societal renewals.

'The residential is political' today (Madden and Marcuse 2016, p. 1), and, as will be shown in the analysis of the 'politics of dwelling' in Red Vienna and Cold War Berlin that follows, it was political in the past as well. From the nineteenth century and far into the twentieth century, two political camps have been shaping responses to the housing question: the liberal camp and the socialist camp. Without denying the multiformity of the respective doctrines, it could be said that the liberal camp considers the market to be the most efficient provider of housing and thus responds to housing crises – be they crises due to a general shortage of housing, a lack of affordability, or poor living conditions – by selective, often temporarily limited state interventions. In addition, it tends to incentivize private homeownership. The socialist camp, by distinction, foregrounds the state and non-profit co-operatives as key providers of sufficient, adequate, and affordable housing. It regards housing as a social right and fosters public, communal, and co-operative approaches to housing provision. The question of whether housing is a right, a key element of public infrastructure, or a commodity has been negotiated by these camps for over a century, and with it, political beliefs about the very meaning and function of society and the state (Häußermann and Siebel 1996; Madden and Marcuse 2016).

The responses to the housing question in Vienna after WWI and Berlin after WWII clearly embody manifestations of these two camps, manifestations this book takes as a point of entry into a more general study of the making and remaking of political beliefs – ideologies – in and through residential and urban space. This undertaking implies that we understand ideologies not as merely manipulative and false beliefs and ideas but as political ones that shape the social and material worlds we inhabit (Freeden 2006, 2008; Freeden et al. 2015b). Ideologies do so by serving as maps that allow us to find our way around in the political world, including everyday life and the socio-material environs we inhabit. They imply ontological assumptions about the human condition and, relatedly, the very meaning and function of society and its spaces. Additionally, they typically entail a program of political action or at least ideas about how to change a given society so that it resembles the one prescribed by the ideology in question (Dobson 2007, p. 3). Ideologies understood in this sense were operative in the past, leaving their socio-material traces, and continue to be operative in the present. If, as is currently the case in numerous European countries that used to have robust public welfare programs, investing in homeownership is normalized as a key component of providing for one's own social security, this is hardly a politically neutral fact. Instead, current reconfigurations of homeownership – a type of dwelling indebted to imaginaries of security and protection – are squarely nestled within (neo-)liberal sets of political beliefs that make and remake subjects (in terms of their self-governing), spaces (in terms of the meaning and function of housing), and welfare systems (from public to asset-based welfare) (Gurney 1999; Ronald 2008; Smith 2015; Kohl 2019).

Studying the ideological production of space (Lefebvre 1991) in Red Vienna and Cold War Berlin means looking into the 'hard-wiring' (Freeden 2006, p. 14) of political beliefs through space, including its scope, limits, and legacies. Instead of enlivening political thinking by reinterpreting texts – the 'great books' of 'great thinkers' – this book examines what happens when political ideas of socialism and liberalism 'flow through' a society and 'turn into social levers' used to change dwellings, cities, and citizens (Freeden 2006, pp. 8–9). To reconstruct and make sense of what becomes of political ideas when they 'hit' space and what becomes of spaces when they are 'hit' by political ideas is the general focus of this volume. More specifically, the book is driven by two questions. First, how were political beliefs in and visions of socialism and liberalism entrenched in everyday life through the provision of mass housing in Red Vienna and Cold War Berlin? This question involves taking a closer look at how and why certain elements of socialist and liberal thinking became real through given spaces while others moved to the background, were supplanted, or even foiled by already existing or competing beliefs and practices. Second, how did citizens appropriate and contest the spaces created, including the norms and ideals underpinning them, to make a home for themselves? This question entails studying the alternatives to the dominant pathways taken to rebuilding dwellings, cities, and citizens and the specific critiques these alternatives involve.

What the following analysis will show is, first, that ideologies cannot be reduced to encompassing systems of thought based on single truths. Instead, their meaning is made and remade through space. Although, for instance, all three 'regimes of truth' (Foucault 1980, p. 131) promised radical new beginnings, the translation of these promises into political action and socio-material environs often implied falling back on and renormalizing existing practices and norms. In Red Vienna, for example, an 'episteme of bourgeois suspicion' (Maderthaner and Musner 2008, p. 160) continued to shape the administration of the workers' housing, *despite* the Austro-Marxists' commitment to break with the bourgeois [*bürgerliche*][1] past, which meant empowerment to the upper middle class and deprivation to workers. Second, the analysis here will demonstrate that the boundaries between ideologies, even fiercely competing ones such as East German socialism and West German liberalism, may be astoundingly porous. In East Germany, Marxism ultimately played a lesser role in solving the housing question than did Taylorism, that is, an approach to housing shaped by a commitment to building efficiently and cheaply by means of standardization that was also prominent in 'the West'. Third, taking a closer look at the production of specific spaces may challenge common perceptions of a given regime of truth and their underpinning political beliefs. Whereas the West German response to the housing question is commonly perceived as the embodiment of a social democratic approach to the housing question, it was in fact an early and specific instantiation of a neoliberal response – an ordoliberal response. Fourth, this book will show that although certain political beliefs *did* become hegemonic through space, they did not 'control' space. In all three cases, the ideological making and remaking of dwellings, cities, and citizens triggered contestation or were accompanied by cunning subversions and the emergence of alternative practices and imaginaries. In Vienna, the Wild Settlers considered self-help and bottom-up workers' education to be the more appropriate approach to not only the housing question but also social emancipation. In East Germany, garden colonists gradually appropriated the loosely regulated green land in between large-scale housing estates to make a home for themselves. In West Germany, the government-critical, extra-parliamentary opposition [Außerparlamentarische Opposition, APO] emerged out of the large-scale social housing estates to mobilize against high rents and poor, monotonous living conditions.

Analytically, the subsequent study of the politics of dwelling in Red Vienna and Cold War Berlin is inspired by Henri Lefebvre's production of space (1991) – more precisely, by his identification of three categories that typically shape the making and remaking of space in a dialectical way. The first such category is what Lefebvre calls 'representations of spaces' (conceived space), by which he means the 'space of scientists, planners, urbanists, technocratic

1 The term 'bourgeois' conveys two meanings – a historical and a political one. It serves as a reference to a specific point in time that signified the economic, political and cultural emancipation of the bourgeoisie from feudalism. It also serves as a political term that denotes the 'opponent' in the social emancipation of workers and relatedly, in socialist discourses. In this book, the term is used in both senses. Context decides on the specific meaning of the term in the text that follows.

sub-dividers and social engineers [...]' (ibid., pp. 38–39) – to which I add sets of political beliefs about the meaning of society and its functions, such as Austro-Marxism, Stalin's 'socialism in one country', or ordoliberalism. Yet, as mentioned above, representations of space are never simply inscribed into space as if space were a void receptacle; rather, representations are molded and remolded by already existing, entrenched spatial practices, which Lefebvre refers to as 'perceived space', the second category. These practices 'structure daily life and a broader urban reality and, in doing so, ensure societal cohesion, continuity and a specific spatial competence' (Merrifield 1993, p. 524). And finally, since 'as human beings, as individuals and as social collectivities, we do not always do what we are told, act as we are supposed to or accept the limitations imposed by others' (Zieleniec 2018, p. 7), there is a third category that matters to the production of space: 'spaces of representation' (lived space). This category refers to conscious appropriations of space by users and inhabitants, appropriations that may confirm – but also challenge and subvert – representations of space and entrenched spatial practices (Lefebvre 1991, p. 39). From a Lefebvrian point of view, these three categories interact in the production of space – a production he conceives of as an ongoing, open-ended dialectical, or rather 'trialectical', process. Informed by these analytical categories, the reconstructions of Red Vienna and Cold War Berlin's productions of residential and urban space that follow require us to engage with theories on socialism and liberalism. Yet it also means letting go of given theories in order to turn towards what may from the perspective of political theory seem insignificant: architectural plans, political decision-making and the ensuing policies, social and urban history, sociological and historical accounts of the perceptions and experiences of the spaces built, and accounts of alternative provisions or counter-hegemonic appropriations of residential space.

'Close acquaintance with ideologies', as Michael Freeden puts it, 'is not only knowledge of a major political phenomenon but a step towards comprehending what the social product we call "political thought" is' (2006, p. 17). Freeden conducted pioneering work on rehabilitating the study of ideologies in political theory and encouraged not only the questioning of common assumptions about ideologies but also the transgression of disciplinary boundaries to make sense of the manifold hard-wirings of political ideas in and through society (2008, 2006, 2015). The focus of this book is the socio-*spatial* hard wiring of Austro-Marxism, East German socialism, and West German liberalism through the provision of mass housing. Whereas the production of space is not a key topic in the field of political theory, it is prominently discussed in the field of urban studies.

Interweaving the two fields to deliver a spatial perspective on political ideologies is one key goal of this book. It takes on Freeden's challenge to political theory and theorists: to more often dare to take a closer look at how political ideas are hard-wired in and through society. The *spatial* hard-wiring of political ideas is what I look at, which means charting into terrains outside political theory, my home turf, such as planning, architecture, sociology and history – 'turfs' I have come to be drawn to without having 'grown up' in them academically.

What is typical of my home turf, however, is to shed light on social phenomena from an explicit conceptual angle, in my case the angle of critical theory. The differences between the thinkers and theorists that are referred to throughout the book – Marx, Engels, Benjamin, Lefebvre, Adorno, Berman, Foucault, Buck-Morss, or Kohn – are considerable. But what unites them is a commitment to emancipatory political agendas; a sensitivity towards power relations that stand in the way of the exercise of autonomy, equality, or democracy; a critical distance to equations of 'human progress' with techno-scientific and economic progress; a conception of modernity as an achievement and promise that at the same time undercuts itself – at times disastrously; a conception of paradoxes and contradictions not as a failure but as a key characteristic of social life; an emphasis on the contingency of given realities, not to give in to the slippery slope of relativism but to denaturalize the present; and judgements that – against the backdrop of normative ideals such as autonomy, equality, and democracy – suggest that some social constellations are worthwhile to revisit, actualize in the present, or fight for while others are not. Thus, the historical analysis in this book is decidedly not a mere recounting of what was (if this is at all possible) but a reconstruction of the past from a specific conceptual angle: a 'historico-critical' angle.

Given the book's locatedness at the intersection of political theory and space, it complements existing urban and architectural histories on Red Vienna (Blau 1999; Maderthaner and Musner 2008) and Cold War Berlin (Ladd 2008; Richie 1999; Stangl 2018). The book also adds to existing accounts of mass housing (Madden and Marcuse 2016; Urban 2012) that tend to be concerned with either policy or architectural form but that barely touch on the housing question as a promising lens for looking at negotiations of ideologies at large. Housing research, Christian Kohl argues, often lacks a 'social theory' perspective (2018). It also often lacks a 'political theory' perspective. By taking a profoundly mundane everyday space – housing – as a point of entry into a history of political thinking, this book provides maybe not a novel but certainly a specific perspective on the role of housing in the building, negotiating, and contesting variants of the two ideologies that have shaped European twentieth-century history: socialism and liberalism.

The cases studied are Red Vienna (1919–1934), a municipal experiment in socialism, and Berlin from 1945 until the 1970s – a city that, after a brief history as an undivided city (1945–1949), became a prominent stage for the Cold War. Although different in many respects, three common denominators connect post-WWI Vienna and post-WWII Berlin: 1) a dire shortage of housing; 2) the empowerment (or installment) of new political leaders who promised societal renewal and sought to realize this promise by providing housing and rebuilding capital cities; and 3) a commitment to political beliefs within the range of socialism and liberalism. Socialism in Red Vienna and East Berlin obviously meant different things. In the case of Vienna, it manifested itself as a commitment to majoritarian democracy, the rule of law, and gradual as opposed to radical change; in East Germany, socialism meant, among others, governing through a centralized, authoritarian state. Similarly, the meaning of liberalism varies from context to context: it served as a foil for the emergence of Red Vienna; as both an ideal and a red flag in the debates on the future of Great Berlin (1945–1949); it took a specific shape in West Germany that was informed by *Systemkonkurrenz* [system competition], i.e. the Cold War, with East Germany. The following analysis engages with contexts shaped by common denominators *and* historical, political, and cultural differences. It does so to show that spatializing ideologies occurs by contextual battles over interpretation that lead to idiosyncrasies, shades of grey and spectrums with a view to the very meanings, forms, and functions of a given set of beliefs.

This book strives to increase our awareness of the making and remaking of political beliefs via a specific space and challenges common perceptions of ideologies. It also seeks to challenge common perceptions of housing. First, it shows that East German mass housing is not the 'radical other' of West German mass housing but – with a view to form – a close relative given the shared fascination with and commitment to Taylorist mass production on both sides of the Wall. Second, it shows that the public provision of housing often comes with highly divergent intentions. While Red Vienna tamed capitalism via political power in the service of decommodifying housing, ordoliberal West Berlin used social policies in the field of housing to accelerate the return of a market economy. Third, the book systematically adds a feminist perspective to the making and remaking of political ideologies through space – a perspective that is still often underrepresented in accounts of housing. It reflects on the formation of gender roles and on how given family norms are in some cases reproduced and in some cases questioned by the design of the spaces, its underpinning policies, or through spatial appropriations. Fourth, it shows that the appropriation of green space in cities has a long history, one that offers critical insights into current revivals of garden movements and cooperative movements. Fifth, the book is deliberately historical in nature, not so much to extract lessons from the past as to challenge the focus on the present that is prominent in housing research. Much of the current discussions on 'politics of dwelling', for instance, focuses on the neoliberalization of housing since the 1990 (see, among others, Holm 2014; Kadi 2015; Vollmer and Kadi 2018). Yet as this book shows neoliberal socio-spatial makeovers through the politics of dwelling are not solely a phenomenon of the last decades. West German housing policies in the 1950s are a case in point.

Each chapter of this volume is roughly structured based on the component parts of the trialectical production of space mentioned earlier – representations of space and the 'new men' and societies to come (conceived space), actually existing spatial practices (perceived space), and 'unruly', conscious appropriations of space (lived space). Chapter 2 examines municipal housing built in Vienna during the 1920s by the newly empowered workers' party. The creation and continuous expansion of proletarian spaces were central to the so-called Austro-Marxist project, which pursued a gradual rather than revolutionary transition towards socialism. By the early 1930s, every fourth Viennese household lived in municipal housing. Municipal housing consisted of quasi decommodified apartments and communal facilities such as libraries, theaters, clubs, daycare facilities, sports facilities, and health clinics. The Austro-Marxist elite aimed to turn workers into educated and healthy socialist citizens. Their approach to bringing about new 'socialist men' was, however, strongly informed by the bourgeois past. Everyday life in municipal housing was infused by a pedagogical approach to emancipation, which put more emphasis on abstract knowledge than on practical knowledge and more on discipline than on cooperation. This top-down approach to turning workers into socialist citizens had a competitor: a democratically organized, self-help housing movement called The Wild Settlers. Also committed to the goal of socialism, the Wild Settlers built on the 'equality of intelligence' (Rancière 1991, p. 46) as its starting point, a more egalitarian relationship between the educator (the socialist elite) and the educatee (the workers). The chapter presents the rebuilding of everyday life in the name of socialism as shaped by ideals, contradictions, and contestations. It is a rebuilding that left material traces that shape the city to this very day. Even today, a quarter of Vienna's population live in municipal housing, which the city has never privatized – in stark contrast to global trends.

Chapter 3 focuses on post-WWII Berlin before the onset of the Cold War in 1949. The chapter demonstrates that immediately after 1945, it was visions of nature rather than explicit political ideologies that dominated discourses on urban and societal renewal. The modernist architect Hans Scharoun, whom the Allies had initially entrusted with the task of rebuilding what was called Great Berlin, regarded the bombing of Berlin as not only a disaster but also an opportunity. In line with many others, he considered the metropolis, which had grown rapidly in the nineteenth and early twentieth centuries, unnatural and a key source of moral and social decay. Scharoun suggested destroying more areas of Berlin in order to build decentral city landscapes [*Stadtlandschaften*] in its place, which he regarded as the *sine qua non* for a new beginning for society. The fascination with nature was common among 'progressives' such as Scharoun – who was, at least in principle, committed to emancipatory agendas informed by the values autonomy, equality, and democracy – and conservatives alike, whose critique of modernity targeted not only the metropolis but also modern, emancipatory agendas. Thus, whereas conservatives turned to nature to seek guidance for reestablishing elements of a pre-modern world, such as naturalized hierarchies, progressives took to nature as a source of inspiration for a future-oriented, more egalitarian and democratic society. With the onset of the Cold War, nature ceased to serve as the primary compass for societal renewal, a compass accompanied by political undertones, and was instead supplanted by explicit, political ideologies. As an urban form, city landscapes did, of course, find their way into the reconstruction of East and West Berlin: decentralized, suburban landscapes dotted with mass housing became prominent on both sides of the Wall.

Chapter 4 examines the reconstruction of East Berlin in the name of socialism through the lens of mass housing. Whereas the socialist experiment in Red Vienna came about gradually, the socialist experiment in the German Democratic Republic (GDR) came about by decree. In the early years of the GDR, Stalin's doctrine of 'socialism in one country' ushered in a frantic search for a truly German and at the same time socialist aesthetic vernacular. The historicist rebuilding of East Berlin's *Stalinallee* , which included model mass housing known as 'workers' palaces' [*Arbeiterpaläste*], is a prominent example of this quest. After Stalin's death, palatial mass housing was supplanted by industrialized mass housing. Most East Germans neither slept in monuments nor lived downtown but rather resided in suburban

Plattenbauten [concrete slab buildings] (see also Rubin 2016). The predominance of the *Platte* had less to do with a specific political vision than with economic constraints and a lingering housing crisis that constituted a risk for the East German state's stability and, more generally, the credibility of the superiority of Marxism-Leninism (one-party-rule, a centralized state, and a planned economy) over the liberal-capitalist West. Standardization and prefabrication – two key features of Taylorism that Stalin and his East German acolytes had initially rejected as alienating, dehumanizing capitalist practices – became acceptable and even crucial for turning the GDR's formal promise of a right to public housing into a substantive one. The housing question was ultimately solved in East Germany, a fact that was widely appreciated by the East German citizenry well beyond the fall of the Berlin Wall. Yet in between the concrete slab towers, there emerged spaces that were infused by musings of everyday life beyond standardization, prefabrication, and social control: allotment gardens, which this chapter discusses as spaces that were located simultaneously within and outside of the socialist state.

Chapter 5 explores West Germany's (the Federal Republic of Germany, FRG) reenvisioning of Berlin and its politically loaded take on the housing crisis. It shows that while nature continued to serve as a guideline for urban and societal renewal well into the late 1950s, it was integrated into explicitly liberal narratives. The housing of the future was to emerge in city landscapes, that is, in large green areas speckled with residential high-rise towers. Political elites regarded city landscapes to be ideal urban forms to facilitate the practice of freedom, the unfolding of individuality, and the nurture of healthy (nuclear) families. Although strikingly similar to socialist mass housing after Stalin at the level of urban form, mass housing in the West was underpinned by political norms that differed starkly from the norms that informed mass housing in the East. Decommodification was the core rationale behind East German housing policies, while recommodification was the basis of West German housing policies. Based on a close analysis of housing policies in the 1950s, the chapter presents West Germany's post-WWII liberalism as an early and very specific form of neoliberalism: ordoliberalism. Its core constituents are the free market and an enabling rather than redistributive state. Both shaped West German housing policies, whose central goal was to eventually facilitate the acquisition of a privately owned, single family home. The chapter also examines spaces of everyday life that engaged critically with the norms inscribed into West German mass housing. In the late 1970s, the *Märkische Viertel*, one of West Berlin's largest housing developments, turned into a site of protest against the market logic that underpinned West German mass housing more generally. Also in the 1970s, *Kommune 1*, a commune in the midst of Berlin, became a recurrent focus of public debate given its experimentation with gender roles and family norms that challenged the ones that had been entrenched by post-WWII housing policies.

The conclusion summarizes the main findings regarding the relationship between political ideas or visions and actual everyday spaces. In addition, it builds a bridge between past and present – a present shaped by the return of the housing question as a key social question (an affordability question) *and* as an ecological question. The book concludes with Benjamin-inspired, postcard-like messages from the past – interventions – whose purpose is to trigger reflection on the present. The *legacy* of mass housing built in post-WWI Vienna and post-WWII Germany does not, in my opinion, lie in offering lessons for – let alone solutions to – present-day challenges. Instead, its legacy consists in reminding us that how people dwell is and has always been a profoundly political question to which there was never one answer but many. The answers given to the question in the past continue to shape the present – physically or ideationally or both. This book reveals the negotiations, contestations, and contingencies that underpinned mass housing in Red Vienna and Cold War Berlin and concludes with opening a discursive space: What are the scopes and limits of state and market-based approaches to housing? How 'private' is the unbroken dream of the privately owned, single family home, a dream that implies 'emancipation' from mass housing? What is the actuality of debates on high rise versus low rise, on loose city landscapes versus dense metropolises in light of current socio-ecological challenges – debates that had already shaped the remaking of Red Vienna and Cold War Berlin? What are the scope and limits of civil-society-driven housing provision? And how can we account for the unbroken relevance of the question famously asked by the architectural historian Dolores Hayden more than 40 years ago (1980): What would a non-sexist city be like?

References

Benjamin, Walter. 1968/2007. 'Theses on the Philosophy of History'. In *Illuminations*, eds. Walter Benjamin and Hannah Arendt, 253–264. New York: Schocken Books.

Blau, Eve. 1999. *The Architecture of Red Vienna. 1919–1934*. Cambridge, MA: MIT Press.

Dobson, Andrew. 2007. *Green Political Thought*, 4th edn. Hoboken, NJ: Taylor & Francis.

Foucault, Michel. 1980. 'Truth and Power'. In *Power/Knowledge*, ed. Michel Foucault, 109–133. New York: Pantheon Book.

Freeden, Michael. 2006. 'Ideology and Political Theory', *Journal of Political Ideologies* 11 (1): 3–22. DOI: 10.1080/13569310500395834.

———. 2008. *Ideologies and Political Theory: A Conceptual Approach.* Oxford: Clarendon Press.

———. 2015. *The Political Theory of Political Thinking: The Anatomy of a Practice.* Oxford: Oxford University Press.

Freeden, Michael, Lyman Tower Sargent, and Marc Stears (eds.). 2015b. *The Oxford Handbook of Political Ideologies.* Oxford: Oxford University Press.

Gurney, Craig M. 1999. 'Pride and Prejudice: Discourses of Normalisation in Public and Private Accounts of Home Ownership', *Housing Studies* 14 (2): 163–183. DOI: 10.1080/02673039982902.

Häußermann, Hartmut, and Walter Siebel. 1996. *Soziologie des Wohnens.* Weinheim/Munich: Juventa.

Hayden, Dolores. 1980. 'What Would a Non-Sexist City Be Like? Speculations on Housing, Urban Design, and Human Work', *Signs* 5 (3): 170–187.

Holm, Andrej. 2014. 'Berlin's Gentrification Mainstream'. In *Doing Urban Space*, ed. Sandra Maria Geschke, 171–188. Bielefeld: transcript.

Kadi, Justin. 2015. 'Recommodifying Housing in Formerly "Red" Vienna?', *Housing, Theory and Society* 32 (3): 247–265. DOI: 10.1080/14036096.2015.1024885.

Kohl, Sebastian. 2018. 'Why Housing Studies Still Lacks Social Theory and What To Do About It', *Housing, Theory and Society*, 35: 2, 231–234. DOI: 10.1080/14036096.2017.1366943.

———. 2019. *Homeownership, Renting and Society: Historical and Comparative Perspectives.* London/New York: Routledge.

Ladd, Brian. 2008. *The Ghosts of Berlin: Confronting German History in the Urban Landscape.* Chicago: University of Chicago Press.

Lefebvre, Henri. 1991. *The Production of Space.* Oxford: Blackwell.

Madden, David J., and Peter Marcuse. 2016. *In Defense of Housing: The Politics of Crisis.* London/New York: Verso.

Maderthaner, Wolfgang, and Lutz Musner. 2008. *Unruly Masses.* New York: Berghahn Books.

Merrifield, Andrew. 1993. 'Place and Space: A Lefebvrian Reconciliation', *Transactions of the Institute of British Geographers* 18 (4): 516. DOI: 10.2307/622564.

Rancière, Jacques. 1991. *The Ignorant Schoolmaster.* Stanford, CA: Stanford University Press.

Richie, Alexandra. 1999. *Faust's Metropolis: A History of Berlin.* New York: Carroll & Graf.

Roberts, John. 2006. *Philosophizing the Everyday. Revolutionary Praxis and the Fate of Cultural Theory.* London: Pluto Press.

Ronald, Richard. 2008. *The Ideology of Home Ownership.* London: Palgrave Macmillan UK.

Smith, Susan J. 2015. 'Owner Occupation: At Home in a Spatial, Financial Paradox', *International Journal of Housing Policy* 15 (1): 61–83. DOI: 10.1080/14616718.2014.997432.

Rubin, Eli. *Amnesiopolis: Modernity, Space and Memory in East Germany.* Oxford: Oxford University Press, 2016.

Scott, James. 1998. *Seeing Like a State.* New Haven: Yale University Press.

Stangl, Paul. 2018. *Risen from Ruins: The Cultural Politics of Rebuilding East Berlin.* Stanford, CA: Stanford University Press.

Urban, Florian. 2012. *Tower and Slab: Histories of Global Mass Housing.* Abingdon, NY: Routledge.

Vollmer, Lisa, and Justin Kadi. 2018. 'Wohnungspolitik in der Krise des Neoliberalismus in Berlin und Wien: Postneoliberaler Paradigmenwechsel oder punktuelle staatliche Beruhigungspolitik?', *Prokla* 48 (2): 247–264.

Zieleniec, Andrzej. 2018. 'Lefebvre's Politics of Space: Planning the Urban as Oeuvre', *Urban Planning* 3 (3): 5–15. DOI: 10.17645/up.v3i3.1343

2 Municipal Socialism and Housing in Red Vienna (1919–1934)

Abstract
In Vienna after WWI, the newly empowered Austro-Marxists took it upon themselves to bring about "new socialist men" by democratic means. The provision of much-needed housing was key to this undertaking. Within less than a decade, the Austro-Marxists did solve the housing question by building municipal housing, which has been shaping Vienna ever since. The Austro-Marxists' specific approach to turning citizens into new men was, however, deeply indebted to bourgeois traditions and pedagogy: the imparting of knowledge 'from above'. An alternative to the latter did exist in the form of the 'Wild Settlers', a housing movement that was also committed to the goal of socialism but opted for 'revolutionary practice' (Marx) instead of bourgeois pedagogy to achieve this goal.

Keywords: Red Vienna, municipal housing, Austro-Marxism, settlement movement, democratic socialism

'Which type of man should we educate?' asked Otto Bauer, the leader of the Social Democratic Workers' Party (Sozialdemokratische Arbeiterpartei, SDAP) and main theorist of Austro-Marxism, in a speech delivered to Viennese workers in 1929:

> [a] type of man who grows up in overcrowded apartments where everyone sleeps next to someone else, where everyone wishes to escape from others, where everyone is happy when they do not see anyone anymore, as they are so tightly locked up together; men who spend their leisure in inns, numbing themselves with beer and wine [...], men whose potential and natural talents are poisoned and destroyed by alcohol; or do we want to educate a type of man who flourishes in sunlight and air, a type who perfects himself in tranquility, which is essential to intellectual maturing

Haderer, M., *Rebuilding Cities and Citizens: Mass Housing in Red Vienna and Cold War Berlin*. Amsterdam: Amsterdam University Press 2023
DOI: 10.5117/9789463724944_CH02

> yet unavailable in overcrowded apartments; a type of man who flourishes whenever the objective condition for intellectual development and growth is provided, that is, a place that is no longer a mere bedding but a real dwelling? [my translation] (1976d, p. 608)

Bauer's question to the workers was rhetorical. The decision to educate and thus to provide for the second type of man – that is, men who would flourish physically and intellectually – was made as early as 1919, the year Vienna became the first European socialist metropolis. Instead of regarding access to decent housing as a privilege, the Social Democrats[1] stipulated housing as a right (Bauer 1976b, pp. 118–119). Within a decade, 382 *Gemeindebauten* [municipal housing blocks] were constructed, equipped with communal facilities such as kindergartens, libraries, theaters, cooperative stores, public gardens, sports facilities, social clubs, and polyclinics. *Neue Menschen* [New Men] (Adler 1924) were expected to flourish in the new housing complexes, men and women surmised to actualize the promise of socialism.

The following analysis looks into the interplay between a specific vision of socialism – Austro-Marxism, which opted for a 'slow revolution' (Bauer 1927/1978) and against the 'dictatorship of the proletariat' (Marx 1969) – and the politics of dwelling in Red Vienna (1919–1934). It will show that the democratically empowered SDAP *did* manage to appropriate the city and to reshape it in the name of the proletariat. 'Workers' palaces' began to perforate Vienna, that is, proletarian *Gegenbauten* [counter buildings] emerged in the capital that was strongly shaped by the aristocracy and the bourgeoisie, which proudly demarcated the working class's presence in and relevance the city (see section 2.1). The Austro-Marxists' endorsement of a 'slow revolution', which is widely and in many respects rightly regarded as more indicative of social democratic reform than socialist revolution, did translate into a clear message: that decent housing is a right, not a privilege, a message that has been shaping the city to this day (see section 2.2). Although Red Vienna clearly emancipated workers from squalor, the city's political elite held fast to a certain degree of suspicion toward the proletariat. As will also be shown in this chapter, two approaches to social emancipation were within reach in the Austro-Marxist context: one that endorsed bourgeois pedagogy and its commitment to impart knowledge 'from above', and another one that experimented with 'revolutionary practice', of which self-help settlement housing was but one example (see section 2.3). As

1 The terms Social Democrats and Austro-Marxists were used interchangeably in the context of Red Vienna.

revealed by a closer look at the endorsed dwelling culture in Red Vienna, it was the former approach to emancipation that was to gain the upper hand and reaffirm itself in an idealization of forms of living that would in many respects be infused by bourgeois norms and ideals more so than by socialist ones, let alone socialist feminist ones (see section 2.4). Red Vienna, a term that was initially employed by the Christian Social opposition to frame the SDAP-governed city as a Bolshevik threat (Wasserman 2014, pp. 1–2), was short-lived. Black Vienna, an antimarxist and antisemitic alliance of Christian Socials, German Nationals, and National Socialists which had mobilized against Red Vienna throughout its existence, was to ultimately bring an end to the experiment in democratic municipal socialism but not to one of its legacies: the decommodification of one quarter of the city's housing stock.

2.1 Whose City? Appropriating the City, Creating Proletarian Spaces

'Little red bricks' were to 'build the new world', as suggested by a Viennese workers' song (Nussbaum 2007, p. 51). Yet what was the old world that the new world was supposed to supplant? As a result of a late but rapid period of industrialization, the population of Vienna and its conurbation quadrupled in the nineteenth century from 440,000 in 1840 to two million in 1910. Unskilled or semi-skilled laborers left the crisis-ridden agricultural hinterland of Bohemia, Moravia, and Galicia for the metropolis in search of new sources of livelihood in the fields of industry, commerce, and domestic service (Lichtenberger 1993, pp. 69–71; Maderthaner and Musner 2008, p. 25). Most of the immigrants settled on the city's fringes, an area once shaped by viticulture and small trades that was quickly overhauled by the modern city's own logic and needs: the functional differentiation of urban space expressed, among others, by rectilinear suburbs (Lichtenberger 1993, p. 63; Maderthaner and Musner 2008, p. 24).

Vienna's rapid increase in population was not matched by an increase in housing. Between 1830 and 1850, the population grew by 40 percent. In the same period, the housing stock increased by only 10 percent. As a result of this lingering imbalance, overcrowding, unsanitary living conditions, exorbitant rents, the permanent threat of eviction, and the possibility or reality of homelessness shaped everyday proletarian life (Lichtenberger 1993, p. 74). Some of those who could not secure a roof over their heads made public spaces their home, risking the police, who would relocate them to stables and municipal prisons (Maderthaner and Musner 2008, p. 32) or drop them off in the 'open field' of the metropolis's far periphery (Lichtenberger 1993, p. 63). Others were compelled to subject themselves to a double form of exploitation as producers *and* consumers. As revealed by a famous undercover report from 1888 by the founder of the SDAP, Victor Adler, the workers at the Wienerberger brick factory not only worked 18 or more hours per day for a poor wage but also spent the latter on overpriced, dismal habitats provided by their employer (Adler 1989).

The great majority of workers, however, lived in suburban tenement housing, the so-called *Zinsburgen* [rent-bearing castles], that is, sub-standard housing for which landlords charged disproportionally high rents. Whereas the housing's exterior, its historicist facades, suggested a socio-aesthetic unity between the bourgeois center and the proletarian periphery, the housing's interior spoke a different language: one of social marginalization and exploitation. In the words of Max Winter, an important figure in the emerging field of social reportage at that time, the apartments inside the 'castles of usury' were little more than 'narrow, overcrowded dungeons', 'air-deprived holes that force people and children out into the hallway, the staircase or the court yard', since there was space for neither privacy nor play (Winter 1982, pp. 94–95). The prototypical building type in working class districts was the so-called *Bassena* house, whose long, dark gangways provided access to 10 or 20 *Kleinstwohnungen* [smallest apartments], shared toilets, and a communal water faucet, the *Bassena*. The gangways also served as air shafts for kitchens whose windows opened into the buildings' interior instead of the courtyard or the street. Despite the apartments' limited space – a standard apartment consisted of a kitchen, a room, and sometimes of a *Kabinett*, which was an additional small room – over 50 percent of the tenants sublet to subtenants who contributed to the rent [see Illustration 2.1]. Due to the lack of rent control, the rent was often higher than that for luxury apartments in the prestigious *Ringstrasse* when calculated per square meter (Gulick 1948, p. 410).

The structural reasons for the housing misery were mainly rooted in pre-WWI liberalism. From the 1860s to the 1890s, a newly self-empowered upper-middle class – the Bourgeoisie [*Bürgertum*] – challenged the Viennese court's conservatism and conceived of itself as the redeemer of economic but also political and cultural modernity, the Enlightenment. This self-understanding as modernizer and harbinger of emancipation in the name of universal rights, such as the right to vote, to private property, and to education, was manifest, among others, in the *Ringstrasse*'s 'buildings of splendor', such as the university, the parliament, and the museums.

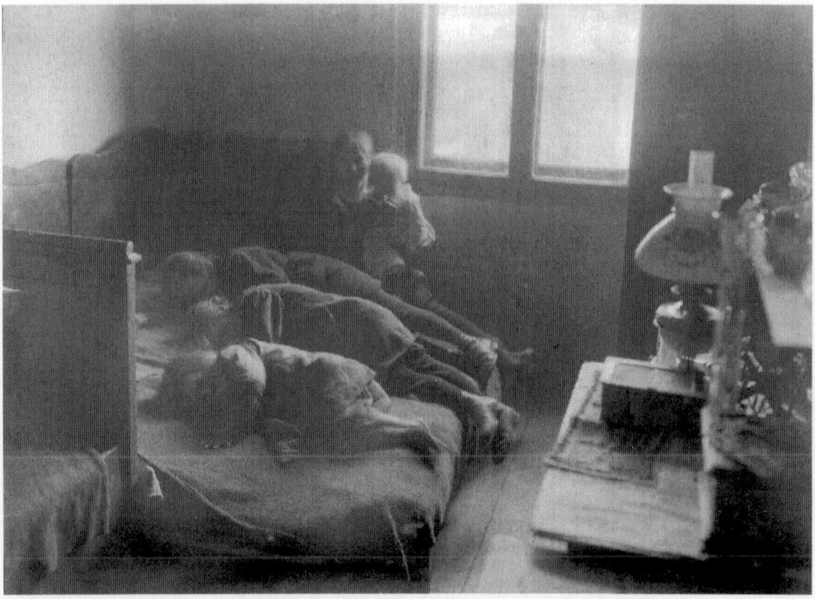

2.1 Housing Conditions in Vienna around 1900. © Verein für die Geschichte der Arbeiter*innenbewegung (VGA), Vienna

Encircling the Viennese court, the *Ringstrasse* and its buildings symbolically challenged the authority of the nobility and its holding fast to feudalism, yet also entrenched a new frontier: a frontier between the 'winners' of political, cultural, economic and technological modernization, the upper-middle class of the inner city, and its 'losers', the lower-middle class of the inner suburbs and the proletariat of the outer suburbs.

At the municipal level, the bourgeoisie's political focus was predominantly on the provision of technical infrastructure, which was essential to the unfolding of industrial capitalism. Vienna did not undergo a spatial makeover as radical as the Parisian one, a makeover directed by Baron Haussmann who demolished the historically grown city and replaced it with a clearly legible, rational urban form. Instead, Vienna's liberal modernizers put more emphasis on overhauling the city to facilitate economic growth than on accommodating all urban dwellers' social needs. Considering the city as an urban body whose 'respiratory' and 'circulatory' functions were in need of (technical) attuning to ensure the organism's health, the city was increasingly split up into functionally divergent zones, such as residential, industrial, and mixed-use zones, to be nourished by 'arteries' of technical infrastructure, such as streets, canalization, gas and water. The latter reached out into the city's periphery, overlaying it with an orthogonal grid system regardless of local topography (Blau 2001, p. 214).

Vienna's second building ordinance of 1859 stipulated the grid as fundamental tenet for planning the expanding city. This was much to the dismay of Vienna's famous city builder, Camillo Sitte (1843–1903). In contrast to Otto Wagner whose students were to shape municipal housing in a prominent way, Sitte was an outspoken critic of modern city planning and a proponent of organic city building. He equated modernity's formulaic uniformity in the form of the grid with torturing the human genius to death and suffocating 'all joyful sense of life' (Schorske 1981, p. 63), a 'risk' he sought to counteract by an architecture indebted to a rebuilding of local 'organic' communities (Harvey 1989, pp. 276–278). The success of the grid went hand in hand with a legal innovation brought about by the bourgeoisie: the introduction of private property and thus the independence of land and its use from both the state and the aristocracy. By means of the grid, land could be parceled up and its use could be maximized regardless of topography, which made it particularly attractive for private investment and speculation (Maderthaner 2006, pp. 183–189). Accordingly, the checkerboard of the industrial suburb was no less a reflection of the hegemony of profit[2] than of the proletariat's dwelling conditions. One such checkerboard is the Viennese workers district *Favoriten*, which the social critic Max Winter described in a newspaper article on the conditions of the working class in 1901 as follows:

> Favoriten is a town unto itself. Someone took a sheet of drawing paper, ruler and pencil, and drew horizontal and vertical lines. He started from Favorita, now known as Theresianum, colonized with his pencil the bare country road that ran toward Himberg, tore down the poplars on the right and left side, filled in the ditches, and made buildings, factories, and tenement blocks arise on their banks. The blocks were hatched in red on the plan but were sober grayish-brown buildings in reality. [...] No monuments decorate them, no ornamental fountain gladdens the eye; even the sole public buildings, the schools, are gloomy like everything else. This raw brick of a factory with its ridiculously even line of windows – four stories one above the other – is the only variation in the picture. Everything covered with smoke and dust, everywhere the roar of industry. Nowhere

2 The building ordinance of 1859 allowed for 85 percent of the lot to be built up, which resulted in a desperate lack of green spaces (Gulick, 1948, p. 410).

is there light of place to relax. Everything bleak, everything gloomy, all gray on gray – that is Favoriten. (Arbeiter Zeitung 1901)

Ironically but also tellingly, the pencil that 'colonized' the country for the sake of economic modernization belonged to Sicard van Sicardsburg and Eduard van der Nüll, two architects less known for their work in proletarian *Favoriten* than in the bourgeois *Ringstrasse* (Maderthaner and Musner 2008, p. 35). In *Favoriten*, Sicardsburg and van der Nüll created an urban fabric that abstracted from its inhabitants' history and needs. In the *Ringstrasse*, they materialized history, namely that of the bourgeoisie, by inscribing the latter's newly found identity into the urban landscape. Whereas the *Ringstrasse*'s monumentalism bore testimony to the bourgeoisie's hard-won freedom to express their vision of history, displayed by the historicist facades and buildings that freely cited styles from different epochs, the proletarian rectilinear suburbs reflected the fact that the bourgeoisie's appropriation of history and its triumphant procession of democratization, universal law, and culture came with its own particular *aporia*: the disregard of the history of those whom economic modernization had subjected to urban life, the industrial proletariat. As the historians of Vienna's fin-de-siècle proletarian counter-culture, Lutz Musner and Wolfgang Maderthaner, put it:

> [...] the anti-hierarchical theme in bourgeois discourse is not only a rejection of the feudal culture of the nobility, but at the same time a devaluation of popular culture, which is denounced as 'low', 'vulgar' and 'impure'. The bourgeois 'purifies' himself in this explanatory model, unaware, as it were, of the historical contingency of his origin, of the socially polymorphous, of the sensual, erotic components of popular culture. (2008, p. 60)

For the proletariat, it would take a few more decades until they themselves would be in a position to reclaim history and build their own *Gegenbauten* [counter buildings] not only in the name of democratic empowerment but also in the name of social equality. Until then, a physical frontier between city and suburbs remained entrenched. As Carl Schorske writes in his book on Viennese modernism: 'Where a Baroque planner would have sought to join suburb and city – to organize vast vistas oriented toward the central, monumental features – the plan adopted in 1859, with few exceptions, suppressed the vistas in favor of stress on the circular flow' (Schorske 1981, p. 32).

In 1873, the bourgeoisie's hailing of economic modernization, techno-scientific progress, and rationalistic individualism became tainted by a massive credit crunch. From within the cracks caused by the crisis, two political contenders emerged: one that was at least partially orientated toward the pre-modern past, the Christian Socials, and the other oriented toward a more modern future, the Social Democrats. Despite being ideological opponents, the Christian Socials and the Social Democrats shared one common denominator: the reliance on mass politics instead of elite politics, which had gradually been made possible through several stages of electoral reform. From 1897 to 1919, the Christian Socials took the political reins into their hands after successfully mobilizing their political clientele of shopkeepers, tradesmen and craftsmen, and civil servants who were severely affected by the economic crisis. Whereas the liberal upper-middle class of the *Ringstrassen* era pushed for an encompassing modernization that included the economic no less than the cultural and political realm, the Christian Socials mobilized their lower-middle class clientele by means of cultural pre-modern romanticism and political conservatism, while simultaneously and maybe contradictorily continuing important aspects of the inherited laissez-faire capitalism. More specifically, spearheaded by the populist and anti-Semitic mayor Karl Lueger, Vienna's Christian Socials promised to heal the pains caused by modernization by returning to Christian patriarchal values and an economy based on *Stände* [corporations] instead of finance and industry. Although Lueger especially presented himself as an outspoken critic of economic liberalism, he and his party continued many of its legacies. Although the Christian Socials socialized some of the city's technical infrastructure, they turned a blind eye to a key social infrastructure: housing. Moreover, they continued to finance municipal projects predominantly by credit and thereby exacerbated the already enormous municipal debts. Finally, they generated the majority of the municipal tax income, 75 percent, by taxing basic consumption and rent, a tax system that heavily and negatively impacted lower social strata (Maderthaner 2006, p. 228).

The Christian Socials' ambivalent balancing of their critique of modernity, celebration of tradition, *and* endorsement of technological modernization was embodied, among others, by their municipal showcase project, the *Stadtbahn* [city railways]. Whereas the *Stadtbahn*'s architecture suggests deep roots in Vienna's urban traditions, its financing was informed by principles of modern economic liberalism and its construction was based on the latest innovations of technology and engineering (Maderthaner 2006, pp. 225–226). Similar to the *Ringstrasse*, the *Stadtbahn* also reentrenched spatial patterns of social segregation. As mentioned before, the *Ringstrasse* symbolically challenged the inner-city palaces of the nobility by encircling them with buildings representative of liberalism's cultural, economic, and political achievements. Yet simultaneously, it also redrew a dividing line between the inner city and the suburbs: the inner suburbs for the lower-middle class and the outer suburbs for the proletariat. Similarly, the *Stadtbahn,* while connecting the inner suburbs with one another, also recreated a socio-spatial division: between the lower-middle-class inner suburbs and the proletarian outer suburbs (Maderthaner 2006, p. 226).

To be sure, the Christian Socials were well aware of the dire need for investment in social infrastructure such as housing. In 1894, the liberal reformer Eugen Philippovich published a study, which became widely known, on the Viennese proletariat's housing conditions. Replicating the existing widespread suspicion of proletarian culture, Philippovich not only noted that working class housing was 'missing everything, which we are used to consider as the basis for a healthy bourgeois life' but also warned that ignoring these conditions would ultimately lead to social regress in the form of 'barbarism, bestiality and rowdyism' (Philippovich 1894). The Christian Socials, however, were rather unmoved by the report. Since workers were neither part of their core clientele (in fact, their electoral base were the owners of *Mietskasernen* [tenement housing]) nor represented a political threat since they were deprived of the right to vote,[3] they had little incentive to substantially improve the workers' poor housing conditions. Accordingly, the few investments in housing that were made during the Christian Social era were, same as in the liberal bourgeois one, typically driven by considerations of charity instead of justice (Weihsmann 1985, p. 98).

It was not until the Social Democrats had transformed Vienna into their political stronghold in 1919 that the city was appropriated by and for the 'Fourth Estate'. The counter buildings that challenged both the *Ringstrasse*'s 'buildings of splendor' and the *Stadtbahn*'s negotiation of tradition and modernity were the *Gemeindebauten*. Initially through an ephemeral 'culture of resistance' (John 1996, p. 239) in the form of anarcho-syndicalist strikes, riots, or mass demonstrations whose object of appropriation was the street itself, Vienna's proletariat repeatedly and sometimes violently claimed the city for itself by intentionally trespassing the boundaries between center and periphery.

In 1919, the year the proletariat empowered the Social Democrats to take control of municipal politics, the ephemeral politics of place-making

3 In fact, the Christian Socials had no interest in empowering workers politically through electoral reform, as doing so would have weakened the political influence of the lower-middle class, the Christian Socials' core clientele.

2.2 Opening Ceremony of a Municipal Housing Block: "Long Live Vienna!" © Verein für die Geschichte der Arbeiter*innenbewegung (VGA), Vienna

subsided and made way for a lasting politics of place-making [see Illustration 2.2]. Public housing equipped with a public infrastructure was destined to serve as a field of experimentation for the redemption of history's ultimate rationality: the realization of socialism. Whereas Marx insisted that as long as capitalism dominates, workers are bound to remain deprived of a 'dwelling in the light', a dwelling they can look upon as their own home (Marx 1844/1978a, pp. 94), his (unorthodox) Austrian followers deemed that having access to a decent home already under conditions of capitalism was crucial for initiating socialism. Austro-Marxism meant, among others, a literal 'war of position': the erection of proletarian spaces in a city shaped by the (interests of the) bourgeoisie. The latter was meant to be a stepping stone towards a 'war of maneuver' (Gramsci 2008, p. 234): the claiming of not only the local state, Vienna, but the national state, Austria, in the name of democratic socialism.

2.2 For a 'Slow Revolution': Austro-Marxist Theory and Housing Policies

Austro-Marxism is best understood as a theory for practice. It is, as Bauer explained, an 'intellectual force that maintains unity' by bringing together 'the capacity for realistic adaptation of all our day-to-day struggles to the particular conditions of time and place, and a constant orientation of all partial struggles to the great goal of the seizure of power by the working class, and thereby to the great inspiring goal of socialism [...]' (1927/1978, p. 47). Influenced by the teachings of Carl Grünberg, who taught in Vienna before becoming the first director of Frankfurt's Institute of Social Research, the Austro-Marxists – most prominently Otto Bauer, Max Adler, Karl Renner, and Rudolf Hilferding – are proponents of a materialist conception of history 'whose object is not abstraction, but the given concrete world in its process of development and change' (Bottomore and Goode 1978, pp. 9–10). Although the Austro-Marxists' scientific work was rather diverse in focus,[4] it was united by two common concerns: the pursuit of Marxism as a social science and the reconciliation of theory and practice. In contrast to Grünberg's students at the Frankfurt School, the Austro-Marxists were deeply enmeshed in everyday politics through their affiliation with the SDAP, a mass party also based on trade unions and cooperatives that had united Austria's workers' movement since its inception in 1888/1889 by Victor Adler. As is implicit in Bauer's definition of Austro-Marxism, the goal of this particular strand of Marxism was – akin to Marx's 'Theses on Feuerbach' (1845/1978) – not only to understand the laws of history but to also alter them. For this purpose, Vienna served as the Austro-Marxists' laboratory, and democratic socialism was the object of their experiment.

Despite the SDAP's strong political position in 1919, the year it emerged as a party with an absolute majority in Vienna and as the strongest political party at the federal level, the SDAP deferred a fundamental overhaul of

4 See T.B. Bottomore and Patrick Goode's introduction in their edited book *Austro-Marxism* (Bottomore & Goode, 1978, pp. 1-44) or Anson Rabinbach's *Vom Roten Wien zum Bürgerkrieg* (Rabinbach, 1989, pp. 39-46). Otto Bauer was the SDAP's main theoretician as well as prominent leader of the SDAP. Max Adler was dedicated to clarifying and vindicating the theoretical foundations of Marxism and was influenced by Ernst Mach's positivism as well as neo-Kantianism. Adler's goal was the pursuit of Marxism as a critique of knowledge applied to the science of society, the demonstration of an 'inner intellectual kinship' between critical idealism and Marxism as a social science. Adler, similar to Bauer, belonged to the left wing of the SDAP who held fast to the idea of a socialist revolution. Karl Renner focused on the relationship between law and the economy. Rejecting Kelsen's pure theory of law, Renner showed how legal forms change their function in response to changes in the economic structure and society at large. Similar to Hilferding, Renner argued for the 'state penetration of the economy', that is, for the extension of the state's welfare functions and the rational organization of the economy under public ownership. Renner and Hilferding belonged to the reformist wing of the SDAP, conceiving of the 'state penetration of the economy' as revolutionary in itself. Rudolf Hilferding challenged the Austrian marginalist school founded by Carl Menger (the most well-known offspring of this school are Friedrich Hayek and Ludwig von Mises). Hilferding rejected Menger's conception of economics as a science of human action that is built on a rational model instead of an empirical basis. He argued for a state-controlled, centrally planned economy instead.

capitalism to the future, to when it would also secure an absolute majority at the federal level. The SDAP understood itself not as one political party among many but as a unique redeemer of a historical truth: the implementation of socialism. However, the party abstained from revolutionary politics and, influenced by Austro-Marxism, pursued a 'politics of *hineinwachsen*' [politics of growing into] vis-à-vis socialism, that is, a politics of a 'planned organizing activity, proceeding step by step toward a clearly conceived goal' (Bauer 1919/1978, p. 150). Thus, instead of considering the replacement of the bourgeois state with a temporary dictatorship of the proletariat as the *only* promising path towards socialism, the Austro-Marxists opted for a 'slow revolution' instead: the creation of a socialist hegemony that would abolish capitalism *gradually* and *from within* the existing liberal-democratic institutions. Max Adler explains:

> Social Democracy cannot be reduced to its political character. It is considerably more than, as one might assume at first sight, one party among many. Social Democracy is the conscious society in the midst of its own becoming already within the state, a society which transitions from its merely natural form to its conscious, planned existence, that seeks to supplant any merely given and contradictory community with a community of law that guarantees solidarity. [my translation] (1924, p. 92)

To be sure, in the early years of the Austro-Marxist project, the choice for a politics of *hineinwachsen* was less a reflection of a timid concession to reformism than one of a strong commitment to bringing about socialism by winning over the hearts and minds of the opposition (see also Wasserman 2014, pp. 47–73). First, the SDAP feared that a 'dictatorship of the proletariat' would lead to economic sanctions by the anti-socialist *Entente* powers, sanctions that would further undermine the country's already utterly difficult economic standing and thereby increase the likelihood of a capitalist counter-revolution (Bauer 1924/1978, p. 163). Second, the party believed since its inception that in the long run, democratic constitutionalism would be the appropriate institutional setting for the proletariat's political empowerment. Democratic constitutionalism was also defended because, as Bauer argued (before twentieth-century history would prove his point), a dictatorship of the proletariat would run the risk of turning into a 'bureaucratic dictatorship' spearheaded by a 'caste' of soviets who suggested to speak and administer in the name of the people while de facto circumventing the latter's immediate control (Bauer 1936/1978, p. 203). The party did not support a 'dictatorship of the proletariat' no less than experiments in building republics of councils

[*Räterepubliken*], such as the Bavarian or the Hungarian one. Third, the party was also opposed to a revolutionary overhaul because it deemed its basis – the workers – to be lacking the maturity necessary for securing the long-term success of socialism, a concern that left its traces in Vienna's *Gemeindebauten* and its underlying policies, as will be shown below. 'Our party,' argued Bauer,

> comprises the most diverse proletarian strata, strata that display highly diverging levels of cultural development and degrees of class consciousness. Our party has the duty to accept the proletarians the way capitalism has educated them: with all the ignorance and lack of culture the capitalist social order has condemned them to; with all the vices of the oppressed capitalism has bred them with. Yet due to the proletarian movement, the praxis of the proletarian class struggle, a continuously growing part of the proletariat is striving to overcome the lack of culture they used to live with. [my translation] (1927/1976, p. 497)

To be sure, despite the SDAP's preference for a gradual and peaceful revolution, it did not entirely discard the possibility of a dictatorship of the proletariat and thus the use of force. To assuage the increasing tension between the party's radical[5] and reformist wings, the SDAP's *Linzer Programm* approved the use of 'defensive violence' (Rabinbach 1989, p. 52; SDAP Deutschösterreichs 1926). The defense of violence was considered to be legitimate in case the opposition decided to violently resist the systemic changes the SDAP was determined to undertake once it had achieved one of its main political objectives: an absolute majority in parliament. The objective itself was laid out by Bauer in 1924: 'If we succeed in diverting only 320,000 voters from the bourgeois parties and in winning them for our party, then we shall obtain the absolute majority in parliament, then we shall govern Austria' [my translation] (Bauer 1976a, p. 960).

For a socialist hegemony to emerge by democratic means, the SDAP pursued three main strategies: the continuous expansion of the party's electorate to gradually secure the party's dominance in parliament, a precondition for the social revolution 'from within' (Bauer 1976a, p. 965); the gradual socialization and democratization of industry and, more generally, the economy (SDAP Deutschösterreichs 1926); and the spiritual and intellectual

5 To make the picture regarding the meaning of 'radical' in the context of the SDAP more complex: Otto Bauer, for instance, was from the left wing of the SDAP but against the use of force.

preparation of the workers for their historic mission to bring about socialism (Adler 1924), an aspect I will elaborate on in the context of the politics of dwelling. Special emphasis was put on the 'reform of consciousness'. As Adler explained, ideology was not to be conceived of as 'insignificant or unreal' but as 'one of the most powerful and fateful realities of history' (Adler 1930/1978, p. 260). For a radical change to be possible and, once achieved, lasting, one 'must first and foremost break through that intellectual state of affairs in which the revolutionary class still thinks the thoughts of the old classes [...]' (Adler 1928/1978, p. 143), an undertaking that took place in a pulsating and explosive field of force shaped by proponents of 'progressivist' Red Vienna and proponents of 'conservative' Black Vienna (Wasserman 2014).

Adler concerned himself with the 'intellectual preparation' for socialism and Bauer with preparatory legislative and administrative work. According to Bauer, the revolution consists of two momenta: '[t]he political revolution [...], the work of one great hour [...], that abolishes political oppression, but allows economic exploitation to continue' and the 'social revolution, [...] the outcome of the old, but well-considered activity of many years'. According to Bauer, the social revolution 'can neither be accomplished in street battles nor in civil war' but only through *'creative legislative and administrative work'* [emphasis added] (Bauer 1919/1978, p. 151). Yet despite the SDAP's unprecedented political success in 1919, it was still far from the 'quick' political revolution Bauer had hoped for. Since the SDAP had not managed to secure an absolute majority in 1919 at the federal level, the party entered into an internally contested coalition with the Christian Socials, a coalition that ended shortly after it had begun. Bauer had – as became evident in the late 1920s – fatally built his hope on a *Gleichgewicht der Klassen* [an equilibrium between classes], that is, in a political constellation in which neither 'the bourgeoisie' nor 'the proletariat' were expected to be in full control of the state but dependent on one another and required to make mutual concessions (Bauer 1976c, pp. 743–751). This hope was anchored in Bauer's specific understanding of the post-WWI central European state. According to him, the state was neither shaped by class interests, as suggested by Lenin, nor was it a neutral institution, as implied by nineteenth-century liberals. Instead, Bauer conceived of it as the outcome of a complex and intricate compromise between different classes. Therefore, it was assumed that socialism could only be achieved in the long run due to the proletariat's ever growing institutional, cultural, and numerical presence. The socialist housing complexes, community facilities, clubs, co-operatives, pedagogical institutions as well as the party's paramilitary organization, the *Republikanische Schutzbund*, were ultimately expected to serve as a bulwark against the hegemony of the right at the federal level. It was the SDAP's hope that the sheer presence of a continuously growing workers' movement would deter the oppositional forces from making purely partisan decisions and from using their influence on the local state against the Social Democrats, a hope that was ultimately proven as illusory (Rabinbach 1989, pp. 50–51).

One of the first crucial 'creative legislative and administrative' steps the SDAP took to anchor its hegemony at the municipal level was housing reform. The strategies that undergirded the socialists' general vision of a politics of *hineinwachsen* also shaped their housing policies. First, to gradually expand the party's electorate, they introduced rent control that was designed in such a way that it would protect not only workers from exorbitant rents but – in their pursuit to expand their electorate – also the lower-middle class typically mobilized by the Christian Socials. Second, to move a step closer to the ideal of a right to housing (a right that the SDAP intended to expand not only to citizens in need but to all citizens), Vienna's SDAP socialized, or rather 'municipalized', vast areas of land, parts of the existing housing stock, and the construction industry to boost the public provision of housing. Finally, to ensure that the SDAP's affiliates would become socially, intellectually, and culturally adequately prepared for socialism, the municipal housing blocks were designed as spaces of socialization and education, as spaces that would afford their inhabitants and users with a foretaste of socialism (Bauer 1976b).

If the introduction of universal suffrage in 1918 was one of the Social Democrats' greatest victories in the period between the party's founding in 1888/1889 and the end of WWI, the institutionalization of tenancy protection – first introduced in 1917 and made permanent in 1922 by the Federal Rent Control Act – was one of Labor's key achievements during the First Republic (1919–1934). The right to vote politically enfranchised workers; while rent control reversed the power relations between landlords and tenants, power relations that fueled competing political camps and, on the urban scale, socio-spatial segregation. Favoring the interests of tenants over those of landlords, the new law curbed land speculation, protected tenants against arbitrary notice and rent increases, and redefined how rent was to be calculated. Rent was no longer to be conceived of as one fixed sum stipulated by the landlord or the free market but as the sum of four different components: net rent, maintenance costs, administrative and operative costs, and a proportional share in taxes. Of these components, only the net rent was fixed, namely at 50 percent of the prewar rent. As a result of high inflation after 1919, *de facto* net rent ended up constituting only a miniscule fraction of the prewar rent: 1/28,800. The extremely low net rent basically amounted to the 'confiscation' of the landlords' net income (Gulick 1948, pp. 442–444), which made land speculation and private construction largely unprofitable. In some areas, the price of land dropped to about four percent of the prewar price (Gulick 1948, p. 445). These developments, coupled with the fact that in 1922 Vienna also became a federal state equipped with extra fiscal prerogatives a municipality does not have, put Vienna in an advantageous financial situation to acquire the land and build the industry necessary to realize its comprehensive public housing program. By 1928, the municipality owned approximately one-quarter of the total area of Greater Vienna (Blau 1999, p. 141). As a contemporary of the Social Democrats, Friedrich von Hayek, one of the early thinkers and proponents of neoliberalism, correctly stated, rent control initially further decreased instead of increased the housing stock, since low rents made investing in housing unattractive (Hayek 1930/2001). Nonetheless, the Social Democrats decided against free market logics. In contrast to Hayek, who saw the post-WWI housing crisis as a *temporary* problem to be adjusted on the free market by price movements, the Social Democrats conceived of it as a *chronic* problem that had plagued the lower social strata throughout the Liberal and Christian Social eras. According to the Austro-Marxists, it was not the market but the local state, the city, that should provide and secure sufficient and adequate housing.

Rent control helped the city to municipalize land, but given the depleted budget the Social Democrats inherited from their political predecessors, it was still lacking the required funds for constructing the *Gemeindebauten*. Thus, before the communal dwellings could become a reality, another 'creative' legislative and administrative step needed to be taken: the overhaul of the tax system and, more specifically, the introduction of diverse new taxes on 'luxuries', especially the *Wohnbausteuer* [housing construction tax]. Entrusted with the task of creating an 'inflation-proof' revenue system, Hugo Breitner and his Social Democratic associates revised the inherited tax system and, in pursuit of a radical redistribution of existing wealth, decided to shift the main burden of taxation onto the rich and well-to-do by introducing taxes on property, business, as well as luxury items and services, such as cars, horses, dogs, amusement, exquisite food, and servants (Gulick 1948, pp. 362–366). One key component of the general overhaul was the introduction of the housing construction tax whose purpose was to generate direct funds, namely about 40 percent of the total funds needed for the construction of public housing. The remaining funds came from other municipal and federal resources. Introduced in 1923, the highly progressive housing construction tax was calculated on the basis of the yearly rent for apartments and commercial spaces. Over 40 percent of the total

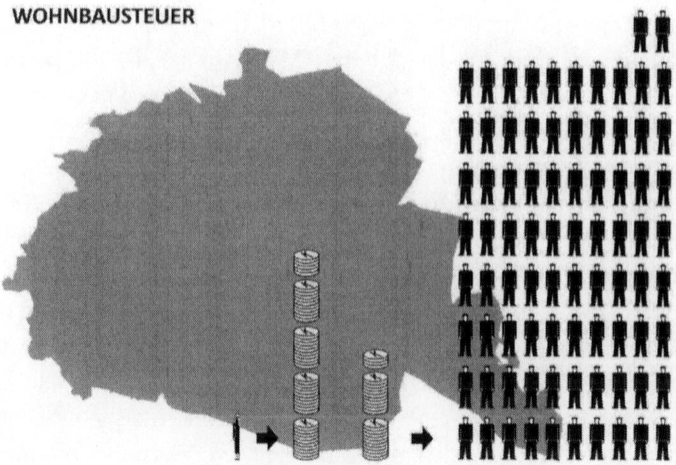

2.3 Housing Tax Isotype. Copyright: © Sophie Hochhäusl

funds generated by the so-called 'Breitner tax' came from taxing rental properties whose yearly rent amounted to more than 10,000 crowns. These were typically luxury apartments and prime commercial spaces, which constituted only 0.5 percent of the city's total rental stock. The yearly rent for the great majority of the city's rental units, 86 percent, amounted to about 1,200 crowns. The tenants of these units were typically working class or lower-middle class. Despite representing the great majority of tenants, the funds generated by taxing them amounted to only 24 percent of the total funds created by the new tax (Danneberg 1929, pp. 65–68). Put simply, the construction of public housing was to a considerable part financed by the wealthy [see Illustration 2.3]. Unsurprisingly, the opposition made up of the Christian Socials and the Great German People's Party [*Großdeutsche Volkspartei*, GDVP] was appalled by the new tax and equated it with 'tax sadism' and 'housing bolshevism' (Maimann 1981, p. 68). The socialists, by contrast, sought to make sure that the tax would be publicly remembered long past its introduction. Accordingly, a publicly visible inscription can be found on every *Gemeindebau,* an inscription that reads: 'Built from the funds of the Housing Construction Tax'.

In 1923, the first five-year construction program was finally inaugurated: 25,000 apartments were built and finished one year ahead of schedule. The first building program was followed by a second one in 1927, ushering in the erection of additional 30,000 public housing units. In conjunction with the housing built before 1923, the SDAP created a total of 64,000 apartments during the Red Vienna period (Danneberg 1929, pp. 27–29). By 1934, the city government was Vienna's biggest landlord, furnishing low-cost housing for eleven percent of the total population (Maderthaner 2006, p. 381). Before the introduction of rent control, the average rent amounted to about 25 percent of a workers' average wage; after rent control was introduced, it was equal to as little as two percent of a medium wage (Danneberg 1929, p. 59). To ensure that rents would be low in the long run, the cost spent on housing was non-recoverable, that is, the *Gemeindebauten* were built on *fonds perdus* (Danneberg 1929, pp. 61–63)

The Social Democrats transformed the municipality into the city's largest landlord but also its largest employer. To curb unemployment in addition to reducing the housing shortage, the city created jobs for 30,000 people, predominantly in the 'municipalized' construction industry (Gulick 1948, p. 401). Accordingly, large parts of the taxes collected for housing construction were reinvested in the local economy in the form of public expenditures. Consequently, and ironically, these expenditures sustained rather than abolished existing capitalist relations of production. Instead of transforming the latter into socialist ones, the Social Democrats sought, at least in the medium term, to render capitalism more 'humane' by reigning in – instead of expanding – Taylorist rationalization and industrialization. As the historian Thomas Hughes explains:

> Taylor's fundamental concept and guiding principle was to design a system of production involving both men and machines that would be as efficient as a well-designed, well-oiled machine. He said, 'in the past, man has been first; in the future the system must be first,' a remark that did not sit well then with workers and their trade-union leaders and that today still rankles those who feel oppressed by technology. (Hughes 1989, p. 188)

In contrast to Taylor, for the Social Democrats, man clearly came first. Considerations of securing dignified labor and of curbing unemployment played a role in the Social Democrats' decision against rationalizing the economy; and so did the fear of an anti-socialist backlash in response to the possibility that a radical technological restructuring might usher in a temporary shortage of goods. To avert such a scenario, Bauer stipulated '[t]he task of socialism' to be one of instituting a 'more just distribution of goods, without doing harm to the production of goods' (Bauer 1919/1978, pp. 148–149). This 'just distribution of goods' was expected to provide workers with a foretaste of socialism. Maybe in anticipation of the risk that foretasting might lessen the taste for the end goal of socialism, the Austro-Marxists complemented their medium-term strategy of redistribution with a strategy of educating the people on the 'cultural ideal of a higher form of societal organization' (Bauer 1928, p. 281). Unsurprisingly, the pedagogical strategy to anchor the long-term perspective of socialism in people's minds and souls found its way into and shaped the 'everydayness' of dwelling.

2.3 Building for 'New Men': Two Approaches to Social Emancipation

In the communal housing blocks, the 'socialist principles of solidarity' were expected to turn into a 'vivid reality' (Braunthal 1948, p. 494). Yet what were the principles underlying the architecture of the *Gemeindebauten* and its related 'politics of dwelling'? Given the Social Democrats' official celebration of public housing as a site of a socialist culture in the bourgeois city, one would assume that the SDAP had a well-defined concept of what socialist housing should look like and a concrete program for the concept's realization. However, in lieu of a programmatic conceptual vision, one is left with, on the one hand, a vague manifesto for the 'new socialist men' (Adler 1924) and, on the other hand, rather general guidelines as to how to create a 'socialist' built environment. The general guidelines, laid out by the city, were mainly informed by repudiating existing building practices and housing conditions. Courtyards within building blocks were not to be merely for private use but also for public use. Apartments were not to be cut off from daylight and fresh air, which was often the case in traditional tenement housing for space-saving and profit-maximizing reasons. More generally, the new socialist dwellings were not to be sites of diseases but places of physical well-being and decompression. Therefore, apartment units were to be complemented with communal recreational and educational facilities (Blau 1999, pp. 176–177). Apart from the city's stipulation of these general guidelines, it was largely up to the commissioned architects to shape the *Gemeindebauten* and their vicinity and by doing so develop a 'new cultural standard of living' (City of Vienna 1923).

Given that the 400 communal housing blocks were designed and built by 200 architects committed to different styles, it is hard to imagine how the *Gemeindebauten* could have represented anything other than stylistic eclecticism. The fact that the municipality abstained from defining an architectural vision for the housing program *prima facie* was subject to much criticism, even from within the SDAP's own ranks. The prominent economist, philosopher, and member of the Vienna Circle, Otto Neurath, expressed one of these critiques. In 1925, he sought to convince representatives of the municipality to commit to a *Gesamtarchitekturplan* [general architectural plan], a plan that would replace the already ongoing piecemeal building activities within the given urban structure. According to Neurath, the urban form of the immanent 'new age' ought to replace the urban form of the past. In his opinion, the 'spirit of calm objectivity' in the form of clear lines and surfaces was destined to supplant the hegemonic aesthetic of the ornamental and decorative. Although Neurath confirmed that a truly *proletarian* aesthetic can only emanate *after* the proletariats' full empowerment, that is, after the realization of a new social and economic order that redefines men's feeling, thinking, longing, he was convinced that *any* new proletarian aesthetic would seek its inspiration from modern technology and rationalization instead of petty bourgeois, feudal, or monarchic traditions (Neurath 1926a, p. 63).

The reason for Neurath's conviction that the proletariat would ultimately be drawn to functionalism and rationalism was rooted in his optimistic perspective on history and technology. Neurath believed socialism to be informed by industrial and technical centralization, tendencies that are already immanent to capitalism (Pfoser 1982). Since these tendencies shaped workers' consciousness in fundamental ways, workers would, once they were politically empowered, appropriate the axioms undergirding large-scale industries, such as rational organization, and transpose them to the private sphere. In other words, instead of being dominated by industrial-capitalist functionalism, *emancipated* workers would have successfully appropriated industrial-capitalism's 'normative power of facticity' (Hösl and Pirhofer 1982, p. 158) and thereby gradually obtained the 'goal of happiness' [*Glücksziel*] (Neurath 1926b, p. 51). To be sure, while Neurath was enthusiastic about rationalization, he did not embrace it blindly. On the contrary, he stressed the importance of always carefully and systematically evaluating the extent to which rationalization would be beneficial or harmful to the workers' physical and psychological well-being. Any decision on rationalization had to be based on the findings of such evaluations (Blau 2013; Pfoser 1982). On the urban scale, Neurath wanted to see the workers' appropriation of modernization reflected at the aesthetic level in the form of a *Generalarchitekturplan* [general architectural plan]. A 'brainchild of art', as one might call it, the general architectural plan for Red Vienna was to complement the city's existing *Generalregulierungsplan* [general development plan], a 'brainchild of engineering'. Whereas the general development plan represented the metropolis only in two dimensions, by outlining its technical and social infrastructure, such as streets, canalization, electrification, or zoning, the general architectural plan also envisioned the city aesthetically as a three-dimensional 'cultural, political, and aesthetic unity' informed by rationalism and functionalism (Arbeiter Zeitung 1923).

The municipality, however, remained unconvinced of Neurath's commitment to capitalize on the *social* potential implicit in economic and technological modernization and to represent it aesthetically by adopting a *Maschinenästhetik* [machine aesthetic] for the city at large. Thus, instead of entrusting city building to affiliates of modernism such as Neurath, who sought to break with traditional aesthetics in search of a new aesthetic language inspired by technological innovation while also being concerned with real human needs, the municipality chose architects who, as the architectural historian Friedrich Achleitner put it, drew on the vocabulary of the old to think new thoughts. In short, in place of post-WWI 'radical modernism' as envisaged by Otto Neurath and others, Otto Wagner's nineteenth-century legacy of 'moderate modernism' was to shape Red Vienna in general and the *Gemeindebauten* in particular, an *aesthetic* legacy that coincided in many regards with the Austro-Marxists' *political* legacy.

Almost all of Red Vienna's architects were trained in Otto Wagner's school of architecture and were thus heavily influenced by his principles of city planning and building. For Wagner, striking a balance between modern urban life, locality, and history was key to urban planning and design. Yet in contrast to his contemporary Camillo Sitte (1843–1903), a radical critic of modernity, Otto Wagner (1841–1918) was forward-looking and was committed to building for *modern* men. Unlike the modernists of the 1920s, however, Wagner did not seek to invent new forms *ex novo* but instead aimed to gradually stake them out by creatively working with given local, material, and financial parameters. A key question he encouraged his students always to ask themselves before embarking on a new architectural project was:

> How will this solution relate to modern men, to the assignment, to the genius loci, the climatic conditions, the materials at hand, and the financial means? Only thus can you hope to elicit true appreciation, and only then will the works of architecture that today are met for the most part with incomprehension or a certain tentativeness become generally understandable, original, and even popular. (Wagner 1988, p. 160)

Similar to Neurath, Wagner was also a critic of the one-sidedness of the development plan, which he believed reduced the modern metropolis to a conglomerate of different economic and infrastructural functions squeezed into a rational grid system. In 1892/1893, Wagner proposed an alternative development plan, one that recognized the city not merely as an economic entity but also as a cultural and architectonic one. Yet in contrast to what modernists such as Neurath would suggest, Wagner's alternative development plan was committed to paying attention to 'the poetry of the past' (Marx 1852/1978, p. 597) and not only to that of the future – that is, to custom, use, and habit. Although Wagner's development plan was also never realized, it was revealing of his architectural outlook, which his students later adopted for Red Vienna's *Gemeindebauten*. For him, the two most important tasks of city-building were the meticulous realization of function and the latter's consecration by art (Wagner 1911, p. 2). Despite Wagner's emphasis on time and place, he did not lose sight of the city in its totality. In fact, the expanding metropolis, the *Grossstadt*, was the architectonic unit he was most interested in, a unit he envisioned as a cluster of interrelated wards of 100,000 to 150,000 inhabitants, each ward with its own civic structures, amenities, as well as places and buildings informed by local conditions and history. Yet, while constituting unique spatial units, the individual wards were connected to one another by a grid that connected them to a thoroughly rationalized entity: the continuously growing modern metropolis (Wagner 1911) [see Illustration 2.4].

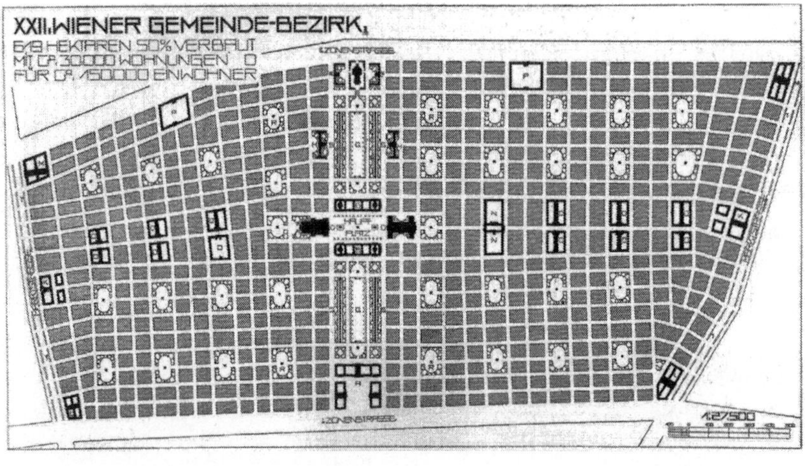

2.4 Otto Wagner's Vision of the Modern Metropolis

Despite the fact that also Wagner's concept for an entirely new metropolis was never realized, important aspects of it found their way into the design of the *Gemeindebauten*. It was Wagner's students who took the metropolis as their model, interweaving the multiform, multipurpose spaces of the 'new' Vienna with those of the old, to recast the metropolis as one in which workers had prominent homes: multiform, multipurpose *Rote Höfe* [red building blocks] (Blau 1999, 238–249), as the municipal building blocks were called.

In the absence of a concrete vision for a city in which 'new men' were to flourish and dwell, it was up to the creativity of the entrusted architects to engrave democratic socialism into urban and residential space. Redeeming the promise of democratic socialism spatially meant that they had 'to build against the existing building ordinances while safely remaining within them' (Blau 1999, p. 172). People's palaces became to perforate the bourgeois city. A closer look at the four main building types that were ultimately adopted – the perimeter block, the infill [*Lückenverbauung*], the residential quarter, and the superblock – reveals that the Wagner-inspired architects *did* indeed find ways to mark the beginning of a new era. As the architectural historian Eve Blau puts it: 'Intricately interwoven with the historical spaces of Old Vienna, the spaces of the New Vienna not only call into question the traditional socio-spatial relationships they describe but also generate a discursive space in the city that is tangible, public and perpetually unresolved' (1999, p. 339).

The most common building type was the *Block- und Randverbauung* [perimeter block building]. Whereas the existing urban grid determined the boundaries of the lot, Red Vienna's architects decided to build the housing complexes along the lot's outer margins to transform its center into public and communal spaces in the form of parks, playgrounds, and paddle pools. In defiance of the logic of profit maximization, which resulted in buildings that covered up to 85 percent of the land, the *Gemeindebauten* only consumed up to 50 percent of the available space to ensure that the courtyards – whose use was, historically speaking, the prerogative of landlords – would be big enough to serve recreational and communal purposes. Apart from creating spaces of socialization, the building block's vast communal spaces also served the purpose of providing the apartments with daylight and fresh air, essentials that inhabitants of traditional proletarian tenement housing were often deprived of (Weihsmann 1985, pp. 126–128).

The *Lückenverbauung* [infill building] was another building type that was adopted, one that was the most literal spatial embodiment of the Austro-Marxists' politics of 'growing into' socialism. Since the municipality owned more gaps in between buildings than free-standing large lots and, since it did not dispose of effective expropriation laws that would have provided the city with access to larger lots, about 50 percent of Red Vienna's municipal housing took the form of infills. Because the inherited building ordinances prescribed that any new buildings had to blend in with their surrounding in terms of height and use, the city and its architects sought to be creative and to nonetheless visually demarcate a difference between public and private housing. For this purpose, two strategies were adopted. Wherever possible, the city gradually and over time purchased adjacent tenement housing to provide architects with additional space to be transformed into communal and public space. If this strategy was not possible, it commissioned architects and craftsmen to decorate the facades of the *Gemeindebauten* with *Kunst-am-Bau* [art on the building], that is, with art whose purpose was to foreground the municipal housing's public function (Weihsmann 1985, p. 126).

If the infill buildings symbolized the SDAP's aim of gradually growing into socialism, the size of Red Vienna's residential quarters and superblocks embodied the party's yearning for a politics of scale. Residential quarters were built in working-class districts with poor local infrastructure. Along with public housing, new social, cultural, and commercial hubs were created, which transformed entire areas once designated as industrial zones into multifunctional urban quarters. Instead of inserting itself into the city center, the residential quarters created socialized urban islands on the city's industrial fringes (Blau 1999, p. 282). The superblock, by contrast, operated not on the outskirts of the old city but in the city's heart. It typically spanned several city blocks; bridged or incorporated streets, accommodated parks, and communal facilities; and housed hundreds – sometimes thousands – of people. Similar to the residential quarter, the superblock reversed the hegemonic differentiation of functions prescribed since the nineteenth century not by altering existing planning principles but by using architecture *strategically* to create an environment in which social functions that had been torn apart – functions such as dwelling, work, leisure, and circulation – would be reintegrated.

The most famous superblock is the *Karl-Marx-Hof* – Red Vienna's flagship. 'Long after we are gone, these stones will speak for us', so were the words of Karl Seitz, Vienna's mayor from 1923 to 1934, at the block's opening ceremony in October 1930. The *Karl-Marx-Hof* was built on unused city land in between a bourgeois residential area and an industrial area. It accommodated 5,500 people in 1,325 apartments and was equipped with two central laundries, two bathhouses, two kindergartens, a youth center, a dental clinic, a health insurance office, a polyclinic clinic, a pharmacy, a post office, several physicians, coffee shops, clubs, and 25 stores–all within a total area of 35.5 acres. The building itself covered only 18.4 percent of land; the rest was used for extensive gardens and parks (Nussbaum 2007, pp. 51–52) [see Illustration 2.5].

By committing to both the metropolis and inner-city workers' palaces, the SDAP opted against an alternative vision for housing the proletariat, one that existed in Vienna since 1915: self-help settlements at the metropolis' periphery. Whereas historically, settlement movements typically subscribed

2.5 Karl Marx-Hof (1930). © Bildarchiv Austria

to bourgeois, picturesque, anti-urban values, the Viennese movement was an anti-picturesque, co-operative, self-help movement that was inextricably bound to the cultivation of food and the construction of makeshift housing (Hochhäusl 2011, 2019). Due to the catastrophic living conditions during and in the immediate aftermath of WWI, urban dwellers left the city to squat on and live off public land. By 1918, 6.5 million square meters had been turned into arable land and more than 100,000 people lived in makeshift shelters (Blau 1999, p. 90). Politically, the settlers had close ties to the Social Democrats who actively supported them until 1923, the year the first mass housing program was launched, by dedicating 30 percent of all fiscal means for housing to the construction of settlements (Hochhäusl 2011, pp. 30–31) [see Illustration 2.6].

Ultimately, the city withdrew its funding for settlements and concentrated on the construction of inner-city housing instead. In contrast to what one might suspect, the decision for building housing in the *Grossstadt* [metropolis] instead of the *Gartenstadt* [garden city] was driven less by ideological concerns than by legal and financial ones. First, the funds created by the housing construction tax were legally bound for reinvestment in inner-city housing. Second, the municipality did not dispose over the land needed for developing settlements on a grander scale, as the green girdle surrounding Vienna belonged to the province of Lower Austria. Third, the construction costs for suburban settlements were considerable higher than for inner-city *Gemeindebauten*, since the former also necessitated the provision of

2.6 Viennese Settlement Movement, Rosenhügel around 1921. © AH! Vienna

additional infrastructure such as streets or canalization (Gulick 1948, p. 490; European Planning Studies 1995).

Yet by deciding against the settlement movement, including its visions of the city and dwelling, for reasons that might have been financially and legally sound, the SDAP also decided against an alternative approach to democratic socialism: one that was committed to building the latter from the bottom up. The socio-economic theory that undergirded the settlement movement was influenced by English guild socialism, which conceived of settlers not only as passive recipients of (local) state-provided housing but also as active and involved producers and administrators (Cole and Vernon 1980). Guild socialism pleaded for state ownership of industry, including the building industry. It also stood for workers' control through delegation of (local) state authority to workers' guilds, including building and consumer guilds, that were organized along democratic lines. One of the movement's key figures was again Otto Neurath who, in 1920, became the Chief Secretary of the Austrian Settlement and Allotment Garden Association, a governing body that, in 1922, counted 50,000 members and oversaw 230 affiliated clubs (Hochhäusl 2011, p. 28). Having been involved in the attempt to establish the Bavarian Soviet Republic in 1919, Neurath was committed to building socialism from the bottom up. He considered workers' self-organization, their participation and co-operation in housing construction, and administration as essential for their socialization, a form of socialization informed by immediate practical, self-educative, and self-empowering experience instead of expert-imparted knowledge (Neurath 1926a, 1926b, 1928).

During Neurath's leadership, the settlement movement pursued three overlapping strategies to bring about socialism by democratic means: an economic, a political, and an educational one. On the economic level, the settlers established a *Gemeinwirtschaft* [communal or co-operative economy] that revolved around collective ownership, shared infrastructure, and the contribution to the building process by unpaid labor. The communal economy's implementation went hand in hand with political efforts to strengthen the settlers' fiscal, judicial, and legislative power at the municipal level. While seeking a certain degree of autonomy from the city, the settlers also worked closely together with it to draw, for instance, on existing infrastructure. With regard to the educational strategy, the settlement association organized classes in agriculture, horticulture, vegetables and fruit growing, cooking, canning, and the keeping of small animals. It also provided lectures on architectural and urban topics, such as the construction of settlements or the emergence of garden cities. Since many settlers were unemployed workers and had a distinctly industrial and urban background, they offered classes aimed at equipping workers with the skills necessary to create a livelihood co-operatively and, at the same time, to educate and empower themselves (Blau 2013; Hochhäusl 2011, pp. 28–32, 2019).

Neurath was at the helm of the settlers' association, and he was also the founder of the settlers' school. Given his quest for democratizing knowledge, Neurath invented pictorial statistics. He hoped that by translating statistical information into a visual language consisting of self-explanatory signs and symbols, he would enable *all* people to 'participate in a common culture' and thereby help to eliminate 'the canyon between educated and uneducated' (Survey Graphic 1937). Neurath was minutely aware of the fact that historically, statistics were an instrument of domination. More often than not, they were used to study and exploit the working class by, for instance, evaluating the advantages to be gained from rationalization. In order to end the workers' subjection to the statistical meta-form of knowledge, Neurath's goal, inspired by Marx's *A Workers' Inquiry* (1938), was to create a visual language that would allow the uneducated to use statistics for their own advantage: to better understand their own working and living conditions and, consequently, to identify possible solutions to their own problems (Neurath 1979, pp. 293–294; Pircher 1982, pp. 164–165).

In 1923, the settlement association organized the 'Viennese Small Garden, Settlement, and Housing Exhibition', which put pictorial statistics, pamphlets, and even entire houses on display. The exhibit demarcated a new position on urbanism, one that incorporated the perspective and history of people who had so far been mere objects instead of subjects, let alone agents of urbanization. The exhibit also demonstrated a new way of *depicting* urbanism by using socio-political maps informed by graphic rules and graphic vocabulary, maps whose goal was to ensure that the visitor, regardless of his educational background, would find 'reflected his problems, his past, his future – himself' (Survey Graphic 1933). With both the settlement association and the settlement school, Neurath sought to overcome the workers' subjection to urbanization and the abstracting, 'colonizing' knowledge that pertained to it. The cornerstone of his 'method' of emancipation was the *experience* of self-efficacy and self-empowerment, an experience that was to be made through enabling praxis, such as house building, subsistence farming, and, more generally, the co-operative organization of everyday life.

Although Neurath and his ideas were respected within the SDAP, they did not become hegemonic. The SDAP opted for a different strategy to prepare for socialism: the public provision of housing. While in 1919, Bauer still deemed self-organization, self-administration, and self-government to be essential for bringing about democratic socialism (Bauer 1976e, pp. 118–131), the SDAP's policies would soon reveal a proclivity for the emancipation of workers through political representation. This strategy, as underscored by the architectural historian Eve Blau, also left material traces, among others, in building typology. The *Rote Hof* [red building blocks], understood as a type, stands for what the SDAP and its architects conceived of an ideal and representative dwelling for workers and future socialists. Two key characteristics shape the *Rote Hof*: the integration of various spaces, namely public space (such as streets, courtyards, civic institutions), semi-public space (communal spaces, such as libraries or clubs), and private space (apartments) and, relatedly the reconciliation of different spatial uses and functions (such as dwelling, recreation, play, communication, cultural and political organization, education, consumption, and circulation). The SDAP celebrated the *Rote Höfe* as *Volkswohnpaläste* [people's palaces] and as *the* antidote to *Zinsburgen* [rent-bearing fortresses] that were typical of the Liberal and Christian Social era (Blau 1999, pp. 218–227). Clearly, the question of how people live was part and parcel of the fierce struggles over political and cultural hegemony in post-WWI Vienna (Wasserman 2014) and left discursive, but also material traces.

There is no doubt that Red Vienna's municipal housing *does* embody emancipation from precarious, overcrowded, and poor living conditions. And yet, the people inhabiting the 'people's palaces' were neither involved in deciding upon the municipal housing's parameters nor consulted concerning their needs and desires. Thus, the *Gemeindebauten* clearly embody an appropriation of the city *for* the proletariat by the party and party-appointed experts rather than an appropriation of the city *by* the proletariat *for* the proletariat. In part, the SDAP's proclivity to bring about democratic socialism 'from above' and in an ordered way was driven by a fierce opposition constantly lying in ambush and waiting for tensions within the workers' movement and the possibility to capitalize on them. Yet, this proclivity is also indicative of a gulf between the Social Democratic decision-makers (and their indebtedness to bourgeois norms in some respects) and its proletarian electoral basis. This gulf shaped the approach to building types. It also shaped debates about dwelling culture – a debate in which the very meaning of social emancipation was, once more, negotiated and, ultimately, also defined.

2.4 The Lures of the Past in the New Socialist Dwelling Culture

The emergence of the *Rote Hof* as Red Vienna's model type building was coupled with the crystallization of the *Gemeinde-Wien*-type apartment. Similar to the *Rote Hof*, the building guidelines for the new apartments were mainly informed by *re*-visions of existing sub-standard living conditions in proletarian tenement housing instead of visionary takes on the dwelling culture to come. Rooms were to be lit and ventilated directly instead of indirectly; each apartment was to be equipped with its own access (instead of shared access) to running water and washrooms; apartments were to be furnished with electricity, gas, tiled floors in the kitchen, and hardwood floors in the other rooms (Blau 1999, pp. 167–177; Gulick 1948, p. 450). Yet what was clearly not informed by a 'new socialist age' was the gradually hegemonized dwelling culture. Instead of challenging dominant bourgeois dwelling traditions, the SDAP's political elite largely rendered bourgeois domestic culture – the culture the elite itself was socialized into – the *conditio sine qua non* of dignified human dwelling (Sieder 1988, p. 418). Norms of privacy, kitchen design, the forms of social control exercised in the communal housing blocks, approaches to education (be it education on reproduction or aesthetics), and allocation policies were deeply steeped in the poetry of the 'bourgeois' past and hardly bore the inscription of a socialist future (although visions of the latter existed, including visions for dwelling).

One important feature of bourgeois dwelling culture is privacy. The semi-privacy of the proletarian dwelling, a dwelling that typically accommodated extended families and that was not strictly divided from the dwelling of neighbors, was increasingly superseded by the privacy that characterized dwellings of the bourgeois nuclear family. This *Wendung nach Innen* [turn toward the interior] (Sieder 1988, p. 416) entailed, among others, the abolition of the semi-private gangways that connected apartments in traditional tenement housing and the creation of hallways inside the apartments. Both innovations had the effect of pushing living areas further back into the interior of the dwelling. By dispensing with the gangways, the city officials and architects not only eliminated the inconveniences of sharing water and toilets and exposure to neighbors' noise and their kitchen smells but, in the process, also abolished a place that was crucial for the formation of informal practices of mutual support and solidarity, especially among women. Without romanticizing the difficult and precarious living conditions in traditional tenement housing, oral histories from the 1980s show that, facilitated by an architecture that fostered semi-privacy over privacy, certain elements of the tenements were remembered positively. Among the positive memories are the mutual support of neighbors and family members regarding household chores and child-rearing; the informal exchange of information and knowledge on issues such as health, birthing, child-rearing, housework, and the labor market among peers as opposed to information and knowledge imparted upon workers by city-appointed experts; and a degree of protection against domestic violence by the apartments' semi-privacy, which increased the social pressure on potential perpetrators (Sieder 1988, pp. 271–274, 418, 423).

Although generally speaking, the SDAP elite paid only limited attention to existing proletarian culture, in its first housing program (1923), it accommodated the proletariat's preference for multifunctional *Wohnküchen* [live-in kitchens], kitchens that served not only the purpose of cooking but also that of living, dwelling, and socializing. As one observer noted in the SDAP's periodical, *Arbeiter-Zeitung,* in 1924: 'Whatever time the Viennese worker has during the day, [it] is spent in the kitchen, and if there is no dining table available to sit at, [he] will perch on a coal box or bench' (Fuchs, 1924). Yet by the time the second building program was launched in 1927, traditional proletarian dwelling culture had again been largely sidestepped. In an attempt to 'westernize' the Viennese dwellings, that is, in an effort to make them more akin to their modernist German counterparts, a commitment to rationalization had also finally found its way into the Viennese working class kitchen. As a matter of fact, by 1927 the proletarian *Wohnküche* was largely replaced by Margarete Schuette-Lihotsky's *Arbeitsküche* [work kitchen], a functional kitchen informed by Taylorist time and motion studies, one that no longer served social or recreational purposes but solely that of (presumably) time- and labor-saving cooking (Blau 1999, pp. 198–199; Hochhäusl

2.7 Replica of Schütte-Lihotzky's Frankfurter Küche, Museum of Applied Arts (MAK), Vienna. © Gerald Zugmann, Vienna

2013; Oldenziel and Zachmann 2009). The task of meal preparation, which in traditional working-class housing was shared among several (female) family members and neighbors, became a task to be fulfilled in private and solitude by women [see Illustration 2.7].

This happened even though a real-world experiment in socializing (as opposed to further privatizing) reproductive labor existed. In 1925, the municipality funded the one-kitchen house called *Heimhof*, tenement housing for professional, middle-class women. At the *Heimhof*, cooking, cleaning, and laundry washing were taken care of by professional, paid house staff. Because the service costs at the *Heimhof* were high and because there was resistance against the *Heimhof* also by women who conceived of the professionalization of reproductive work as an attack on their identity, the city decided against rolling out the *Heimhof* experiment on a large scale and normalizing the professionalization of reproductive labor (Gruber 1991, pp. 51–52).

In the *Rote Höfe* [red building blocks], cooking was to remain an individualized affair *and* a female one. Laundry washing and child rearing, by contrast, became a more communal affair *and* was reshaped by disciplinary power. In the communal *Waschküchen* [laundry kitchens], women were supervised by city-appointed male *Waschmeister* [laundry foremen] who made sure that the female inhabitants stuck to a predetermined washing schedule and the pace of the available machines. If they failed to do so, they would forfeit their right to use the communal facilities. When looking at oral history, the communal laundry facilities were commonly remembered as sites of stress and hazing (Pirhofer and Sieder 1982, pp. 354–355). In terms of child support, the city did provide childcare facilities in almost every larger municipal housing block. Yet it also stepped up the standards for child rearing. Critical of traditional practices of parenting in proletarian families, practices that made, as Otto Bauer worried, '*husbands* [emphasis added] often only know the dark sides of family life', leading to their escape into inns (Bauer 1976e, p. 120), the SDAP set up services such as *Mutter- und Eheberatungsstellen* [counseling for mothering and marriage] in municipal housing blocks. The main target group was, again, women, and they were instructed by specialists in hygiene and pedagogy. 'The more we take care of our youth, the less we have to take care of the old', so said Julius Tandler, Red Vienna's city councilor at the Department for Welfare and Public Health. 'What we spend on the welfare of pregnant women and newborns, we will save on prisons and asylums [my translation]'. To avoid 'short-sighted humanism', unproductive demographic expenses had to be eliminated by means of sterilization if necessary (quoted in Maimann 1981, p. 79). Thus, taking care of the health of oneself and one's family was not merely a matter of individual well-being but one of social responsibility: the health of the entire *Bevölkerungskörper* [population body] was at stake (Tandler 1928, p. 14). To ensure that the transmitted knowledge on health and hygiene was applied at home, *Fürsorgerinnen* [welfare workers], housing inspectors, and teachers were entitled to report 'un-orderly families' to the city. In extreme cases, the Department for Welfare and Public Health intervened and separated children from their families to accommodate them temporarily or permanently in municipal foster homes (Gruber 1991, pp. 71–73).

Concern for the 'population body' also informed the municipalities' allocation policies. The apartments were allocated based on a point system, which took criteria such as overcrowding, disability, residence, and citizenship into account, as well as marital status, pregnancy, and the number of children. Although the SDAP had promised to provide accommodation for the homeless and disabled in particular, its actual allocation praxis gave preference to young families because they constituted the most important demographic stratum for bringing about the 'new men' and also because it was an effective way to de-normalize the extended family and normalize the nuclear family model (Gruber 1991, pp. 61–62).

This entrenchment of – instead of break with – an 'episteme of bourgeois suspicion' (Maderthaner and Musner 2008, p. 60) toward proletarian culture also underpins discussions of and on the aesthetic of the proletariat in prominent Social Democratic outlets. Numerous architects and pedagogical reformers were displeased with the proletariat's proclivity for sentimental knickknacks, embellishments, and ornaments. One of them was Richard Wagner, a newspaper editor and educator who openly expressed his disgust with the 'junk amassed in proletarian dwellings', junk that makes the inhabitant 'tread on eggshells to not hurt himself' in one of the Social Democrats' main periodicals on pedagogy. According to Wagner, 'the pictures of saints and royalty, the postcards and artistically vulgar reproductions, and, particularly, the homemade antimacassars used to prettify the furniture' were clear materializations of an 'education to submissiveness'. To countervail the latter, Anna Bloch, another pedagogical reformer, suggested systematically anchoring fine art in proletarian homes: not by putting up canonic paintings on walls but by storing them in dust-free folders:

> [E]ach proletarian household should own a collection of artistic paintings to be kept in folders as dust free as possible to ensure that they are available whenever the proletarian is need of emotional edification. On such occasions, these treasures should be retrieved and pondered at in a quiet corner of the apartment. (1928)

Workers had a penchant for sentimental knick-knack and kitsch. Numerous socialist reformers, however, wanted to see this penchant gradually supplanted by a new proletarian aesthetic, an aesthetic informed by rationalism and functionalism. An austere, uncluttered interior, unburdened by history and memory was presented as an aesthetic ideal, an ideal that was, in addition, often coupled with the (pseudo-)feminist argument[6] that rationalism

6 I refer to this claim as '(pseudo-)feminist' because neither Taut nor Schuster nor Schacherl sought to actually evaluate whether a minimalist interior would indeed lessen the burden

and functionalism would automatically lessen the burden of household chores (Taut 1926; Schuster and Schacherl 1926).

Otto Neurath belonged to the proponents of a rationalist and functionalist dwelling culture. In line with other socialist reformers, he was critical of the proletariat's love for the sentimental, which, for Neurath, clearly mirrored a 'lack of class consciousness' – an uncritical embrace of the capitalists' obsession with appearance and possession. According to Neurath, in a truly socialist society, both had to be gradually overcome (Neurath 1926a, p. 62). However, in contrast to most reformers within the SDAP, Neurath did not consider the implementation of a new, proletarian aesthetic to be a matter of pedagogy. Instead, a new proletarian aesthetic was only likely to emanate on the basis of an encompassing *social* transformation that involved the active and creative participation of workers in shaping *all* fields of social life. Only if the organized proletariat were *actively* and *practically* involved in the construction of a proletarian counter-culture, an involvement that would encompass the construction of housing and the building of furniture, would workers experience their own capacities and with them, self-empowerment and emancipation. Neurath:

> The internal transformation of things and men [...] will only fully unfold where proletarian majorities or proletarian co-operatives are builders and where the organized working class has control over the production of furniture or influences the latter in decisive ways. Only on a social basis, a new form of life, a new experience of art can emerge. From art education alone, especially from an introduction to art history, hardly anything essential can be derived for the formation of a proletarian way of life as long as the proletariat has not yet become mature for the conscious creation of the present. [my translation] (1926b, p. 52)

Neurath decidedly abstained from interpreting the proletarian culture as backward and, by doing so, refrained from uncritically assuming a distance between the knowledgeable and the ignorant, a distance many of his fellow reformers had reiterated. In fact, in an attempt to make sense of why, for instance, the modernist *Maschinenästhetik* – an aesthetic he himself had hailed as that of the future – had difficulties warming the hearts of the proletariat, he conceded that modern rationality itself might be the problem.

of homemaking. Historically speaking, the rationalization of homemaking often raised the standards for homemaking and, by doing so, increased the time spent on reproductive work instead of reducing it (see, for instance, Ingeborg Beer, *Architektur fuer den Alltag*, 1994).

From a worker's perspective, it is this type of rationality that not only increases efficiency and thus production but also unemployment and hence precariousness (ibid.). The architect Josef Frank, another socialist proponent of rationalism and functionalism, struck a similar self-critical chord. Frank noted that the call for abolishing sentimentality was typically put forth by men and women who were scientifically or artistically engaged, in other words, by men and women whose everyday professional activities were emotionally rewarding. Frank concluded that, given their situation, creative men might have no need to extend sentimentality into their domestic sphere. Yet for industrial workers, the situation was fundamentally different. Because their work was usually deprived of pathos and sentimentality, it was understandable that they would yearn for the accommodation of both in their domestic sphere (Frank 1927, p. 49; Blau 2013).

Among Red Vienna's reformers, a deeper and sympathetic understanding of the working class's aesthetic predilections was often missing. The hegemonic position was one that depreciated existing working-class culture and that conjointly construed workers as objects of reform instead of agents of change. Although this depreciating position was criticized within the SDAP's own ranks – Neurath and Frank were two cases in point (Blau 2013) – in general, the party did not divert from its steered course of top-down socialization. Given that socialism was the goal of the Austro-Marxists' slow revolution, why was so little immediate political power given to the expected redeemers of the promise of socialism, the workers? As Max Adler explained, '[t]he burden of future democracy does not rest on politics, but on pedagogy' (1922, p. 185).

One reason for the SDAP's choice of pedagogy over politics was the concern that political action, especially if uncoordinated, could provoke the opposition, lead to a civil war, and thereby jeopardize the party's long-term goal of obtaining socialism by democratic means (Rabinbach 1989, pp. 55–60). Another reason for this choice was the fact that the party elite assumed its political basis to be lacking the necessary maturity for bringing about and sustaining socialism, an assumption coupled with an idealist notion of education that deemed insights into the laws of morality to be the *conditio sine qua non* for social transformation. Max Adler:

> 'To know in order to live' – with this phrase science assumes control of humanity's moral and social spirit, in whose ever-growing strength the full force of reality lives more powerfully than in the development of the intellect. [...] The leap from the realm of natural necessity into the realm of freedom is only accomplished by the practical action which deliberately

> subordinates the *comprehended* [emphasis added] regularities of nature to man's own self-imposed goals. (1904/1978, pp. 77–78)

Max Adler introduced a gap between knowing and living, between the comprehension of the laws of morality and their implementation in action, a gap that also involved a temporal component: a component that, in the name of 'growing into socialism' and progress, lent itself to pedagogical reform without an endpoint.

Adler's intellectual adversary was, once again, Neurath, whose philosophical hero was not Kant but Epicurus. Influenced by Epicurean materialism, Neurath was convinced that realizing socialism was neither a matter of morality nor of pedagogy but solely a matter of social action and (conscious and unconscious) dynamics (Pfoser 1982). Yet, as already mentioned above, it was not Neurath's rationale for praxis but Adler's rationale for the primacy of knowing over doing that was backed up by Bauer's socio-political outlook and, more generally, the SDAP's approach to social emancipation. As noted by Bauer (1976b), the main pathway out of the workers' alleged immaturity and their lack of culture was the proletarian class struggle. However, the class struggle that Bauer envisaged was less informed by a 'revolutionizing practice' – a practice that stressed 'the coincidence of the changing of circumstances and human activity' (Marx 1845/1978, p. 144)[7] – than by the idealist notion of *Bildung*, education built on a distance between theory and practice, between the educator and the ignorant.

In the context of Red Vienna's housing policies, experts in the fields of medicine, hygiene, child rearing, art, and architecture were to encourage workers to aspire to 'higher knowledge' and to seek pleasure in 'real art' (Gruber 1991, pp. 87–96). If necessary, encouragement was to give way to discipline. Thus, instead of asking the question of 'who is educating the educator', the Austro-Marxists opted for the *traditional* pedagogue and sought to alter social circumstances by spreading knowledge 'from above' – certainly not in all aspects of social life[8] but with a view to housing. Adler stressed the importance of breaking the 'intellectual state of affairs

7 Karl Marx: 'The materialist doctrine that men are products of circumstances and upbringing, and that, therefore changed men are products of other circumstances and changed upbringing, forgets that it is men who change circumstances and that it is essential to educate the educator himself. Hence, this doctrine necessarily arrives at dividing society into two parts, one of which is superior to society. The coincidence of the changing of circumstances and of human activity can be conceived and rationally understood only as revolutionizing practice' (Marx 1845/1978, p. 144).

8 Otto Glöckel, for instance, *did* break with traditional school teaching by introducing reform pedagogy.

in which the revolutionary class still thinks the thoughts of the old classes [...]' (Adler 1928/1978, p. 143), a break with 'the old' that the 'front men' of Austro-Marxism themselves did not always deliver on.

2.5 Red Vienna Turning Black

The proletarian basis had little influence on the chosen political and educational direction. Despite this situation and the discontents expressed regarding educating the uneducated, workers largely *did* support the decisions made by their party's leaders. They legitimized the steered course with their votes, with loyal party membership, and membership in the manifold cultural organizations. From 1919 to 1927, the SDAP's Viennese electorate increased from 54 percent to 60 percent (Holtmann 1996, pp. 126-7). Even in 1932, the year the National Socialist Workers Party [NSDAP] gained in popularity considerably and secured 17 percent of the votes, the SDAP remained the strongest party in city hall, securing 59 percent of the votes (Frei 1984, p. 59). Party membership was widespread. In the period from 1919 to 1929, it doubled at the federal level and quintupled in Vienna (Holtmann 1996, p. 127). Similarly, involvement with the party's numerous cultural and social organizations was popular, particularly in Vienna. By the early 1930s, the SDAP's loose network of more than 40 cultural organizations registered an aggregate of some 400,000 members, noteworthy for a city of less than two million (Gruber 1991, p. 81). There is no doubt that the SDAP greatly enhanced workers' quality of life by introducing social legislation and municipal institutions that provided for people from 'cradle to grave' – public provisions meant to secure a slow revolution towards socialism. Yet in contrast to the party's expectation, the provided *foretaste* of socialism under capitalism did not elicit the expected appetite for 'real' socialism. In fact, the vast majority of the SDAP's members showed little interest in a socialist revolution. Much to the dismay of Bauer, *Interessenssozialismus* [interest-driven socialism], socialism that aimed at quality-of-life improvements trumped *Gesinnungssozialismus* [conviction-driven socialism], that is, socialism that pursued the realization of the 'cultural ideal of higher form of societal organization' (Bauer 1928, p. 281). What marked the beginning of the end for Red Vienna was, however, not a lack of desire for a socialist revolution among the SDAP's electorate, a party that had also won the sympathy of the liberal upper-middle class (Wasserman 2014), but a chain of events that gradually shifted the tide in favor of the antimarxist opposition consisting of Christian Socials, German Nationals and National Socialists.

15 July 1927, for instance, marks one caesura in the Austro-Marxist experiment in general and Bauer's trust in political stability through an equilibrium between the classes in particular. In response to an acquittal of members of the mainly Christian Social, German National but also National Socialist paramilitary group *Österreichische Heimwehr,* who had killed a child and a member of the SDAP's paramilitary organization, members of the socialist paramilitary group *Schutzbund* took to the street to protest against the state's move toward *Klassenjustiz* [class-based judiciary]. During those protests, the seat of the judiciary, the *Justizpalast,* was set on fire, followed by violent and fatal confrontations between Social Democrats and the police. The events of 15 July 1927 had a disastrous impact on the Austro-Marxist experiment. It meant the death knell to the idea of a slow revolution towards socialism as well as to the hope for a peaceful competition for hegemony between progressives (socialists and members of the culturally liberal – often Jewish – upper-middle class) and conservatives (e.g. Catholic) as well as reactionary forces (fascist forces supported, among others, by Catholic and German National sympathizers with fascism) (Wasserman 2014).

Without doubt, the SDAP had created an impressive 'bulwark' of socialist organizations and infrastructure such as housing, public facilities, health care, cultural organizations, and educational institutions. Yet the turmoil in 1927 painfully disclosed a chink in the SDAP's armor: the Social Democrats had confounded the widespread popular support for the party and its social and cultural institutions with the party's actual political power and effectiveness. As Bauer remarked self-critically in 1936: 'If the working class had hoped to achieve a socialist order of society by utilizing democracy, it must now recognize that it has first to fight for its own dominance to build up a socialist social order before a complete and lasting democracy will be possible' (Bauer 1938/1978, p. 186).

In light of the opposition's gain in influence in the late 1920s, a gain that meant the normalization of anti-democratic, corporatist, and fascist norms and values, the SDAP found itself in a position in which its fight for socialism became secondary to its fight for democracy. In March 1933, the Christian Socials finally catapulted themselves into a position of ruling by decree under the aegis of Chancellor Engelbert Dollfuss, preparing the path for Austro-Fascism. The SDAP's last major attempt to resist the by then dominant reactionary forces in Vienna was in mid-February 1934. Using the *Gemeindebauten* as barricades, members of the *Schutzbund* fought the *Heimwehr* over the course of a few days. Yet it did not take long for the 'Red Fortresses' to fall in the civil war and with them not only the Austro-Marxist experiment in democratic socialism in Vienna, but democracy in Austria *tout court.*

What are the key insights from the preceding analyses of the Austro-Marxists' response to the housing question as a key social question? Red Vienna's 400 communal housing blocks embody a 'politics of place making' that was driven by considerations of social equality and the demand for the recognition of a class that had been the backbone of Vienna's modernization and yet had been deprived of modernization's fruits. By appropriating spaces and cultural markers of the imperial and bourgeois city, the *Gemeindebauten* not only symbolized the proletariat's political enfranchisement, they also generated important dialectical spaces between Old and New Vienna (Blau 1999, p. 15). Key political questions were projected onto the urban: whether housing is a right or a commodity; whose interests are written into urban space and which interests are sidestepped; who has access to the scientific, cultural, and educational achievements of modernity and what is to be made of these achievements. To be sure, the Social Democrats did not simply project these questions onto the urban fabric, they also sought to answer them. One of their answers was the municipal housing program. The introduction of the Federal Rent Control Act and the Breitner taxes brought an end to the free-market housing policies of pre-WW1 regulation. The creation of vast courtyards and parks for public use inside building blocks repudiated the principle of profit maximization. And the democratization of access to the cultural, educational, and medical facilities called into question the bourgeoisie's monopoly on culture and knowledge.

Yet the appropriation of bourgeois culture for the masses must also be seen in a critical light. It implied the failure to thoroughly question and evaluate the conditions of production and the signification of modern culture and science. While repeatedly evoking the emergence of a new 'socialist language' or the flourishing of 'new men', in numerous respects – such as dwelling culture, gender roles, family norms, the approach to and understanding of education – the SDAP did not always succeed in critically questioning or redefining inherited norms and understandings. It can be argued that Bauer and Adler's repeated emphasis on the reform of consciousness as an essential step toward breaking with inherited traditions, the type of reform the SDAP finally adopted, did not quite live up to the method of reform that one of their intellectual forefathers had in mind: 'the ruthless criticism of everything existing' to obtain a clearer picture of the meaning of one's own actions (Marx 1844/1978b, p. 13). With a view to social emancipation, the SDAP largely reentrenched inherited dividing lines between the erudite ('traditional intellectuals') and the ignorant (the workers). The Social Democratic elite's reluctance to support workers' self-organization and their spontaneous praxis, which existed as well and of which Otto Neurath was one proponent, stood in the way of the emergence of 'organic intellectuals', intellectuals who could have directed – and thus advanced – the aspirations of their *own* class (Gramsci 2008, pp. 6–7).

Without defending the SDAP's reluctance to subject its own organizational structures to a critical inquiry with a view to power and class relations, one might nonetheless try to make sense of this reluctance. It is clear that the Social Democrats' vision of the reform of consciousness as well as their vision of a social revolution clearly differed from those of Marx, who stated that proletarian revolutions have to

> [...] criticize themselves constantly, interrupt themselves continually in their own course, come back to the apparently accomplished in order to begin it afresh, deride with unmerciful thoroughness the inadequacies, weakness and paltriness of their first attempts, seem to throw down their adversary only in order that he may draw new strength from the earth and rise again more gigantic before them, recoil ever and anew from the indefinite prodigiousness of their own aims, until the situation has been created which makes all turning back impossible, and the conditions themselves cry out: Hic Rhodus, hic salta! (1852/1978, pp. 597–598).

In light of Marx's criteria for a socialist revolution, most importantly, the criteria of permanent (self-)critique, it is obvious that the SDAP's experiment with democratic socialism fell short of Marx's notion of a revolution. Yet the fact that the SDAP's elite eschewed (open) critical self-reflection is perhaps not only a sign of weakness but also a reflection of the difficult historical and political circumstances the Austro-Marxist experiment was embedded in. The party operated in a climate in which Christian Social, German National and National Socialist forces were keen on identifying differences and chasms within the workers' movement in order to widen them (Wasserman 2014). Although the *Gemeindebauten* turned out to be symbols of reform rather than revolution, they embodied a clear political answer to the housing question: that access to decent housing is a right (not a privilege) and that the provision of housing is a key public (and not merely private) task. Although Vienna's housing stock is by no means exempt from wider trends of neoliberal urban restructuring (Kadi 2015; Bärnthaler et al. 2020), to this day, about one-quarter of Vienna's population does still live in municipal housing, the most affordable form of housing, which the city has so far refused to privatize *despite* global trends to do so.

References

Adler, Max. 1904/1978. 'Causality and Teleology [From: Kausalität und Teleologie im Streite um die Wissenschaft]'. In *Austro-Marxism*, eds. Tom Bottomore and Patrick Goode, 76–78. Oxford: Clarendon Press.

———. 1922. *Die Staatsauffassung des Marxismus: Ein Beitrag zur Unterscheidung von soziologischen und juristischen Methoden*. Vienna: Wiener Volksbuchhandlung.

———. 1924. *Neue Menschen: Gedanken über sozialistische Erziehung*. Berlin: Laub.

———. 1928/1978. 'The Sociology of Revolution [From: Zur Soziologie der Revolution]'. In *Austro-Marxism*, eds. Tom Bottomore and Patrick Goode, 136–146. Oxford: Clarendon Press.

———. 1930/1978. 'Ideology as Appearance [From: Lehrbuch der materialistischen Geschichtsauffassung, Chapter 11]'. In *Austro-Marxism*, eds. Tom Bottomore and Patrick Goode. Oxford: Clarendon Press.

Adler, Victor. 1989. 'Zur Lage der Wienerberger Ziegelarbeiter'. In *Vision und Wirklichkeit: Ein Lesebuch zum Austromarxismus*, ed. Alfred Pfabigan, 18–24. Vienna: Löcker.

Bärnthaler, Richard, Andreas Novy, and Basil Stadelmann. 2020. 'A Polanyi-inspired Perspective on Social-ecological Transformations of Cities', *Journal of Urban Affairs* 1–25. DOI: 10.1080/07352166.2020.1834404.

Bauer, Otto. 1919/1978. 'Political and Social Revolution [From: Der Weg zum Sozialismus]'. In *Austro-Marxism*, eds. Tom Bottomore and Patrick Goode, 146–151. Oxford: Clarendon Press.

———. 1924/1978. 'Problems of the Austrian Revolution [From: Die österreichische Revolution]'. In *Austro-Marxism*, eds. Tom Bottomore and Patrick Goode, 156–167. Oxford: Clarendon Press.

———. 1927/1976. 'Sozialdemokratie, Religion und Kirche'. In *Otto Bauer. Werkausgabe, Vol. 3*, 449–531. Vienna: Europaverlag.

———. 1927/1978. 'What is Austromarxism?' In *Austro-Marxism*, eds. Tom Bottomore and Patrick Goode, 45–48. Oxford: Clarendon Press.

———. 1928. 'Klassenkampf und Ideologie', *Der Kampf. Sozialdemokratische Monatsschrift* 21 (7): 281–288.

———. 1936/1978. 'The Dictatorship of the Proletariat [From: Zwischen zwei Weltkriegen]'. In *Austro-Marxism*, eds. Tom Bottomore and Patrick Goode, 201–203. Oxford: Clarendon Press.

———. 1938/1978. 'Fascism [From: 'Der Faschismus', Der Sozialistische Kampf]'. In *Austro-Marxism*, eds. Tom Bottomore and Patrick Goode, 167–186. Oxford: Clarendon Press.

———. 1976a. 'Der Kampf um die Macht'. In *Werkausgabe: 2*, ed. Otto Bauer, 947–967. Vienna: Europaverlag.

———. 1976b. 'Der Weg zum Sozialismus'. In *Werkausgabe: 2*, ed. Otto Bauer, 89–131. Vienna: Europaverlag.

———. 1976c. 'Die österreichische Revolution'. In *Werkausgabe: 2*, ed. Otto Bauer, 489–866. Vienna: Europaverlag.

———. 1976d. 'Mieterschutz, Volkskultur und Alkoholismus'. In *Werkausgabe: 3*, ed. Otto Bauer, 593–608. Vienna: Europaverlag.

———. (ed.). 1976e. *Werkausgabe: 2*. Vienna: Europaverlag.

Blau, Eve. 1999. *The Architecture of Red Vienna. 1919–1934*. Cambridge, MA: MIT Press.

———. 2001. 'Die Kodifizierung von Identität und Differenz'. In *Otto Wagners Großstadt als Form und Idee*, eds. Moritz Csakz and Peter Stachel, 209–243. Vienna: Passagen Verlag.

———. 2013. 'ISOTYPE and Modern Architecture in Red Vienna'. In *Use Matters: An Alternative History of Architecture*, ed. Kenny Cupers, 15–34. Hoboken: Taylor and Francis.

Bloch, Anna. 1928. Zur Rundfrage: Das Bild im proletarischen Heim. *Bildungsarbeit. Blätter für Sozialistisches Bildungswesen*) 1:50–51.

Bottomore, Tom, and Patrick Goode. 1978. *Austro-Marxism*. Oxford: Clarendon Press.

Braunthal, Julius. 1948. *Auf der Suche nach dem Millenium, Bd. 2*. Nürnberg.

Cole, G.D.H., and Richard Vernon. 1980. *Guild Socialism Restated*. Somerset: Taylor and Francis.

Danneberg, Robert. 1929. *Die Wohnungspolitik der Gemeinde Wien*. Wien: Gesellschafts- und Wirtschaftsmuseum.

Frank, Josef. 1927. 'Der Gschnas fürs G'muet und der Gschnas als Problem'. In *Bau und Wohnung*, ed. Deutscher Werkbund, 49–57. Stuttgart: Wedekind & Co.

Frei, Alfred Georg. 1984. *Rotes Wien*. Berlin (West): DVK-Verlag.

Gramsci, Antonio. 2008. *Selections from the Prison Notebooks*. New York: International Publishers.

Gruber, Helmut. 1991. *Red Vienna*. New York: Oxford University Press.

Gulick, Charles Adams. 1948. *Austria from Habsburg to Hitler*. Berkeley, CA: University of California Press.

Harvey, David. 1989. *The Condition of Postmodernity. An Enquiry into the Origins of Cultural Change*. Oxford: Blackwell.

Hayek, Friedrich von. 1930/2001. 'Wirkungen der Mietzinsbeschränkungen'. In *Wirtschaft, Wissenschaft und Politik*, ed. Friedrich von Hayek, 208–223. Tübingen: Mohr Siebeck.

Hochhäusl, Sophie. 2011. *Otto Neurath – City Planning*. Innsbruck: Innsbruck University Press.

———. 2013. 'From Vienna to Frankfurt Inside Core-House Type 7: A History of Scarcity through the Modern Kitchen', *Architectural Histories* 1 (1): 24. DOI: 10.5334/ah.aq.

———. 2019. 'Traveling Exhibitions in the Field: Settlements, War-Economy, and the Collaborative Practice of Seeing, 1919–1925'. In *Neurath Reconsidered: New Sources and Perspectives*, eds. Jordi Cat and Adam Tamas Tuboly, 141–176. Cham: Springer International Publishing.

Holtmann, Everhard. 1996. 'Die Organisation der Sozialdemokratie in der Ersten Republik, 1918–1934'. In *Die Organisation der österreichischen Sozialdemokratie 1889–1995*, eds. Wolfgang Maderthaner and Wolfgang C. Müller, 93–167. Vienna: Löcker.

Hösl, Wolfgang, and Gottfried Pirhofer. 1982. 'Otto Neurath und der Städtebau'. In *Arbeiterbildung in der Zwischenkriegszeit. Otto Neurath – Gerd Antz*, ed. Friedrich Stadler, 157–161. Vienna: Löcker.

Hughes, Thomas P. 1989. *American Genesis: A Century of Invention and Technological Enthusiasm, 1870–1970*. New York: Viking.

John, Michael. 1996. 'Straßenwalle und Exzesse'. In *Wien – Prag – Budapest*, eds. Gerhard Melinz and Susan Zimmermann, 230–244. Vienna: Promedia.

Kadi, Justin. 2015. 'Recommodifying Housing in Formerly "Red" Vienna?', *Housing, Theory and Society* 32 (3). 247–265. DOI: 10.1080/14036096.2015.1024885.

Korthals Altes, Willem, and Andreas Faludi. 1995. 'Why the Greening of Red Vienna Did not Come to Pass: An Unknown Chapter of the Garden City Movement 1919–1934', *European Planning Studies*, 1995.

Lichtenberger, Elisabeth. 1993. *Wien, Prag: Metropolenforschung*. Vienna: Böhlau Verlag.

Maderthaner, Wolfgang. 2006. 'Von der Zeit um 1860 bis zum Jahr 1945'. In *Wien. Geschichte einer Stadt*, eds. Peter Csendes and Ferdinand Opll, 175–544. Vienna: Böhlau Verlag.

Maderthaner, Wolfgang, and Lutz Musner. 2008. *Unruly Masses*. New York: Berghahn Books.

Maimann, Helene (ed.). 1981. *'Mit uns zieht die neue Zeit. Arbeiterkultur in Österreich 1918–1934'*. Vienna: Habarta & Habarta.

Marx, Karl. 1844/1978a. 'Economic and Philosophic Manuscripts of 1844'. In *The Marx-Engels Reader*, ed. Robert C. Tucker, 66–125. New York: Norton.

———. 1844/1978b. 'For a Ruthless Criticism of Everything Existing'. In *The Marx-Engels Reader*, ed. Robert C. Tucker, 12–15. New York/London: Norton & Company.

———. 1845/1978. 'Theses on Feuerbach'. In *The Marx-Engels Reader*, ed. Robert C. Tucker, 143–144. New York: Norten & Company.

———. 1852/1978. 'The Eighteenth Brumaire of Louis Bonaparte'. In *The Marx-Engels Reader*, ed. Robert Tucker, 594–617. New York/London: Norton & Company.

———. 1938. 'A Workers' Inquiry', *The New International* 4 (12): 379–381.

———. 1969. 'The Class Struggle in France: 1848–1850'. In *Selected Works*, ed. Karl Marx. Moscow: Progress Publishers.

Neurath, Otto. 1921. Erziehungsaufgaben des Sozialismus. *Bildungsarbeit. Blätter für sozialistisches Bildungswesen*, 1921.

———. 1923. Neu-Wiens Gesamtarchitektur – eine Aufgabe des Proletariats. *Arbeiter Zeitung*, October 28.

———. 1926a. Bauformen und Klassenkampf. *Bildungsarbeit. Blätter für sozialistisches Bildungswesen* XIII (4): 61–64.

———. 1926b. Rationalismus, Arbeiterschaft und Baugestaltung. *Der Aufbau* (May): 49–52.

———. 1928. Proletarische Lebensgestaltung. *Der Kampf*, 1928.

———. 1933. Museums of the Future. *Survey Graphic*, 1933.

———. 1937. Visual Education: A New Language. *Survey Graphic*, 1937.

———. 1979. 'Statistik und Sozialismus'. In *Otto Neurath – Wissenschaftliche Weltauffassung, Sozialismus und logischer Empirismus*, eds. Otto Neurath and Rainer Hegelsmann, 288–294. Frankfurt: Suhrkamp.

Nussbaum, Andrea. 2007. 'Kleiner roter Ziegelstein, baut die neue Welt'. In *Karl-Marx Hof. Versailles der Arbeiter*, ed. Gerold Kriechbaum and Genoveva Kriechbaum, 50–79. Wien: Holzhausen Verlag.

Oldenziel, Ruth, and Karin Zachmann (eds.). 2009. *Cold War Kitchen: Americanization, Technology, and European Users.* Cambridge, MA: MIT Press.

Pfoser, Alfred. 1982. 'Das Glück in der Vernunft – Überlegungen zu Otto Neuraths Kulturtheorie und zur austromarxistischen Lebensreform'. In *Arbeiterbildung in der Zwischenkriegszeit. Otto Neurath – Gerd Antz*, ed. Friedrich Stadler, 168–172. Vienna: Löcker.

Philippovich, Eugen. 1894. Wiener Wohnungsverhältnisse. *Archiv für soziale Gesetzgebung und Statistik* 7:215–277.

Pircher, Wolfgang. 1982. 'Bemerkungen zu "Statstik und Sozialismus"'. In *Arbeiterbildung in der Zwischenkriegszeit. Otto Neurath – Gerd Antz*, ed. Friedrich Stadler, 162–167. Vienna: Löcker.

Pirhofer, Gottfried, and Reinhard Sieder. 1982. 'Zur Konstitution der Arbeiterfamilie im Roten Wien: Familienpolitik, Kulturreform, Alltag und Ästhetik'. In *Historische Familienforschung*, eds. Michael Mitterauer and Reinhard Sieder, 326–368. Frankfurt am Main: Suhrkamp.

Rabinbach, Anson. 1989. *Vom Roten Wien zum Bürgerkrieg.* Vienna: Löcker Verlag.

Schorske, Carl E. 1981. *Fin-de-Siecle Vienna. Politics and Culture.* New York: Vintage Books.

Schuster, Franz, and Franz Schacherl. 1926. Proletarische Architektur. *Der Kampf* XIX:34ff.

Sieder, Reinhard. 1988. Zur alltäglichen Praxis der Wiener Arbeiterschaft im ersten Drittel des 20. Jahrhunderts. Habilitation, Universität Wien, Wien.

Tandler, Julius. 1928. 'Gefahren der Minderwertigkeit'. In *Das Wiener Jugendhilfswerk*, ed. Franz Breunlich, 1–22. Vienna: Verlag des Jugendamtes der Stadt Wien.

Taut, Bruno. 1926. Die Frau als Schöpferin der Wohnung. *Der Aufbau. Österreichische Monatshefte für Siedlung und Städtebau* (2).

Wagner, Otto. 1911. *Die Groszstadt: Eine Studie über diese.* Wien: Schroll.

———. 1988. *Modern Architecture: A Guidebook for his Students to this Field of Art.* Santa Monica, CA: Getty Center for the History of Art and the Humanities.

Wasserman, Janek. 2014. *Black Vienna: The Radical Right in the Red City, 1918–1938.* Ithaca, NY: Cornell University Press.

Weihsmann, Helmut. 1985. *Das rote Wien: sozialdemokratische Architektur und Kommunalpolitik, 1919–1934.* Vienna: Promedia.

Winter, Max. 1901. Rund um Favoriten: Eine Skizze aus dem Leben der Enterbten. *Arbeiter Zeitung,* December 14.

———. 1982. 'Zinsburgen und Chaluppen'. In *Max Winter. Das schwarze Wienerherz: Sozialreportagen aus dem frühen 20. Jahrhundert*, ed. Helmut Strutzmann, 94–108. Vienna: Österreichischer Bundesverlag.

3 Short-Lived Great Berlin: Tabula Rasa and the Reinvention of Nature (1945–1949)

Abstract

In post-WWII Berlin, utopias of nature dominated discourses on urban and societal renewal. Among architects and planners, the bombing of Berlin was widely perceived as 'history's auto-correction'. Plans were made for further destroying the nineteenth-century industrial metropolis to replace it with a decentralized city landscape [*Stadtlandschaft*]. What sounds politically innocent was in fact an ideological battleground. Conservatives turned towards nature to seek guidance for rebuilding natural hierarchies. Progressives conceived of nature as a source of inspiration for a more egalitarian, democratic society. With the onset of the Cold War, references to nature receded into the background. Yet, as an urban form, the decentralized city had an afterlife on both sides of the Wall – with different normative implications.

Keywords*:* post-WWII Berlin, anti-urbanism, utopias of nature, city landscape, conservatism, modernism

Akin to Austria after WWI, in post-WWII Germany, discourses on reconstruction were infused by the hope that overhauling existing urban environs would contribute to a rejuvenation of society at large. This applied to West Germany no less than to East Germany. Since both 'Germanies' claimed Berlin as their respective capital, the city increasingly turned into a stage for two competing political rationales: state socialism and liberal capitalism. The questions of how to reconstruct the city in general and that of how to provide housing in particular were put center stage in this ideological battle. Building for the 'new man' and, to a lesser extent, for the 'new woman' became a site of *Systemkonkurrenz* [system competition], i.e. the Cold War. Human flourishing and progress was promised by both 'regimes of truth' (Foucault 1980, p. 131). As will be shown in chapters 4 and 5, this promise was

Haderer, M., *Rebuilding Cities and Citizens: Mass Housing in Red Vienna and Cold War Berlin.* Amsterdam: Amsterdam University Press 2023
DOI: 10.5117/9789463724944_CH03

soon to be foiled by the 'logic of urbanism': a state-administered, technocratic rationality that affected urban reconstruction as much as the provision of mass housing. 'Urbanism', as Lefebvre explains, 'claims to be a system [that] pretends to embrace, enclose, possess a new totality. It wants to be the modern philosophy of the city, justified by (liberal [or, as I would add, socialist]) humanism while justifying a (technocratic) utopia' (2003, p. 153). Yet, *before* the beginning of the Cold War and the gradual normalization of the logic of urbanism, plans for Berlin's reconstruction resulted from *joint* efforts between the Western Allies and the Soviets. Shortly after 1945 and with the approval of the Western Allies, the Soviets entrusted the modernist and politically untainted architect Hans Scharoun with the task to work out a plan for Berlin's reconstruction. Similar to other modernists inspired by Le Corbusier, Scharoun and his Collective's Plan involved the dissolution of the nineteenth-century industrial metropolis. The latter was problematized by progressives, such as Scharoun, who suggested dissolving the metropolis into a city landscape that would do away with the existing city and its malaises, including its underpinning property relations and the lack of influence of citizens on their everyday environment, and facilitate the emergence of a new, more egalitarian and democratic society. The metropolis was also the bogeyman of post-WWII conservatives (not only political but also cultural conservatives) and reactionaries who conceived of it as a key source of moral decay. However, in the few years before the onset of the Cold War, Berlin and Scharoun's planning collective's vision of Great Berlin got the upper hand in the struggle for interpretation over urban and societal reconstruction, in which appeals to nature played a prominent role. As heirs of the modernist movement of the 1920s shaped by Le Corbusier, and as close affiliates of the German architectural movement, *Neues Bauen* [New Building], Scharoun and his planning collective argued that for human flourishing and progress to be possible, the social, technological, and aesthetic had to be reconciled and adapted to existing landscapes. Cold War politics quickly brought an end to the dissolution of the metropolis into a city landscape, which Scharoun had conceived of as a profoundly egalitarian and democratic urban form. Yet, as Margaret Kohn puts it, '[e]ven an unsuccessful movement [or vision for urban reconstruction] may reveal democratic possibilities' (2003, p. 10). For this reason, I outline Scharoun's take on Berlin's reconstruction in what follows, a take on modernist city planning that represents an alternative to the ultimate boiling down of modernist ideals to techno-scientific modernization and the 'logic of urbanism' (Lefebvre 2003, p. 153). In addition, this chapter shows that appeals to nature as guidance for urban and societal reconstruction were prominent in Germany after WWII (see section 3.1), appeals that were hardly politically neutral. In fact, they were infused as much with conservative – if not reactionary – 'retrotopias' (Bauman 2017) (see section 3.2) as they were with egalitarian, democratic utopias, of which Scharoun's vision for Great Berlin is but one example (see section 3.3).

3.1 The Bombing of Cities as 'History's Auto-Correction'

In post-WWII German discourses, the year 1945 has often been referred to as the *Stunde Null* [Zero Hour]: a point in time that embodies a severing of the strings with the past and the opening of the horizon toward a radically different future. Urban planners, architects, public intellectuals, and political leaders were desperate for a new beginning and hoped to turn catastrophe into opportunity. Since war destruction meant to a large extent *urban* destruction, the desire to not simply rebuild cities but to reform and improve them and their inhabitants dominated post-WWII debates and fantasies on urban renewal. Post-WWII German cities were certainly places of despair. In Berlin, half of its overall housing stock was in ruins; thousands of people lived in makeshift homes and fed themselves on the yield of urban land. In addition, 500,000 displaced persons poured into the capital each month in search of a new home, which put already dismal housing conditions under additional pressure (Reiche 1989, p. 37) [see Illustration 3.1].

At the same time, the 'landscapes of ruins' were repeatedly perceived as history's justified reckoning with a civilization that had transgressed too many 'no-trespass' boundaries. Karl Scheffler, a painter and art critic, suggested conceiving of the Allied bombing as 'history's auto-correction' (Baumeister 1947), a drastic assessment that was by no means a singular one. In fact, the post-WWII discourses on urban and social renewal were dominated by a *Zivilisationskritik* [critique of civilization] whose vanishing point was a reconciliation with nature, a reconciliation that was informed by the desire to leave behind the excessive industrialization and technologization that had informed WWII. The metaphor of nature overgrowing human-caused destruction was prominent after 1945 – prominent and perceived as liberating. As the author Max Frisch put it: 'And all of a sudden one can imagine how it continues to grow, how a jungle covers our cities, a silence of thistle and moss, a soil without history accompanied by the twitter of birds, by spring, summer and fall, the breath of years no longer counted' [my translation] (Frisch 1965, p. 35).

A key component of the discourse on 'history's auto-corrections' was the destruction of the nineteenth-century metropolis. After the emergence of the metropolis in the wake of industrialization and particularly after 1945, its density, pace, crowds, commercial activities, and living conditions

3.1 Berlin in Ruins, Budapester Straße (1945). © ullstein bild

had been considered anathema by both conservative (if not reactionary) architects, planners, and social reformers and progressive ones. Against this backdrop, Scheffler's opinion of the bombing as 'history's auto-correction' (Baumeister 1947) was less a teleological point than a view that was widely held especially by planners and architects in post-WWII Germany: that despite all the despair and tragedy, the massive destruction of urban centers such as Berlin constituted an opportunity for urban reconstruction on an unprecedented scale (Glaser 1989, pp. 11–15). The planners' and architects' anticipation of and excitement about the possibility of a thorough urban overhaul was accompanied by the political elites' and the reformers' hope that society could be rejuvenated if only Babylon, the 'city of chaos' (the dense, nineteenth-century metropolis), was finally replaced by Jerusalem, the 'city of order' (city landscapes). These visions came predominantly in two forms: one that refuted modernity, including the egalitarian and democratic agenda; and one that held fast to 'progressive' modern agendas while taking issue with other legacies of modernity.

3.2 The Metropolis, A Moloch

On the conservative and reactionary side, the post-WWII critique of the modern metropolis harked back to Oswald Spengler's famous pre-war diagnosis of the modern city as the root cause for – and locus of – the decline of culture (a discourse that was also prominent in post-WWI Vienna, see Wasserman 2014), a diagnosis expressed in his book, *The Decline of the West* (1928). In Spengler's view, the metropolis marks the 'end of organic growth and the beginning of an inorganic and therefore unrestrained process of massing without limit'. Its inhabitants are intellectual nomads, 'petrified historic beings' whose dwellings are

> mere premises which have been fashioned, not by blood but by requirements, not by feeling but by the spirit of commercial enterprise. So long as the hearth has a pious meaning as the actual and genuine centre of a family, the old relation to the land is not wholly extinct. But when that too follows the rest into oblivion, and the mass of tenants and bed-occupiers in the sea of houses leads a vagrant existence from shelter to shelter [...] then the intellectual nomad is completely developed. (Spengler 1928, p. 100)

By 1945, the hearth had undoubtedly lost its alleged pious meaning as the center of the family. Those who had been naturalized into working the hearth – women – were forced to break with 'nature' and to take to rubble clearing instead. In the immediate post-WWII years, the so-called *Trümmerfrauen* [rubble women] concentrated on street-clearing instead of homemaking and thus prepared the path for urban reconstruction. After the rubble was cleared, political incentives were laid to encourage women to return to their 'natural selves' as keepers of the hearth not in the agrarian sense Spengler had envisaged but in the industrial setting Ford had devised: women as caretakers (and later also as consumers).

One of Spengler's closest acolytes was Hans Sedlmayr, whose book *Verlust der Mitte* [Loss of the Middle], published in 1951, influenced West German planning debates well into the late 1950s. According to Sedlmayr, modern man is shaped by 'total dysfunction'. His relation to God, to himself, to others, and to nature is upside down. A state of *Bodenlosigkeit* [abysm] marks the human condition. Instead of men conceiving of themselves as the crown of creation, as the master and center of nature, they transform themselves into something cold and brutal. 'Fathomless architecture' (Sedlmayr 1951, p. 170), which Sedlmayr equated to *modernist* architecture, was an example of this coldness and brutality – modern architecture as the epitome of man's dysfunction. Echoing but also reinforcing the post-WWII zeitgeist, the conservative author was convinced that ultimately '[i]norganic, mechanic thinking will be refuted by the earth itself', that 'the culture of earth' will regain momentum and gradually reconstitute natural relations, the basis of any 'higher culture [...] that reconciles art with the sacred and that sets an end to dreams of man's autonomy'. (Sedlmayr 1951, pp. 244, 247)

Thinkers of 'extreme reaction' (Adorno 1950, p. 124), as Theodor Adorno referred to Spengler and his post-WWII acolytes, construed the nineteenth-century metropolis as a Moloch that was ridden with moral, social, and political decay – a social construct that was to be rolled back and replaced by 'natural', more 'humane forms' of living. After 1945, this perception of the metropolis was particularly echoed by the German settler movement. To be certain, in the immediate aftermath of 1945, given the dire food and housing shortage, settlements were supported by *all* political and social camps. Gradually, however, the post-WWII settlement movement became, in contrast to settlement movement in Vienna after WWI, closely affiliated with the anti-modernist conservative and Catholic camps. It lobbied for the normalization of settlements and smallholdings as the most promising pathway towards re-rooting the family and 'crisis-proofing uprooted men' (Harlander 1992, pp. 21–22). According to the conservative and reactionary critics of the metropolis, the unpropertied 'men of the mass' – meaning the inhabitants of traditional tenement housing or of modern 'dwelling machines' – would be particularly seducible and prone to sympathize with left- or right-wing radicalism (Harlander 1992, p. 22). The only remedy against the dangers of extremism and 'massification', the assumption went, was the privately owned, single family home, a home built on land that would be big enough to facilitate subsistence farming. Only if the family was reestablished as the 'fruitful cell of life' of society would the healing of the wounds of modernization be certain (Katholischer Siedlungsdienst e.V. 1956, p. 7). Yet much to the dismay of the proponents of settlements and smallholdings who wanted the private and suburban single family home to emerge as the only form of dwelling worthy of public funding and the title of 'social housing' (Harlander 1992, p. 26), mass housing made a return after 1945. Especially in West Germany, however, mass housing did not supplant the ideal of the single family home but was instead conceived of as an intermediary step.

3.3 Great Berlin: A New Beginning through Greening the City

The 1946 exhibit *Berlin plant – erster Bericht* [Berlin is Planning–First Report] by Hans Scharoun and his Planning Collective provided an answer to the question of how to reconfigure post-WWII urban everyday life that differed considerably from conservative critiques of the nineteenth-century metropolis. Appointed by the Soviets in 1945 as the Director of the Department of City Building and Housing for Greater Berlin, the politically untarnished, modernist architect and former *Ring*[1] member Hans Scharoun was entrusted with the task of developing a plan for building a new, democratic city. In 1946, he and his planning collective presented their plans for public scrutiny and debate in the ruins of Berlin's City Castle.

For Scharoun, 'the mechanical decentralization' (Scharoun 1946/1974, p. 158), as he paraphrased the bombing of Germany's cities, represented an unprecedented and, in a way, exciting possibility to reconstruct life along new aesthetic and socio-political lines. Yet in stark contrast to the anti-modern, conservative 'nature fetishism' embodied by reactionary social critics, political leaders, and representatives of the settlement movement, Scharoun's appeal to nature was radically modern. It was informed by the hope of finally bringing about a new architectonic order that would go hand in hand with a new social order. Similar to the Austro-Marxists' promise of building (for) 'new men', Scharoun envisioned a *Neue Stadt* [New City] and a *Neue Wohnung* [New Dwelling] as steppingstones toward a new society (Scharoun 1949/1974).

Scharoun and his Planning Collective proposed to erase most of what was left of Berlin in order to recreate the city as a *Stadtlandschaft* [city landscape], an organic entity consisting of 'equal elements, which themselves comprised smaller equal elements', such as the apartment, i.e., the smallest architectural unit [see Illustration 3.2]. One goal of the plan was the equalization of dwelling conditions. Each city district, delimited by four traffic arteries, was to accommodate about 80,000 inhabitants. The districts themselves were to be subdivided into smaller units, 'dwelling cells' that were to accommodate about 5,000 inhabitants each (Scharoun 1946). These dwelling cells (or, as they were also called, neighborhoods) were expected to serve as anchor points for people's experiential horizon:

> The smallest units are to be designed and shaped to mirror the unity of life, the 'life fabric' [*Lebensbau*]. Apart from apartment buildings and single family homes [....], these units have to also provide accommodations for singles, accommodations that are to be connected with guest

1 The *Ring* was an architectural collective founded in Berlin in 1926 whose goal was the promotion of modernist architecture. Its founding members are Mies van der Rohe and Hugo Haering. Scharoun was a student of the latter. Van der Rohe and Haering increasingly represented two different streams within modernist architecture: a rationalist one represented van der Rohe and an organicist one represented by Haering and later also by Scharoun.

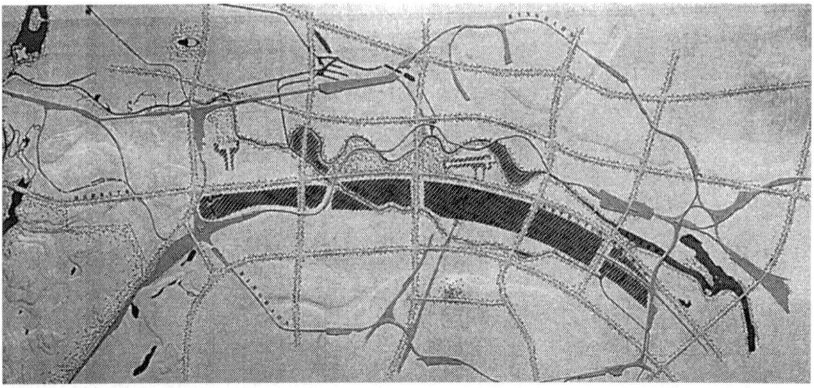

3.2 Hans Scharoun's and his Collective's Plan for Turning Berlin into a City Landscape. © Akademie der Bildenden Künste, Berlin

> houses [...]. Moreover, [the dwelling cell] ought to be equipped with a cultural and social center (to be shared by several dwelling cells), hospital, kindergarten, children's home, cinema, theater, library, research institute [...] The education system is to be present in the dwelling cell through an elementary school and in the city district through a high school. All the available social, cultural, and educational facilities are to make use of the green space located in between the dwelling areas. [...] In this way the new city will emanate organically from social necessities and constitute a *Leistungsform* [performance form]. [my translation] (Scharoun 1946).

Whereas mixed use was a key characteristic of 'Old Berlin', Scharoun's new metropolis was to be organized according to four urban functions: dwelling, working, recreation, and circulation. Embedded in green space and bounded by streets, a traffic system that made the automobile indispensable, the dwelling cells and districts were meant to be located in the proximity of industrial and farming cells but nonetheless separated from them to ensure maximal health and hygiene and to minimize commuter traffic. The Collective Plan proposed neither an encompassing reuse of still existing infrastructure nor a far-reaching reconstruction of Berlin's architectural heritage. The Museum Island, the boulevard Unter den Linden, the Brandenburg Gate, and the Charlottenburg Castle were among the few historical sites that the plan proposed to reconstruct and to equip with additional recreational and representative facilities to architecturally demarcate the city, i.e., a center that was expected to serve as Germany's 'display window' (Geist and Kürvers 1980, 3: 235–236). Thus, instead of being attuned to the historically grown city, the city landscape was predominantly adjusted to local geography, such as the glacial valley of the Spree. Non-organic – that is, socially and historically constructed – specificities and localisms were to be destroyed in order to rebuild the urban environment and urban life based on natural laws.

Although Scharoun's appeal to nature and organicism was informed by the idea that natural laws would be an essential source of inspiration for constructing a well-ordered society, the thrust of his appeal was not an authoritarian one that would have heaved the architect into the position of a chosen figure endowed with the task of reconfiguring the world according to his or her interpretation of natural laws. Instead, Scharoun's plea for organicism was critical and differentiated, a plea that distanced itself from the dominance of abstraction (e.g., urban grids), instrumental reason (e.g., the dominance of exchange value over use value), and social fragmentation (e.g., driven by land and rent prices) that had prominently shaped the modern metropolis. At the same time, Scharoun refrained from dismissing modernity in its entirety and from sympathizing with pre-modern romanticism:

> The notion of 'being at home' is insufficient to counter the discontinuity of the modern society. Science and the perfection of technology create tensions that also interfere with the relationship that art entertains with science. This interference can only be changed if we make use not only of the external but also inner essence of the scientific-technological. Technology and science can contribute to *Gestaltfindung* [the finding of form], if art refrains from imposing *Gestaltzwang* [the constraint to form]. [my translation] (1954/1974, p. 229)

For Scharoun, natural laws and organic forms served as sources of inspiration – instead of prescriptions – for future-oriented instead of reactionary social imaginations. Accordingly, he and his Planning Collective resuscitated the modernist architects' self-understanding as 'social condensators' (Kopp 1978, p. 211), as midwives of change – a self-understanding that was particularly prevalent in the 1920s. Scharoun was fully aware that in order to be effective midwives of social transformation, visions of a new society had to take into account actually existing social processes and realities. Committed to democratic principles, Scharoun was opposed to implementing the New City by decree. '[T]o avoid that [the New City] turns into a mold that acts against its inhabitants', it must be continuously shaped and informed by the 'culture of its inhabitants' (Scharoun 1946/1974, p. 160). Moreover, it must be responsive to people's 'manifold desires, insights, hopes, and fulfillments' (Scharoun

1954/1974, p. 232). Scharoun's commitment to democratic practices was also evinced by his refusal to consider practicability as the most important criteria for evaluating urban plans. For him, the purpose of the Collective Plan for Berlin's reconstruction was to initiate and involve the public in a debate on urban reconstruction instead of presenting citizens with a ready-made plan that was to be implemented. Similarly, although the Collective Plan considered working, dwelling, recreation, and circulation as key urban functions – akin to the 'bible' of modernist city building, the Charter of Athens (1943) – Scharoun and his Planning Collective treated these functions as *social* constructs subject to change instead of permanent objective norms (1946/1974, pp. 160–161).

Against this backdrop, it could be argued that what applies to democracy as a *political* form also applied to Scharoun's specific take on an *urban* form he had inherited from his modernist predecessors: an inescapable necessity to be open to – and to come to terms with – the provisional and transformative. Implicit to the Collective Plan was a political progressiveness understood as a commitment to equality and democracy and, in addition, economic radicalism that questioned the primacy of private property relations. The proposed *Stadtlandschaft* largely disregards existing property relations and seeks their radical revision. As mentioned above, Scharoun also deemed the nineteenth-century metropolis to be an urban form in need of an overhaul. Yet in distinction to the conservative critics of the big city, Scharoun did not believe that merely limiting the modern metropolis' growth by dissolving it into small towns would constitute a sufficient remedy for over-densification, social alienation, and poor living conditions (Scharoun 1954/1974, pp. 228–229). For him, the 'true solution' to the problems caused by the modern metropolis lay in the radical rethinking of building and land policies (Scharoun 1946). He believed that as long as inherited economic and political practices are continued, the social problems caused by the modern metropolis could not be solved. Thus, the declared goal of the Planning Collective was to redefine the economic basis of the city by building the New City on economic policies that aimed at a balanced relationship between the 'fabric of the economy' [*Wirtschaftsbau*] and the 'fabric of life' [*Lebensbau*] (Scharoun 1946/1974, p. 161). As Scharoun put it, '[i]t has always been the case that institutions, once devised by men, weigh down on them as if these institutions were of a higher, inescapable order, as if it were impossible to change them'. It is nonetheless necessary and possible to carry out a 'reevaluation of values' based on the insight 'that justice that has become injustice cannot be eternalized' [my translation] (1946/1974, p. 166).

What Scharoun's post-WWII utopianism stood for was a brief revival of the modernist belief that was so dominant in architectural practices of the

1920s. It was the belief in the possibility of a fundamental makeover that would usher in 'new humans' who would no longer be merely subject to but in charge of processes of modernization, i.e., technological, industrial, or scientific innovation. The new urban dwellers would make themselves at home in the modern world and be able to navigate modernity's perilous potential for both radical transformation in the service of social progress and, the very contrary of the latter, for destroying everything in existence (Berman 1988). Implicitly acknowledging that cities are a collective product, a product through which human beings produce and reproduce themselves (Harvey 2000, p. 159), Scharoun's post-WWII spatial utopia was an exploration of human possibilities that went beyond narrow considerations of feasibility and practicability. Moreover, despite acknowledging the actual and potentially devastating effects of modernity, Scharoun distanced himself from romantic yearnings for a pre-modern past. The Collective Plan was decidedly future-oriented. It sought to reconcile natural science and technology, aesthetics, and politics to the advantage of the 'viability and vitality of all humans' instead of certain 'interest groups' (Scharoun 1946/1974, p. 166).

Although the plan was utopian in the sense that it proposed an urban form that sought to be a pre-vision of a democratic city, Scharoun's utopianism did not lose itself in imaginative play but took existing social, cultural, and technological conditions into account. Given this negotiation between reality and possibility, Scharoun's utopianism is best understood as what David Harvey calls 'dialectical utopianism' (2000, p. 196). The plan held fast to the modern promise of emancipation, to the possibility of progressive '*Menschenbildung* [the formation of men]' that takes the actually existing needs and desires of men as the starting point for future designs of human dwellings (Scharoun 1946/1974, p. 166). Simultaneously, it sought to push the boundaries of what was architecturally, socially, and politically possible.

'[W]hat distinguishes the worst architect from the best of bees is this', wrote Marx: 'the architect raises his structure in imagination before he erects it in reality. [...] He not only effects a change of form in the material on which he works, but he also realizes a purpose [...]' (1887, VII, I). As an architect and city planner, Scharoun clearly did so. In the immediate post-WWII years, Scharoun was still hopeful of successfully straddling the aporetic condition Adorno ascribes to architecture:

> Because architecture is in fact both autonomous and purpose-oriented, it cannot simply negate men as they are. And yet it must do precisely that if it is to remain autonomous. If it would bypass mankind *tel quel*,

> then it would be accommodating itself to what would be a questionable anthropology and even ontology. (1965/1997, p. 16)

Yet within the wider post-WWII climate, Scharoun's position turned out to be increasingly the position of an outlier instead of the mainstream. That the Collective Plan would remain a utopia was already made clear to Scharoun in 1946, when American officers who visited the *Berlin plant* exhibit told the architect that in the Western Zones, existing private property relations the Collective Plan sought to overhaul would remain sacrosanct (Kirschenmann and Syring 1993, p. 177). A phalanx of critics of the Collective Plan soon also formed in the Soviet sector. The reason was not the question of property – in fact, the first housing program of the German Communist Party had already announced the abolition of all obstacles resulting from 'private arbitrariness' for the sake of 'public interest' (Hoscislawski 1991, p. 49) – but rather the question of aesthetic. Despite the fact that the Soviets were initially welcoming of representatives of the New Building due to their typically left-leaning political worldview, the New Building's aesthetic of formalism was, with the onset of Stalinization, construed as an antidote to Stalin's vision of socialist realist aesthetics. Ultimately, only a fraction of the Collective Plan ended up being built in the eastern part of the city.

In December 1949, the ground was broken for the construction of the first dwelling cell. Yet not long after the construction began, the undertaking again came to a standstill. The only part of the Collective Plan that was realized consists of two *Laubenganghäuser* designed by Ludmilla Herzenstein. Located at the *Frankfurter Allee*, a boulevard that was soon to be renamed *Stalinallee* and transformed into the *Magistrale des Ostens* [Magistrale of the East], Herzenstein's apartment buildings – despite their novelty – quickly turned into a fossil of a past urbanism. To cover up the material traces left by East Germany's ideological transition from modernist to socialist realist architecture, fast-growing trees were planted in front of them, poplars, which to this day suggest to the quick passerby an 'undisturbed', socialist-realist, monumental unity.

References

Adorno, Theodor. 1950. Spengler nach dem Untergang. *Der Monat* (20): 115–128.

———. 1965/1997. Functionalism Today. In *Rethinking Architecture*, ed. Neil Leach, 6–19. Oxon, New York: Routledge.

Bauman, Zygmunt. 2017. *Retrotopia.* Oxford: Polity Press.

Berman, Marshall. 1988. *All that is Solid Melts into Air. The Experience of Modernity.* New York: Penguin Books.

Le Corbusier. 1973. *Athens Charter.* New York: Grossman Publishers.

Foucault, Michel. 1980. 'Truth and Power'. In *Power/Knowledge*, ed. Michel Foucault, 109–133. New York: Pantheon Book.

Frisch, Max. 1965. *Tagebuch 1946–1949.* Munich, Zürich.

Geist, Johann Friedrich, and Klaus Kürvers. 1980. *Das Berliner Mietshaus.* Munich: Prestel.

Glaser, Hermann (ed.). 1989. *So viel Anfang war nie.* Berlin: Sieder Verlag.

Harlander, Tilman. 1992. Kleinsiedlung und Selbsthilfe im Wiederaufbau. In *Siedeln tut not: Wohnungsbau und Selbsthilfe im Wiederaufbau. Aachen*, eds. Hermann Gödde, Tilman Harlander, and Katrin Hater, 19–37. Aachen: Einhard.

Harvey, David. 2000. *Spaces of Hope.* Berkeley, CA: University of Berkeley Press.

Hoscislawski, Thomas. 1991. *Bauen zwischen Macht und Ohnmacht: Architektur und Städtebau in der DDR.* Berlin: Verlag für Bauwesen.

Katholischer Siedlungsdienst e.V. 1956. *Heim und Familie. Zehn Jahre katholische Siedlungsarbeit.* Köln.

Kirschenmann, Jörg C., and Eberhard Syring (eds.). 1993. *Hans Scharoun. Die Forderung des Unvollendeten.* Stuttgart: Deutsche Verlags-Anstalt.

Kohn, Margaret. 2003. *Radical Space. Building the House of the People.* Ithaca, NY: Cornell University Press.

Kopp, Anatole. 1978. *L'Architecture de la Periode Stalinienne.* Grenoble: Presses Universitaires de Grenoble.

Lefebvre, Henri. 2003. *The Urban Revolution.* Minneapolis: University of Minnesota.

Marx, Karl. 1887. *Capital.* Moscow: Progress Publishers.

Reiche, Jürgen. 1989. Zukunft nach dem Ende. In *So viel Anfang war nie*, ed. Hermann Glaser, 36–49. Berlin: Sieder Verlag.

Scharoun, Hans. 1946/1974. Vortrag anlässlich der Ausstellung ‚Berlin plant-erster Bericht', September 5. In *Hans Scharoun. Bauten, Entwürfe, Texte*, ed. Peter Pfankuch, 156–168. Berlin: Gebr. Mann Verlag.

———. 1946. Vortrag Scharoun, April 4: Protokoll der 9. Sitzung des BWA. Berlin: Archiv der Akademie der Künste/ SB Nachlass Scharoun (Mag I/2).

———. 1949/1974. Zur Wohnzelle Friedrichshain. In *Bauten, Entwürfe, Texte*, ed. Peter Pfankuch, 184–188. Berlin: Gebr. Mann Verlag.

———. 1954/1974. Vom Stadt-Wesen und Architekt-Sein. In *Hans Scharoun. Bauten, Entwürfe, Texte*, ed. Peter Pfankuch, 228–232. Berlin: Gebr. Mann Verlag.

Scheffler, Karl. 1947. Phantom Großstadt. *Baumeister*, Vol. 44., Issue 1–12 Munich: Verlag Herrmann Rinn.

Sedlmayr, Hans. 1951. *Verlust der Mitte: die bildende Kunst des 19. und 20. Jahrhunderts als Symptom und Symbol der Zeit.* Salzburg: Otto Müller.

Spengler, Oswald. 1928. *The Decline of the West. Perspectives on World History.* New York: Alfred A. Knopf Incorporated.

Wasserman, Janek. 2014. *Black Vienna: The Radical Right in the Red City, 1918–1938.* Ithaca, NY: Cornell University Press.

4 Divided City I: East Berlin and the Construction of Socialism (1949–1970)

Abstract
This chapter examines the reconstruction of East Berlin in the name of socialism through the lens of mass housing. It shows how the search for socialist semantics regarding the rebuilding of housing and the capital city oscillated between the reinvention of national traditions due to Stalin's doctrine of 'socialism in one country' and the outright elimination of this doctrine by standardization and prefabrication. The latter would prevail: the prefabricated concrete tower, the *Platte*, became a symbol of socialism. It signifies a 'liquidating abstraction' (Adorno) and, at the same time, a radical and appreciated commitment to social equality. One prominent counter-space to the *Platte* was the allotment garden, a space that was simultaneously located within and outside of the socialist state.

Keywords: East Berlin, socialism, socialist realism, industrialization, *Platte*, allotment garden

For the Soviets, Hans Scharoun and his collective's plan for Great Berlin turned out to be too modernist. Stalin summoned his East German acolytes to resuscitate national traditions committed to monumentality instead. Ironically, as this chapter shows, it was the socialists, formerly committed to internationalism, who would retap the notion of *Heimat*, which had been dear to the Fascists. 'Socialism in one country' (Stalin 1954) and a return to the 'beautiful, truly German city' were the architectural dictums in the early years of the Cold War, of which the showcase 'workers' palaces' on East Berlin's *Stalinallee* turned out to be a prominent manifestation (see section 4.1). Yet, as will be also illustrated, behind the facades of national traditions and monumentality, new building practices were already being experimented with, practices of Taylorism that emphasized efficiency via rationalization. Once decried as the epitome of worker-unfriendly, dehumanizing 'imperial capitalism', Taylorism was gradually integrated

Haderer, M., *Rebuilding Cities and Citizens: Mass Housing in Red Vienna and Cold War Berlin*. Amsterdam: Amsterdam University Press 2023
DOI: 10.5117/9789463724944_CH04

into socialism, which in East Germany meant Marxism-Leninism (shaped by one-party-rule, a centralized state, a planned economy, and an emphasis on techno-scientific progress). In the immediate post-WWII years, Taylorism was coupled with shock work: the expectation of an above-average work ethic in the service of building socialism (due to a shortage of labor and machinery). Many workers agreed to perform above average in their jobs but failed to move any closer to the promised fruits of their labor nonetheless: a decent standard of living. The lingering hiatus between the promised material bounty and the actual economy of shortage made workers take to the streets. They did so less to question socialism *tout court* than to challenge its East German form, a questioning to which the Soviets responded with tanks (see section 4.2.) In addition to the tanks, the East German elite responded to civil unrest with a promise: a new, comfortable dwelling culture, accessible to all. Similar to the dwelling culture promoted in Red Vienna, the East German dwelling culture was not likely to catapult citizens into a socialist future. Instead, it firmly reanchored dwelling ideals that were prominent in the bourgeois past (see section 4.3). That said, this chapter argues that the East German response to the housing question *did* leave a socialist legacy (see section 4.4.): namely the decommodification of housing. The latter was widely perceived as positive among East German citizens, in contrast to common assumptions about East German socialism as a failed experiment in socialism in every respect (see section 4.5). The chapter also shows that even under authoritarianism, creative appropriations of space did take place, appropriations that, at least initially, operated below the radar of the authoritarian socialist state: allotment gardens, which were both spaces of bourgeois utopias and spaces of counter-culture (see section 4.6).

4.1 Back to the Future: 'Socialism in One Country' and the 'Beautiful German City'

In the spring of 1950, delegates of the East German Ministry of Reconstruction traveled to the Soviet Union to study urban reconstruction. Among them were Lothar Boltz, head of the Ministry of Reconstruction, and Kurt Liebknecht, nephew of Karl Liebknecht, affiliate of Mies van der Rohe, and – after his return from his exile in the Soviet Union – head of the German Building Academy [*Deutsche Bauakademie*] (Hain 1993). What happened in Moscow was a reorientation towards Marxism-Leninism, of which the Sixteen Principles of Urban Design was just one expression, an expression at the aesthetic front. They were announced after the delegates' homecoming,

4.1 Stalin-Allee: Display Window of East German Housing Development. © Bundesarchiv (Germany)

principles that broke radically with modernist architecture and city planning, such as that of Scharoun and his Collective. Based on Joseph Stalin and his acolyte's, Lazar Kaganovitch's urban visions for Moscow's reconstruction, the Sixteen Principles announced the return to architecture indebted to history, monumentality, and national traditions (Kopp 1978, pp. 193–295). Thus, the new 'socialist way of life', a life to be looked upon in awe by the West through the GDR's chosen 'display window of socialism' – the 'workers' palaces' on *Stalinallee* – took its inspiration from the past [see Illustration 4.1].

Similar to the divine city, which needed the profane city as a counterpart for its own contours to be visible, the socialist city was defined by its difference from the suddenly loathed modernist city. It was meant to be a city of centrality and architectonic unity instead of functional division (Principles VI, IX); density instead of decentralization (Principles XII, XIII); community instead of individualism (Principles I, II, X), walkability instead of auto-mobility (Principles VI, VIII), singularity instead of schematic repeatability (Principle XIV). Whereas many modernists sought to dissolve the historically grown industrial city and with it its social, political, and economic shortcomings to pave the way for a radical reconstruction of urban and social life, the Sixteen Principles ordained the reverse: the re-appreciation of the metropolis as the most developed form of human settlement (Principle I) (Bolz 1951, pp. 32–52). Aesthetically, the Sixteen Principles were indebted to Stalin's doctrine and policy of 'socialism in one country' (Stalin 1954). Instead of conceiving of the proletarian revolution as an international undertaking, Stalin broke with Lenin and switched to a *national* approach to building socialism guided by the center of the Eastern Bloc, Moscow. The main function of socialist architecture and city building was no longer to experiment with new forms, as was suggested by modernists, including socialist ones. Instead, architecture was to identify and resuscitate 'progressive national traditions' (Principle X), which citizens would identify with (Principle IX). The new aesthetic doctrine of socialist realism proclaimed to be 'democratic in its content' and 'national in its form' (Principle XIV). It was meant to constitute a clear antidote to modernism's 'play with forms that was lacking in content' and its allegedly one-sided, technical-organizational orientation and cosmopolitanism, which was deemed to be negligent of 'national life' (Bolz 1951, pp. 32–52). Ironically, it was the socialists who retapped the myth of *Heimat*, which was a prominent element of National Socialism, a retapping that constitutes but one example of the less clear-cut severing of the ties to Germany's fascist history than the official socialist rhetoric suggested (Palmowski 2009).

At the Fifth Congress of the Central Committee of the Socialist Unity Party of Germany (Sozialistische Einheitspartei Deutschlands, SED) in 1951, the 'war' against modernism was finally officially declared. Modernism was equated not only with the uprooting and destruction of national culture but also with American anti-humanism and capitalist imperialism (Hain 1996b, p. 79) – a line of argument brought forward by socialists and previously by fascists. The SED trusted in *gesundes Volksempfinden* [the people's healthy sentiment] instead and declared the representation of the latter as the main tasks of art in general and architecture in particular (Hain 1996b, p. 86). In her seminal work *Dreamworld and Catastrophe* (2002), the philosopher Susan Buck-Morss captures the turn from modernist to Stalinist aesthetics as follows: a 'culture of monumentality' began to supplant a 'culture of mobility'. The latter is characterized by having freed itself from human immobility for the sake of constant motion and creative tempo, 'because only the very idea of movement has a great potential for development'. By contrast, 'the culture of monumentality' is shaped by a repudiation of movement, change, and cosmopolitanism, characteristics that, from the perspective of Stalinist aesthetic, betrayed the motherland. This culture of monumentality, Buck-Morss pinpoints poetically, makes even a 'monument to space flight' appear 'unrelentingly grounded'. No matter how high the pedestal or how soaring its shape, the cosmonaut seems to struggle against gravity in vain' (2002, pp. 121–122).

In a speech delivered to the East German *Volkskammer* [people's chamber] in October 1951, Walter Ulbricht, head of the SED's central committee from 1950 to 1971, declared that from that point on, true socialist architecture was to embody totality, beauty, and national traditions, traditions that reminded people of their struggles for national liberation (1951). Ulbricht's political dictum was translated into architectural practice in the form of East Germany's 'display window', the *Stalinallee*. Hermann Henselmann, the housing project's chief architect, believed his task as a city builder was to:

> ... express the ideas of socialism by means of architectural images that draw on popular symbols of people's social life and, simultaneously, to take the unity of urban and artistic concepts as a starting point, a unity the *Stalinallee* is a part of. The core idea behind these buildings is that the creative power of man is able to raise victory above rubble, war, and misery. It is this idea that should become effective by means of a pathos that strengthens the belief in one's own capacities and that awakens one's will to act. [my translation] (Henselmann 1991)

To be sure, socialist realism was implemented from above. Yet, as Simone Hain shows, the implementation fell on fertile ground in East Germany. After WWII in particular, heroic attempts to rescue social totality in the form of art (including architecture) and politics *did* resonate with the masses. After 1945, people were desperate for a better future and, more specifically, desperate for the reconstitution of respect for one's self and one's country. For the great majority of people, transcending the sober post-WWII reality by means of founding a 'new society' based on tradition and the protective shell of the collective was considerably more attractive than – as suggested by many modernists – inventing society from scratch (Hain 1996b, pp. 88–94). Ultimately, modernism would make a prominent return in East Germany in the 1960s, namely in the form of highly standardized, prefabricated concrete slab towers, the (infamous) *Plattenbauten*. Yet in the early 1950s, the course was still set for socialist realism, of which the 'workers' palaces' on Berlin's *Stalinallee* are a prominent example.

4.2 Constructing Socialism with Taylor, Defending it with Tanks

On September 6, 1950, the National Reconstruction Law [*Aufbaugesetz*] was passed. It anchored the Sixteen Principles (§ 7); determined the cities where the reconstruction efforts were to be focused (§ 2); and equipped the state with an extensive right to expropriate (§ 14). The new law also provided the basis for a large-scale mobilization campaign, the National Reconstruction Work [*Nationales Aufbauwerk*], launched in January 1951. The National Reconstruction Work (re-)introduced public competitions modeled after the Russian Stakhanov movement[1] that incorporated Taylorist work methods in order to increase productivity at construction sites and in workplaces. The SED hoped that stepping up the productivity of workers would countervail the limited economic output that had resulted from ongoing structural reforms, such as expropriation, nationalization, and high taxation on private industry.

On November 25, 1951, the party released a nation-wide appeal in the socialist daily *Neues Deutschland* to volunteers for rebuilding the capital of Germany 'more beautifully and generously' than it had ever been before (Neues Deutschland 1951). The provision of housing on Berlin's *Stalinallee* was the National Reconstruction Work's first focus. The choice to link the mobilization campaign to housing construction instead of other social domains was driven not only by humanitarian considerations (as suggested by the official rhetoric) but also by strategic concerns. For one, mobilizing people to volunteer for something they were in dire need of was promising. Moreover, mass participation in housing construction and, more generally, in the reconstruction of the capital was meant to demonstrate to the West the socialist regime's decidedness in its efforts to begin anew as well as the popular support it gained in doing so.

Yet before the actual construction of the *Magistrale des Ostens* [Magistrale of the East] could begin, the rubble had to be cleared and recycled: 'Only if scrap metal is collected by the inhabitants of Berlin *above target*, founded by steel workers *above target*, milled by the millers *above target*, transported by the rail-workers *above target*, will we have modern high rises at the end' [my translation, emphases added] (Neues Deutschland 1951). The rhetoric employed to motivate people to participate in the National Reconstruction Work suggested that the redemption of the promise of socialism would be imminent. All that was allegedly needed for the ultimate advent of socialism (and thus the comprehensive satisfaction of human needs) was a collective commitment to above-target productivity. The impending major leap forward in human history was also depicted as being dependent on a

1 In 1935, a miner in the Soviet Union, Alexei Stakhanov, was coronated as a socialist 'model worker' due to his (alleged) 'above-average productivity'. By showcasing outstanding workers, Stalin hoped to achieve two purposes: to increase worker productivity and to underline the superiority of the socialist economic system.

shared understanding of progress, which was already lying dormant and thus only in need of being woken up. As the SED put it: 'As soon as the people [*Volk*] start to speak its own language, to speak the language of progress, any cultural feat [*Kulturtat*] is possible' (Neues Deutschland 1951). But to bring about above-target productivity and 'cultural feats' already *before* the full emergence of a shared language of progress, the party had to resort to other means: 'shock work' in the form of socialist competitions and the introduction of Taylorist production methods.

At 5:00 pm on November 25, 1951, the bells for the first major collective undertaking in rubble clearing sounded and 45,000 volunteers started their shifts on *Stalinallee*. Floodlights lit up the rubble clearance sites, loudspeakers amplified songs composed for the purpose, and party-appointed poets and painters documented the operations and their heroes. Among the first voluntary reconstruction workers were high-ranking officials, among them the SED Secretary General Walter Ulbricht, East Germany's premier minister Otto Grotewohl, and East Berlin's mayor Friedrich Ebert, all of whom sought to demonstrate unity between the governing and the governed (Nicolaus and Obeth 1997, p. 172) [see Illustration 4.2].

Inspired by Soviet-style socialist competitions, the Committee for the National Reconstruction Work, together with the SED's mass organizations, organized competitive rubble clearance and reconstruction operations, especially on weekends and holidays. They encouraged local construction businesses to outperform one another in clearing construction sites, adults to top one another's number of voluntary shifts worked, and children to compete with one another in 'building their own future'. 'Activists' were expected to emerge from these competitions, that is, outstanding volunteers whose performance would exceed existing work norms. The possibility of obtaining one of the emerging apartments on *Stalinallee* was among the 'material lures' that were expected to entice people to outperform one another for the collective goal of socialism (Nicolaus and Obeth 1997, pp. 128–130).

And activists *did* emerge. They also broke existing work norms, norms that were set by socialist specialists in Taylorism who dissected and calculated the workers' body movements to increase efficiency. The East German elite was particularly fascinated by a particular Taylorist masonry system. Heralded by the famed and medaled Soviet activist called Schawlugin, the masonry system was described as follows:

> Schawlugin's team of five consists of two men and three women. Schawlugin himself works closely with a woman. She prepares the bricks for

4.2 Rubble Clearance, Berlin (1945). © ullstein bild

> the outer brick row, spreads the mortar with a shovel, which the mason redistributes with his ladle before finally laying the bricks. Schawlugin concentrates exclusively on the exterior brick row [...] he only performs tasks that require skill [...]. The second, less skilled mason also teams up with a woman and lays the interior brick row. The third woman, the last 'man' in the team, lays the bricks in between the outer and interior row. [my translation] (Planen und Bauen 1950)

Schawlugin's work method was soon to be employed on *Stalinallee*, whose construction sites fulfilled the double purpose of displaying a collective, above-average work ethic and showcasing a commitment to Taylorist efficiency.

Apart from increasing efficiency, Taylorism also offered a promising path toward expanding the workforce by bringing in (unskilled) female labor. Without doubt, the SED considered the integration of women into the workforce as an essential step toward women's emancipation. Yet instrumental reasons such as increased economic output often weighed more than the realization of the socialist principle of gender equality (Schmidt 2007). In fact, the above description of the Schawlugin method itself highlights the gender *in*equality: *skilled* labor was to remain in male hands and *unskilled* labor in female hands.

The questions of why and how Taylorism – a mode of production that clearly had its origins in the United States, the heartland of 'capitalist imperialism' – was imported and normalized by socialists, will be explored in more detail below. For now, suffice it to say that the reason Taylorism was embraced in East Germany already at this point was that socialists, no less than capitalists, saw in Taylorism the possibility of generating social harmony by means of producing material bounty (Kopstein 1997, pp. 30–31). Efficient production lines were key to the latter. While the hopes attached to Taylorism were similar on both sides of the wall, the success in redeeming the promise was starkly different. In post-war West Germany, as will be shown in the next chapter, Taylorist mass production was complemented by Fordist mass consumption, which ushered in the *Deutsche Wirtschaftswunder* [German economic miracle], of which the 'housing miracle' was one component. By contrast, in East Germany, increased productivity did not bring about the promised material bounty, at least not as quickly and never to the same extent as it did in West Germany. Citizens who were dissatisfied with the standard of living provided by the Plan were simply expected to work harder. 'The way we work today, we will live tomorrow' was an often-repeated slogan in East Germany during the 1950s (Merkel 1996, p. 9).

Historically speaking, the dream of a perfectly harmonized society was often accompanied by the dream of a military society, noted Foucault. The latter's

> fundamental reference was not to the state of nature, but to the meticulously subordinated cogs of a machine, not to the primal social contract, but to permanent coercions, not to fundamental rights, but to indefinitely progressive forms of training, not to the general will but to automatic docility. (Foucault 1977/1995, p. 169)

The SED clearly dreamt of both: of a perfect society and of a military one. And both dreams were staged on *Stalinallee*. On the construction sites, workers built their own 'palaces' because in a socialist society, the proletariat was not only to live decently but prestigiously. They would be trained in building methods but also in motor sports and shooting. Especially the younger workers were later commonly recruited by the *Kasernierte Volkspolizei*

[Baracked People's Police], the military branch of the police. Those young male construction workers who *did* become police were released pompously into their new duties. At roofing ceremonies, a merited construction worker would hand over weapons to the young men – a public orchestration of the perfect harmony so sought after by the regime between workers and the executive (Nicolaus and Obeth 1997, pp. 178–188). Yet the staged and dreamt-of harmony turned out to be imperfect in reality.

On June 16, 1953, construction workers from Block 40 of the *Stalinallee* walked off their jobs in protest against an increase of the productivity quota by 10 percent. This increase was paired with price hikes for food, health care, and public transportation and amounted to a monthly wage cut of about 30 percent (Beier and Köbele 1993). The SED's decision to raise work norms and prices was a response to financial pressures due to inflation, increased defense spending, and declining agricultural and industrial output. While the party insisted that higher productivity was dependent on an enhanced socialist work ethic, workers were fully aware that the root causes of the limited economic output and the low standard of living were political. They were the result of a chronic shortage of material and technology combined with a command economy whose planning was often at odds with the available human and material resources (Nicolaus and Obeth 1997, pp. 199–200). Workers from all over the city and country quickly joined the protesters on *Stalinallee*. The demonstration's peak was on 17 June 1953. A general strike took place in East Berlin and all over East Germany, a strike that was supported by more than one million people in the capital alone (Deutsches Bundesarchiv, 2013) [see Illustration 4.3].

In a frenzy to ward off the possibility of a coup, the SED adopted a dual strategy of disciplining *and* appeasing. On the disciplining side, the SED relied on tanks and show trials to streamline society. In fact, the 1953 revolt proved to be the perfect occasion for enacting a public purge against those alleged 'fascist and capitalist agitators' who dared to sabotage the 'planned construction of socialism' (Nicolaus and Obeth 1997, p. 200; Buck 2004, p. 146). Apart from disciplining, appeasement was also a chosen strategy. It included measures such as the lowering of work norms, prices, and taxes as well as the public display of the government's commitment to finally elevate the standard of living. In a widely advertised exhibition titled *Besser Leben–schöner Wohnen* [Living Better, Dwelling More Beautifully], the German Academy for Building [*Deutsche Bauakademie*] and the Ministry for Light Industry had 30 showrooms display the immanent socialist way of life. To demonstrate that the government *did* care about the people, visitors were encouraged to participate in a survey in which they were to express

4.3 June 17th, 1953, Russian Tanks, Potsdamer Platz, Berlin. © Bundesarchiv

their 'true' needs and desires (Deutsche Bauakademie and Ministerium für Leichtindustrie 1954, p. 75).

4.3 'Living Better, Dwelling More Beautifully': Toward a Socialist Dwelling Culture?

Ironically, similar to the dwelling culture propagated by the Austro-Marxists, there was little that was specifically 'socialist' about the dwelling culture endorsed by the East German government. In East Germany, as in Vienna, the floor plans of the 'workers' palaces' mirrored rather than challenged bourgeois dwelling norms such as privacy, representation, traditional gender roles, and the normalization of dwelling as an independent activity in the form of living rooms (Häußermann and Siebel 1996, pp. 16–19). Thus, epigonism informed the *Stalinallee*'s facades no less than the ideal socialist apartment's interior. In light of the post-1953 promise to improve people's standard of living, the Council of Ministers instructed the German Academy for Building and various ministries to carry out scientific research on traditional national designs of furniture, lighting, and textiles; to select the best designs; to adjust them to the workers' needs; and to accelerate the mass production of furniture (Deutsche Bauakademie and Ministerium fuer Leichtindustrie 1954, 106, 108–110). In contrast to modernists who had stipulated the 'measurement of men' as the 'correct measurement' (Stam 1984), if men are understood as *modern* men who sit, lie, walk, eat, and wash themselves differently from the men in the past (Schuster 1984), the socialists held fast to socialist realism. Socialist realist interior design was to be functional and yet shaped by tradition – ironically, the tradition of bourgeois aesthetics – in order to adequately accommodate the eye in need of rest. As Kurt Liebknecht, head of the German Building Academy, put it in the immediate aftermath of the 1953 unrests, 'The care for men' can never be adequately expressed 'by constantly creating something new [...]'. Instead, it hinges on creating the 'practical-useful' and the 'aesthetic-artistic' on the basis of 'the humanism of classicism, the modesty of *Biedermeier*, and the comfort of *Chippendale*' (Liebknecht 1954, 13, 21, 58).

Bourgeois norms informed the aesthetics of the ideal socialist dwelling as well as the latter's floor plans, at least in the exhibit. In the brochure that accompanied the 'Living Better, Dwelling More Beautifully' exhibit, the importance of representative and interstitial spaces – such as the lobby, the apartment's entrance hall, and the living room – was underlined (Deutsche Bauakademie and Ministerium für Leichtindustrie 1954). As Liebknecht explained, lobbies were also to be built in workers' housing, since they constituted an important 'intermediary' space between the 'higher social significance of the socialist street' and the semi-privacy of the socialist dwelling. As a space of transition, the lobby was conceived of as a space of representation, and thus it was to be equipped with ideally mass-produced marble and stone, tiles, stucco, paint, ornate staircase railings, sculptures, and paintings. Similar importance was given to the apartment's entrance hall. Besides connecting the semi-public space of the building with the private or personal space of the apartment, the entrance hall was to render the visitor with a good first impression of the apartment while simultaneously protecting him or her from the intimate smells and noises of the apartment's 'guts' – the kitchen and the bathroom. As for the living room – the 'largest and most social dwelling space' and the 'center of composition' – the Academy of Building proposed to equip it with mass-produced hardwood floors, lusters, solid wooden doors, painted walls decorated with stucco, and paintings (Liebknecht 1954, pp. 53–58).

Despite the fact that the socialists retained and celebrated numerous features of bourgeois dwelling culture, the *de facto* modest size of the apartments in the workers' palaces revealed the necessity to strike a balance between the goal of mass access to bourgeois dwelling practices and the economic imperative of cost-effectiveness. The average size of the apartments built from 1951 to 1955 was 42 square meters. Due to limited space, multiple dwelling functions were attributed to the living room, which was clearly not the case in traditional bourgeois dwellings. Besides serving the purpose of dwelling, the living rooms in the workers' palaces on *Stalinallee* had to also serve the purposes of sleeping, eating, and working if necessary (Nicolaus and Obeth 1997, pp. 8–9). Cost-effectiveness was also one of the reasons for ultimately eliminating an important feature of traditional working-class culture in East Germany no less than in Red Vienna: the live-in kitchen, i.e., a kitchen used not only for meal preparation but also for socialization. Under the banners of hygiene, efficiency, and women's integration into the workforce, the live-in kitchen had to gradually give way to the allegedly space-saving, labor-saving, and time-saving functional eat-in kitchen, which sometimes amounted to a size of less than five square meters. As the feminist Marlene Grotewohl suggested in an article from 1952: '[T]he utmost rationalization and mechanization of domestic work [is essential to] winning over the female labor force for the great reconstruction work of our country. [...] Every work hour saved in the single household means freeing additional resources for society.' [my translation] (1952, pp. 98–99).

By integrating women into the workforce and by seeking to facilitate the latter by rationalizing and also socializing reproductive labor, especially with a view to childcare, the German Democratic Republic (GDR) clearly and fundamentally broke with one core element of the bourgeois family ideal: women's economic dependency on men. On the economic front, gender equality in East Germany was considerably further advanced than in post-war West Germany, where the ideal of the housewife and consumer reigned supreme well into the late 1960s (Hund 1987; Ghodsee 2018; Kleinschmidt 2008, pp. 131–162). As Jürgen Habermas explains, in the bourgeois tradition, the family was relegated to the private sphere, a sphere free from both the anonymous laws of the market and the political directives of the court. Consequently, the family was considered the locus of the 'private autonomy of the intimate', a space in which family members were able to explore what it means to be human. In theory, argues Habermas, both genders were at liberty to 'humanize their soul and spirit' in the intimate sphere of the private. In practice, however, this humanization in the realm of the private was the prerogative of men. Since *economic* autonomy was a precondition for private autonomy, a precondition met by bourgeois men but not by bourgeois women due to their exclusion from the market, the possibility to humanize one's soul and spirit in the private sphere was clearly a *male* privilege (Habermas 1962/1990, pp. 112–114). Because women were actively integrated into the labor force in East Germany, they *did* manage to secure a precondition for the exercise of autonomy: economic independence (Ghodsee 2018).

Moreover, in East Germany 'humanization' was not meant to be restricted to the private sphere and its spatial correlative, the apartment or the family home, as was the case in traditional bourgeois dwelling culture. Instead, in line with core socialist tenets, East Germany sought to expand the sphere of 'humanization' by complementing the apartment with social spaces, such as locales of mass organizations and recreational, social, and cultural facilities, spaces that were meant to constitute an integral part of any socialist dwelling complex. Accordingly, similar to Red Vienna's *Gemeindebauten*, East Germany's dwelling complexes were to serve, at least in theory, as loci for humanization in the form of *socialization* instead of *individuation*. In practice, East German housing units were not always furnished with the planned political, social, cultural, and recreational facilities. In fact, with the exception of daycare facilities, which were *essential* to bringing women into the workforce, the provision of social spaces was often neglected – the focus being on the numeric increase of apartment units. Financial and material constraints were one reason for the neglect, as was the lingering need for additional housing units.

Social and communal space fell victim to East Germany's economy of shortage, and so did, ultimately, socialist realist architecture. At the All-Union's Conference in December 1954, Stalin's successor, Nikita Khrushchev fulminated against Stalin's architectural excesses and proclaimed that the architects' 'addiction to ornamentation' and the craftsmen's 'tinkering' [*Handwerkelei*] were to be replaced by standardization and typification. Khrushchev's imperative was to 'to build better, cheaper, and faster' in order to solve the housing question (Chruschtschow 1955). The Soviet Union's 'brother states', including East Germany, were expected to align their housing policies accordingly. Thus, at a building conference in 1955, Walter Ulbricht officially ushered in East Germany's revised architectural orientation and a ministerial decision that elevated the industrialization of housing construction to the rank of law (Nicolaus and Obeth 1997, pp. 264–277). This reorientation from socialist realism to modernist functionalism after Stalin's death, the so-called 'great turn' in the construction industry, heralded the era of *Plattenbauten* [concrete slab buildings] which East German socialism's in general, and its public housing policies in particular, are typically connoted with. Similar to West Germany's adoption of modernism in the 1950s, East Germany's return to modernism in the same decade was deprived of the early modernist movement's encompassing *social-political* aspirations: the reconciliation of aesthetics, technology, *and* politics for the sake of human flourishing instead of one-sided, techno-scientific innovation. In East Germany, one-sided, techno-scientific innovation meant a commitment to 'total industrialization', including the total industrialization of the housing question.

4.4 From the Workers' Palace Back to the Dwelling Machine

Already in the early years of the GDR's existence, when socialist realism was still the official aesthetic doctrine, socialists had already experimented with an utterly audacious instantiation of total industrialization: the housing construction machine designed by Ernst Neufert. Neufert was a student of modernism under the aegis of Walter Gropius and, during the years of fascism, an appointee of Albert Speer. Neufert's housing construction machine was devised as a mobile factory. Moving forward like a train on tracks, the machine was designed to 'drop' five-story row houses at any desired length. It was 'fed' with construction material in the front, material that was to be 'digested' in the machine's interior through a pulsing procedure facilitated through a highly specialized crew of workers. The end-product was row housing consisting of units of 10 apartments each, units that could be produced within only a week and all year round, since Neufert's machine's weather-proof casing was designed to render the construction industry independent of seasonal changes (Voigt 1999, p. 29) [see Illustration 4.4].

The socialists' experiment with the housing construction machine was abandoned soon after it had begun. A high number of fatalities among workers brought an abrupt end to this specific dream of 'total industrialization' (Hain 1996a, p. 107). Nonetheless, the experiment bore testimony to a fundamental tension undergirding East German socialism since its inception: the socialist ideal of putting human needs and desires center stage and an awareness that the satisfaction of even the most basic human needs and desires was dependent on rationalization and standardization. As long as the aesthetic doctrine of socialist realism was hegemonic, however, the East German regime had to make deliberate efforts to *hide* new, rationalized technologies behind traditional aesthetic forms. For instance, the ideal socialist realist interior décor was to entail marble, stucco, and tiles, in line with bourgeois dwellings. For cost-saving reasons, it was recommended that the décor be mass-produced using cheap raw material (Liebknecht 1954).

After the 'great turn' in the construction industry, however, the reproduction of historicist forms was finally discarded and functionalist aesthetics was resuscitated. Yet this resuscitation did not entail the resuscitation

4.4 Ernst Neufert's House Building Maschine, 1943. © Neufert Stiftung, Weimar

of modernist *political* ideals, such as the ideal of human emancipation through technology. It simply served the purposes of producing housing more efficiently, quickly, and at a cheaper rate. 'Modernism – Revolution = Modernization', argues the urban theorist Kanishka Goonewardena (2009, pp. 2010–2012), and modernization it was in East Germany. Workers' palaces had to give way to mass-produced concrete slab buildings, the *Plattenbauten*,[2] which were tailored to fulfil the predetermined minimal human functions of sleeping, eating, dwelling, and hygiene.

Although East Germany had already experimented with prefabrication and standardization in the early 1950s, the mass-produced *Platte* as a hallmark of socialism did not emerge until the early 1970s. The latter coincides with the empowerment of Erich Honecker as General Secretary of the SED in 1971 who declared solving the housing question a state doctrine. Consequently, in October 1973, the SED's central committee passed a housing program that foresaw the construction of at least 100,000 new public housing units per year, amounting to a total of 2.8 to 3 million apartments by 1990 (Buck 2004, p. 325). By 1990, 2.2 million new housing units were built throughout East Germany, of which 1.5 units were *Plattenbau* apartments, typically located in large-scale, suburban housing settlements. In East Berlin and in East Germany, every second and fourth household respectively lived in a *Plattenbau* (Liebscher 2009, p. 7). The new form of housing was

2 The term *Plattenbau* or, in short, *Platte* denotes a specific industrial building technique and building type that is informed by certain technical, organizational, aesthetic, and sociological norms, norms this section will elaborate on. In East Germany, most *Plattenbauten* were designed for housing purposes (Richter, 2006, p. 5).

4.5 East Berlin's "Plattenbauten": Marzahn. © Bundesarchiv

expected to finally accommodate 'developed socialist personalities' (Maaß 2006, p. 121) and to mirror a class society of a new kind in which university professors would live next to factory workers and plant managers next to poets. Although East German socialists had initially dismissed the modernist dream of Mies van der Rohe or Walter Gropius as an effigy of capitalism's inhumanity – the technoid dream of solving the housing question by means of industrial rationalization – the SED was ultimately and ironically *the* political force that came closest to normalizing the modernist dwelling machine. Apartments in East Germany's most common *Plattenbau* type, the WBS70, were standardized to such an extent that they could be built and assembled in as little as 18 hours (Stadt und Land Wohnbauten-Gesellschaft mbH) [see Illustration 4.5].

The *Platte* has become a symbol of state socialism. Yet, one may ask, why is this the case? Neither industrialization nor rationalization nor socialism would *necessarily* have resulted in the building of the *Platte*. In fact, industrialization and rationalization were considerably further advanced in the United States than in Europe before and certainly after 1945 (Hughes 1989). Moreover, an explicit decision against industrial rationalization was within the range of socialist options. For instance, the Austro-Marxist administration of Red Vienna (1919–1934) also declared housing as a right and yet consciously chose not to extend the industrial logic into the private space in its construction of workers' housing, as they saw in it an extension of the logic of alienation, as mentioned in the second chapter.

One explanation for why the *Platte* instead of other building types materialized as socialism's *symbol* is that the existing dominant industrial practices of the time – Taylorism and Fordism – outpaced socialist theory. Although fundamental discussions about the nature and direction of the techno-scientific revolution that the *Platte* was a product of *did* take place, their impact on actual building practices was limited. As the urban sociologist Christine Hannemann explains:

> The GDR's construction industry is [...] a great example of the relative lead of practice over theory [...] Since no binding practical conclusions could be drawn from typically politically explosive, meta-theoretical debates [on the future of housing], construction practitioners could apply their professional ideologemes even more audaciously. [my translation] (1996, p. 108)

The ideologemes invoked were strikingly similar to capitalist ones: scientific labor management, rationalization, and automatization.

One of the practitioners and driving forces behind East Germany's techno-scientific revolution was Gerhard Kosel, who was a committed socialist, a student of Bruno Taut, and an émigré to the Soviet Union, where he worked as an architect from 1933 to 1954. Upon his return to Germany, the Ministry of Reconstruction entrusted Kosel with the task to develop the industrialization and rationalization of the construction industry based on his experience in the Soviet Union (Hannemann 1996, pp. 70–71). In his pursuit of the rationalization, centralization, and 'scientification' [*Verwissenschaftlichung*] of the construction industry, Kosel took issue with one of Marxism-Leninism's fundamental principles: to consider science as part of the unproductive superstructure. Kosel, in contrast, fervently made the case for recognizing not only manual and industrial labor but also scientific work as a productive force. He was convinced that the housing question could only be effectively solved if production, technology, and science were closely intertwined. For this to be possible, science had to be socialized by the state (Kosel 1957, pp. 5–7). The state's greatest task, according to Kosel, was to bring about 'encyclopedically educated workers' who were versed in all fields of natural science and steeped in practical experience. Only a highly educated and experienced workforce would be 'well equipped for and adaptable to the industrial economy's constantly changing challenges and conditions' (Kosel 1957, pp. 139–142). Moreover, in Kosel's view, production, technology, science, and – as already suggested by Henry Ford – leisure had to be closely intertwined, as they constituted the *sine qua non* for increased productivity and efficiency. The expected reward for increased productivity and efficiency was human self-realization. For the latter to be possible, the automatic factory had to supplant the mechanic factory, and automatons had to replace experts (Kosel 1957, p. 135). According to Kosel, centralization, including the centralization of the construction industry, was the prerequisite for automatization – a perspective the East German state adopted gradually, especially after the construction of the Berlin Wall in 1961 (Marcuse and Schumann 1992).

Kosel's position exemplifies how Taylorist principles of management and Fordist principles of social politics reappeared in Marxist clothes in East Germany. The emphasis on the importance of scientific innovation for the production process, the deconstruction of the production process and its rational and more efficient reconstruction, the centralization of management and oversight, the decision to use industrial labor over craftsmanship, the creation of a flexible labor force, and the promise of increased leisure were all hallmarks of Taylorism and later of Fordism that found their way into socialism. Yet why did Marx in particular and socialist texts in general play a lesser role in determining certain economic practices than did Taylor and Ford? Certainly, Marx's celebration of industrialization and the full unfolding of the productive forces in his Communist Manifesto found its equivalent in the GDR's initial primary focus on heavy industrialization. Moreover, Marx's argument that the transition from the 'principle of the subjective division of labor' to 'the objective division of labor' (Marx 1887, XV, I) is the precondition for class consciousness was echoed by East German proponents of 'deep' industrialization, centralization, and standardization. To be sure, the socialist embrace of practices that were closely connected with capitalism had less to do with a compromising of their ideological principles than with a fundamental dilemma that all real socialist experiments faced: the limited availability of socialist practices to rely on or fall back on. This situation led to the appropriation of already established practices, with all the ensuing contradictions. In Foucault's terminology, one of the core problems of state socialism was the lack of a 'socialist governmentality', i.e., the lack of a socialist rationalization of governmental practice in the exercise of political sovereignty. Typically, argues Foucault, socialism

> has been connected up to liberal governmentality, and then socialism and its forms of rationality function as counter-weights, as a corrective, and a palliative to internal dangers. [...] We have seen it function [...]

> within governmentalities that [...] fall more under [...] the police state, that is to say, a hyper-administrative state in which there is, so to speak, a fusion, a continuity, the constitution of a sort of massive bloc between governmentality and administration. [...] if there is a real socialist governmentality, then it is not hidden within socialism and its texts. It cannot be deduced from them. It must be invented. (2008, pp. 91–93)

Although one may disagree with the absolutist nature of Foucault's claim given that East German socialism *did* develop elements of a truly socialist governmentality, such as the constitutionally anchored right to housing, Foucault's point touches on something crucial: the legacy of inherited governmental practices, ideas, and rationalities that cuts *across* the political and ideological spectrum.

Kosel belonged to the group of practitioners who sought to anchor a socialist governmentality in the housing sector – not by inventing it *ex nihilo* but by appropriating practices entrenched in capitalist regimes for socialist purposes. Yet by doing so, some of these practices' fundamental contradictions – contradictions from a socialist perspective – were appropriated as well. For instance, the type of knowledge Kosel wanted to 'encyclopedify' was very specific: the productive, positive knowledge of applied, natural science, i.e., knowledge that was quintessential to the techno-scientific revolution. Ultimately, Kosel's proposed encyclopedia was an encyclopedia of 'best practices' that evolved from narrowly defined techno-scientific parameters whose goals were to enhance productivity and to increase leisure. By contrast, Marx's endorsement of an 'all-round development of the individual' pursued neither increased productivity nor leisure but social conditions under which labor would no longer serve as a means to life (or livelihood) but as 'life's prime want' (Marx 1875/1978, p. 531). Against the backdrop of Marx, the East German trajectory of educating citizens to step up production and to expand leisure constituted an extension of capitalist relations of production rather than their overhaul. Marx's vision of social conditions that rendered labor 'life's prime want' clearly went beyond the promise of leisure and its underpinning rationales, the regeneration of labor and, under Fordist conditions, mass consumption. Moreover, in East Germany, Marx's ideal of differential egalitarianism captured in the precept '[f]rom each according to his ability, to each according to his needs' (Marx 1875/1978, p. 531) was replaced by abstract egalitarianism, embodied by a highly standardized and functionalist living environment. In short, Marx's materialist history of need pointed to the possibility of liberating desire. East German socialism promised to redeem the liberation of desire yet entangled itself with practices that socialist theory had criticized and had sought to supersede.

The relative dominance of existing practices over socialist theory is an important explanation for why the *Platte* emerged as a symbol of socialism. It is, however, not the only explanation. An equally weighty factor for the hegemony of the *Platte* as a building form is the East German political elite's decision to opt for centralization. Public housing is one manifestation of the East German government's decision to catapult the state into the position of a technologically oriented planner and social engineer. The national plan determined the number of new units to be produced as well as the availability and redistribution of material resources and labor. Regional and local plans were developed to implement the national plan, without having much impact on what was decided at the national level (Marcuse & Schumann, 1992, p. 96). Although land was never nationalized to the same degree as it was in the Soviet Union, the East German state had easy access to it: by the equivalent of eminent domain, the state could take away land from private owners for state purposes, such as the construction of public housing (ibid., pp. 88–89). The Ministry of Building was the central state institution that oversaw the planning and financing of new housing development as well as the production of material at the state-owned building concerns [*Baukombinate*]. It also administered the standardization of building materials and building types – a degree of standardization unprecedented in liberal capitalist regimes. Due to the standardization of entire buildings, art in the form of architecture and traditional skills in the form of trades were increasingly supplanted by centrally planned civil and industrial engineering. Equally important, the standardization of building types led to the normalization of suburban settlements.

Certainly, industrial buildings had already been coupled with decentralized, suburban settlements in the 1920s. Yet in the GDR, the rigidity of industrial building in the form of building types and the centralized construction industry took urban decentralization to another level. In fact, often the emergence of suburban settlements was less driven by planning than by the spatial requirements of highly industrialized construction sites, requirements determined by crane runways, the operating range of hoists, storage for concrete slabs, and access routes for trucks (Hain 1996a, p. 108; Topfstedt 1988, p. 18). Accordingly, in contrast to early decentralized urban forms, such as the garden cities of the 1920s, the suburbs that emerged with the *Platte* were less imbued by the desire to reconstitute a harmonious balance between city and nature than by what the East German architect Bruno Flierl called *Kranideologie* [crane ideology] (Flierl 1993). Correspondingly, the 'in-between-green' between the *Platten* was clearly not the effect of a given planning ideal, such as the garden city or the city landscape, but a waste product of technological modernization.

4.5 Creative Destruction: The Double Legacy of the Platte

The industrial, functionalist *Plattenbau* settlements can be read as an embodiment of what Marshall Berman calls a 'Faustian model of development'. The East German state assumed the role of an 'organizer' or 'developer', which promised to 'bring material, technical and spiritual resources together, and transform them into new structures of social life' (Berman 1988, p. 74). Yet new creations come with a price. In Goethe's *Faust*, the building of new dams – a symbol of Faust's modern desire to finally reign supreme over nature – resulted in the tragic elimination of the old and hospitable couple Baucis and Philomen and their peasant way of life. In East Germany, the building of a new socialist society and its dwellings meant silencing those who disagreed with the state's equating of human progress and techno-scientific progress, its exploitative approach to nature given its push for heavy industrialization, the substitution of engineering for architecture, the elimination of local construction industries and their knowledge (including knowledge of craftsmanship), *and* the giving up of autonomy to state control (see also Rubin 2016). Throughout modernity, abstract reason in the form of economic and techno-scientific imperatives has repeatedly rendered concerns for the human secondary. This raises the question of whether the promise of modern political projects to reconcile techno-scientific progress with human progress may itself have become unkeepable. In 1947, Horkheimer and Adorno provided an unequivocally clear answer to this question. Abstraction, a key feature of Enlightenment,

> stands in the same relationship to its objects as fate, whose concept it eradicates: as liquidation. Under the levelling rule of abstraction, which makes everything in nature repeatable, and of industry, for which abstraction prepared the way, the liberated finally itself become the 'herd' (Trupp), which Hegel identified as the outcome of Enlightenment. (1947/2002, p. 9)

When applying Horkheimer and Adorno's negative assessment of Enlightenment reason to the East German context, one can certainly argue that the monotonous aesthetic of the *Platte* and *Plattenbau* settlement represented a prototypical micro-example of the Trupp's condition of possibility: people's emancipation from the housing misery was accompanied by the liquidation of – or, less strongly, abstraction from – place, difference, and particularity. To be sure, the discussed social norms implicit in the rigid building types and urban forms severely hampered people's ability to accommodate their own needs and desires in their living environment. Standardized housing and neighborhoods limited individual expression and disadvantaged social relationships that differed from the relationship normalized by the *Plattenbau* apartment's floorplan and by allocation policies, that is, the two-generational nuclear family (Hannemann 2005, pp. 113–116, 175–182; Kahl 2003, p. 69). However, while abstraction is reductive by definition and potentially destructive in practice, often it is also simultaneously and paradoxically creative. Thus, although East German mass housing undoubtedly neglected desires and differences, at the same time it embodied the state's commitment to render housing a right, and with this right a commitment to decommodify the basic need for shelter and the principle of social equality. In other words, the 'creative' dimension of the *Platte*'s implicit logic of abstraction was the reduction of social inequality. Whereas under liberal capitalist conditions the quality, size, and location of housing typically depended on and reflected the tenant's socio-economic standing, East German mass housing – while not eliminating social inequality completely[3] – nonetheless considerably reduced it (Häußermann and Siebel 1996, pp. 171–174). Moreover, 'de-differentiated' housing conditions had not only an equalizing effect on class relations but also on gender relations due to the fact that *Plattenbau* settlements were usually provided with childcare facilities. Although the provision of social and cultural facilities was often less prioritized than the quantitative increase of housing units, childcare *was* provided due to the state's interest in integrating women into the workforce. As a result, the combination of access to the labor market and childcare near one's home allowed East German women to achieve a degree of economic independence (Harth 2010, pp. 136–139; Ghodsee 2018), which would remain out of reach for West German women until the late twentieth century. Thus, one may argue, the legacy of the *Platte* is both 'destructive' and 'creative'. It is destructive regarding its underpinning 'liquidating abstractions' in the form of a built environment shaped by techno-scientific imperatives instead

3 *De jure*, privileges were abolished. *De facto*, however, privileges continued to exist in regard to, for instance, allocation policies (apart from social need, merit was a criterion for obtaining a newly built apartment) and access to high-end housing. In fact, and ironically, many members of the political elite lived in mansions located in upscale suburbs.

of human considerations. At the same time, it is creative because the *Platte* embodies a critical perspective on liberal capitalism's 'emancipation of civil society from politics' (Marx 1843/1978, p. 45). East Germany's constitutionally anchored right to housing and its underlying principle of egalitarianism called into question the logic of the market, its depoliticization of the need for housing, and the 'liquidating abstractions' that shape capitalism, for instance, in the form of spatial segregation along socio-economic lines. Moreover, it provided a critical perspective on the West German welfare state. Article 20 of the West German Basic Law from 1949 defines Germany as a social state, yet only *in principle.* Accordingly, the extent to which the state interferes with the market is highly dependent on the given political, economic, and ideological climate. This dependency, as I will show in greater detail in the next chapter, has informed West German housing policies, including their legacies today, in a major way. Whereas public investment in housing was generally agreed upon right after 1945, by the mid-1950s the West German government decided to slowly but steadily withdraw from the housing sector, a decision that was accompanied by a shift from the public subsidization of housing to the subsidization of individuals in need of housing (Häußermann and Siebel 1996, pp. 153–157). Yet before we turn to the building of liberalism to the west of the Berlin Wall, let us first take a look at the green in between the *Plattenbauten* and the latter's appropriation from below *despite* authoritarianism.

4.6 The Allotment Garden as the Platte's Antidote?

The gradual appropriation of the 'in between-green' by citizens for purposes of gardening and the building of makeshift homes was clearly not part of the SED's plan for building socialism, at least not at the beginning. Given the German garden movement's conservative and reformist history[4] and its political volatility,[5] the government under Walter Ulbricht (1950–1971)

4 The history of the East German allotment gardeners is rooted in nineteenth-century reformist traditions, including *Lebensreform* [reform of life], a social movement that propagated a back-to-nature lifestyle. This bourgeois reform movement sought to care for the working class by bettering the workers' living conditions without, however, generally questioning capitalist relations of production.

5 By the beginning of the twentieth century, a considerable part of the German garden colonies settlement organizations was affiliated with or was even operated by the Social Democrats who, in contrast to the Socialists, entertained a rather pragmatic relationship with the gardening segment of labor. By the 1930s, the National Socialists brought the settlement movement into line

assumed that the increasing popularity of the garden colonies would fade, once the economic situation, including the food supply, had improved. However, they remained popular well past the post-WWII food shortage. Accordingly, Ulbricht decided to resort to punitive measures to eradicate what he deemed to be petty-bourgeois and individualizing 'birthmarks of capitalism'. Some of the measures Ulbricht's government resorted to were expropriation, the centralization of the initially decentralized settler organizations, and sudden, poorly announced land use laws (Dietrich 2003, pp. 28, 76–84). Despite the adverse political climate, garden colonies survived. By the late 1950s, Ulbricht changed his punitive stance to a more accommodating one, a turn that, after the 1953 uprisings, was part of a general political reorientation toward better accommodating the needs and desires of the people. After the Fifth Party Congress of the SED in 1958, the garden colonies were no longer referred to as 'birthmarks of capitalism' but rather as an integral element of the transition from capitalism to socialism. 'Important social tasks' were allocated to the politically diverse yet centralized garden allotment association, the VKSK,[6] such as the 'political-ideological education' of gardeners and the strengthening of the gardeners' efforts to complement the Plan's not always reliable food supplies with fresh, local produce (Dietrich 2003, pp. 28–29, 134–135). In other words, as long as the 'fragmentary knowledge' of the gardeners and settlers – initially disapproved of – could be rendered socially productive and integrated into the 'total knowledge of socialism', at least rhetorically, the garden colonies were officially regarded as acceptable.

In contrast to Ulbricht's initial hesitant stance toward the garden movement, Honecker embraced the garden colonies as an appropriate environment for socialist citizens, an environment in which citizens were engaged in 'meaningful recreational activities' such as working the land and thereby tending to their social, physical, and mental well-being (Dietrich 2003, pp. 29, 221–234). Honecker's acceptance of the garden colonies went hand in hand with his commitment to Fordism. Given the promise of continuously increasing leisure time, 'meaningful recreational activities' had to be provided. Despite Honecker's support for garden colonies and the fact that the state provided the land for them, the state largely refrained from regulating or interfering with how the garden lots were used and

with National Socialism – without facing much resistance from the garden colonists (Dietrich, 2003, pp. 26-27).

6 The abbreviation VKSK stands for *Verband der Kleingärtner, Siedler und Kleintierzüchter*, that is, association of allotment gardeners, settlers, and small animal breeders.

appropriated.[7] One reason for the limited interference was administrative: in contrast to new housing construction, the garden colonies did not fall under the jurisdiction of the Ministry of Building but rather the Ministry of Agriculture, whose regulations concerning land use and development were loose and whose competence concerning building regulations was limited. Another reason was that Honecker concentrated his political attention and economic resources on the construction of new housing, given his promise to solve the housing question by 1990. Finally, Honecker was well aware of the citizens' dissatisfaction with the quality of life in East Germany. Providing recreational spaces such as the garden plots was important for increasing the state's legitimacy, as was refraining from overregulating their use.

What rendered the garden settlements so popular throughout the GDR's existence? The gardens did not escape the logic of the industrial-urban but rather extended it into the rural in the form of materialized leisure that had little to do with traditional rural life. Lefebvre explains this extension as follows:

> [...] the traditional unit typical of peasant life, namely the village, has been transformed. Absorbed or obliterated by larger units, it has become an integral part of industrial production and consumption. [...] The urban fabric grows, extends its borders, corrodes the residue of agrarian life. This expression, 'urban fabric,' does not narrowly define the built world of cities but all manifestations of the dominance of the city over the country. In this sense, a vacation home, a highway, [or] a supermarket in the countryside are all part of the urban fabric. (Lefebvre 2003, pp. 3–4)

The East German garden colonies were clearly part of what Lefebvre calls 'urban fabric'. In addition, they were an extension of the industrial-urban life: gardening was pursued as a hobby rather than as a necessity, the cottage was used as a second home instead of a primary home, the time lived at the cottage was compressed into weekends, holidays, and vacation. Nonetheless, the rural and natural *did* serve as a vanishing point for the needs and desires that functional urban spaces did not cater to (Schretzenmayr 2012, p. 46). One literary example of this is Sarah Kirsch's autobiographic text

7 This applied also to the allocation policies. In order to obtain a garden plot, membership in the settlers' organization VKSK was necessary. Although the state gradually attributed social and political tasks to the initially decentralized VKSK, membership in the organization was less driven by the members' interest in these tasks than their interest in obtaining a garden plot. In fact, most members were unfamiliar with the political statutes of the VKSK (Dietrich, 2003, p. 21).

4.6 Allotment Gardening in Marzahn, 1982. © Bundesarchiv

Allerleihrauh [Cinderella], in which she captures the experience of living in a newly built urban settlement in the metaphor of an egg that 'when dropped from a high-rise, never reaches the ground, but simply disappears' (quoted in Gremler 2007, p. 125). The metaphor of an endless fall conveys a sense of loss of control that Kirsch anchors in (but does not reduce to) the life world of the *Platte*. For her, escaping the city is equal to escaping the state. Kirsch's utopia is a farmhouse in Mecklenburg, a rural place remote from East Berlin in which a myriad of positive memories of summers well spent have their roots. One day, however, a fire ruthlessly destroys the bucolic idyll and with it, the utopian dream of a place outside of the demands of society (ibid.).

Kirsch's perspective was not merely a fictitious or personal one but one that was widely shared. Although moving into new public housing was popular not only because of the housing shortage but also because of the modern amenities it offered that were unavailable in old, inner-city housing (Rubin 2016), the monotony of the built environment was a common criticism (Topfstedt 1988, pp. 16–18; Marcuse and Schumann 1992, pp. 86–87; Kahl 2003). Another complaint was the lack of possibility to participate in the decision-making process that left people at the mercy of the communal housing authorities who oversaw allocation, collected rents, organized exchanges, and took care of maintenance and repair (Marcuse and Schumann 1992, pp. 94–95). As Marc Garcelon put it, one of the ironic paradoxes of sustained Soviet-style party rule was that

> the subordination of particular interests and the individuals' life course to the diktat of 'total administration' did not result in a harmonized society striving in union to realize the 'vanguard's' blueprint of the general will, but rather in the pervasiveness of particularistic orientations and the near obliteration of civic orientations. (1997, p. 322)

As a popular retreat from the city into nature, the garden colony was one site where particularization was lived. Dwelling, according to Benjamin, can be understood as the 'fashioning of a shell' for oneself, as the creation of a frenetically topical space that is detached from any form of instrumentality (Benjamin 2002, H2, 1; H2, 7; I4, 5). Such 'shells' were certainly fashioned in the garden colonies. A closer look at the specific life world of allotment gardeners will reveal some of the particularizations that were at stake.

The interior of the garden sheds, makeshift homes, and cottages, where weekends and summers were spent, often looked like museums of family histories. They were *omnium gatherums*, places filled with old pictures, documents, furniture, and plates, reflective of a frenetic personal topicality that the *Plattenbau* apartment left little room for due to its limited size, fixed layout, and design. Yet family history was not only preserved at the cottages (in the form of knick-knacks) but also relived. Family arrangements that the state had de-normalized, such as the extended family, were often reconstituted in the garden colonies. They were, for instance, an important locus for the bonding between the first and third generations. Against the backdrop of the state's concerted effort to normalize the nuclear family and to socialize children from an early age, the fact that parents often preferred their children to spend their summer vacation with their grandparents at the cottage instead of at a public childcare facility illustrates a critical censure against the state (Dietrich 2003, pp. 11, 16–20).

The gardens themselves were landscapes of different needs and aesthetic tastes. On the one hand, they supplied people with fresh fruit and vegetables that the collectivized farms did not produce enough of. On the other hand, they served as an experimental ground for aesthetic expression that took the form of such things as miniature trains, tunnels, viaducts, and mass-produced gnomes – an aesthetic one might readily dismiss as kitsch that fetishizes the transitory and reproducible and that is indifferent to the original, permanent, and rational. Yet if one refrains from a hasty rejection of kitsch to return to the original meaning of aesthetics, the fruit, vegetable, and paraphernalia-filled gardens might disclose more than mere worship of mass culture. *Aisthetikos* is the ancient Greek word for that which is 'perceptive by feeling' (Buck-Morss 1992, p. 6). The original meaning of the term aesthetics thus goes beyond the narrower sense of art as a beautiful semblance of the rational. Instead, it comprises a wider meaning of art, one that refers to cognition attained not by abstraction but by tasting, touching, hearing, seeing, and smelling – by what Susan Buck-Morss calls the 'corporeal sensorium'. The most immediate purpose of aesthetics understood as perception by feeling is to satisfy instinctual needs such as the need for warmth, nourishment, safety, or sociability. These needs retain an 'uncivilized and uncivilizable trace, a core of resistance to cultural domestication' that surfaces especially when people experience 'culture' as something that stifles 'nature' (ibid.)

Without doubt, in East Germany, culture was often experienced as something that stifled nature, as a result of which the retreat to the garden signified more than mere agro-romanticism. It was a form of 'embodied critique', of 'inarticulate rebellion against the tyranny of the theoretical', to use a phrase by Eagleton (1990, p. 13). The East German state had elevated the modern narcissist fairy tale of the *homo autotelus* to the fairy tale of *societas autotelus* (an elevation undertaken by other modern political enterprises, such as National Socialism), which suggests, at least in the fairy tale's *mythic* dimension, that a new society can be created miraculously out of its own substance. What was thereby forgotten, as Buck-Morss points out, is the fairy tale's wisdom: that the consequences of such an undertaking can be disastrous (Buck-Morss 1992, pp. 7–8). Retreating to the garden was one way in which to come to terms with what were maybe not disastrous but certainly constraining spatial creations by the state: the functionalist, standardized, and typically suburban housing developments. The allotment gardens catered to the needs and desires that the *Plattenbau* apartments and settlements housing blocks left unfulfilled. They nourished people physically and emotionally by (re-)connecting them with a less controlled natural environment, where they could engage in practices and reemploy skills such as subsistence gardening and the construction of makeshift homes, skills that the state had rendered secondary given its emphasis on industrial modernization. There are emotional rewards to craftsmanship, a term by which Richard Sennett designates all those activities that relate people to a tangible world in a non-instrumental way. Yet too often, as Sennett explains further, modern society stands in the way of taking pride in one's work and of gaining satisfaction from 'doing things well for their own sake':

> At different moments in Western history practical activity has been demeaned, divorced from supposedly higher pursuits. Technical skill has been removed from imagination, tangible reality doubted by religion, pride in one's work treated as a luxury. If the craftsman is special because he or she is an engaged human being, still the craftsman's aspirations and trials hold up a mirror to these larger past and present. (2008, p. 21)

Although practical activity was highly regarded in East Germany, centralized industrial modernization *did* remove technical skill from imagination (it also removed the individual decision-making that is typically involved in training one's skills). It continued and even exacerbated (due to centralization) some of the narrow confines that also characterize capitalist production: the reduction of work to wage labor, the increased division of labor due to rationalization, and the emphasis on productivity over workmanship. Given this backdrop, the allotment garden *did* provide possibilities that the stricter, controlled urban environment did not: to engage in non-instrumental activities[8] and to employ one's corporeal sensorium to satisfy one's needs and desires through aesthetic expression, to connect with extended family, and to have social relationships and lifestyles that the stricter controlled urban environment had made difficult.

Yet how unique was the life world of garden colonies to the East German context? To be sure, in many ways the practices of particularization in East German garden colonies resembled those in West German ones. The importance of appearance (and the desire for recognition) attached to the cottages and gardens, the decoration of gardens with products of mass culture, the intensive use and the often utilitarian approach to nature were common on both sides of the Wall (Kropp 2011). Although some of the practices were undoubtedly similar, the degree to which they were an extension or a subversion of a given dominant politico-economic logic depended on the larger social context in which they emerged. In light of the tight regulations of the urban built environment in East Germany, especially in new housing developments where a considerable part of the East German population lived, the garden colonies *did* represent 'another

8 It should be added that this possibility was more available to men than to women, whose activities at the cottages often remained dominated by reproductive work (Dietrich, 2003, pp. 18-19).

space', a 'heterotopic' space that called into question dominant space, at least in some respects. Put differently, it would be reductive to argue that the resemblance or even mimicry of practices entrenched in the West was merely an expression of a yearning for identity with that which was being resembled and mimicked, such as life in the West. Nature served as a vanishing point for the discontents of East German urban dwellers. Similarly, everyday life in the 'West' served as a vanishing point for people who were frustrated with everyday life in the 'East'. That said, there is an obvious gap between wish and reality: yearning for nature does not yet mean enjoying rural life; similarly, yearning for liberal capitalism does not yet mean living a fulfilled life under conditions of liberal capitalism.

Following David Harvey, 'heterotopia [i.e., spatial vanishing points] allow us to see how "otherness", alterity, and alternatives [to hegemonic space] might be explored not as mere figments of the imagination, but through contact with social processes that already exist'. However, at the same time, these explorations leave us clueless as to what a spatio-temporal utopianism might look like and how potential alternatives might be redeemed (Harvey 2000, pp. 184–185). The garden colonies were sites where particularization and individualization occurred relative to the *Plattenbau* apartments and suburban environs. While they reveal needs and desires whose pertinence was heightened against the backdrop of the rigidity and dominance of the *Plattenbau*, they did not yet point toward an alternative politically emancipatory space. However, the garden colonies did point toward the fact that in any social reality, including spatial reality, there is always a dimension of indeterminacy. As Zizek put it following Lacan, there is always a 'surplus of the Real', such as people's self-accommodation of their needs and desires, 'over every symbolization', such as the East German state's provision of built environments for the 'developed socialist personality' (Zizek 1998/2008, p. vvx).

In the particular context of East Germany, the indeterminacy that Zizek underscored manifested itself among others in the form of the heterotopic space of the garden colony, which reflected critically on the dominant space of the *Platte*. In the larger context of 'both Germanies', the *Platte* itself served as a backdrop against which some of the seemingly less visible and harder to pinpoint 'liquidating abstractions' of West German housing policies – the topic of the next chapter – became visible, most importantly its underlying social stratification and gradual stigmatization of need, 'liquidating abstractions' that went hand in hand with West Germany's decision to recommodify housing. Yet before going into the details of West German housing policies, which the *Platte's* normative content, namely social equality, may shed a critical light on, we'll take a closer look at how West Berlin was refashioned as a showcase for building a free, liberal society.

References

Beier, Gerhard, and Bruno Köbele. 1993. *Wir wollen freie Menschen sein: Der 17. Juni 1953: Bauleute gingen voran.* Cologne: Bund Verlag.

Benjamin, Walter. 2002. *The Arcades Project.* Cambridge, MA: Harvard University Press.

Berman, Marshall. 1988. *All That is Solid Melts Into Air. The Experience of Modernity.* New York: Penguin Books.

Bolz, Lothar (ed.). 1951. *Von deutschem Bauen. Reden und Aufsätze.* Berlin (Ost): Verlag der Nation.

Buck, Hannsjörg. 2004. *Mit hohem Anspruch gescheitert. Wohnungspolitik der DDR.* Münster: Lit Verlag.

Buck-Morss, Susan. 1992. 'Aesthetics and Anaesthetics', *October* 62 (8): 3–41.

———. 2002. *Dreamworld and Catastrophe.* Cambridge, MA: MIT Press.

Khrushchev, Nikita. 1955. *Besser, billiger und schneller bauen. Rede auf der Unionskonferenz der Baufachleute der UdSSR in Moskau am 7. Dezember 1954.* Berlin: Dietz Verlag.

Deutsche Bauakademie, and Ministerium für Leichtindustrie. 1954. *Besser Leben – Schöner Wohnen: Raum und Möbel.* Leipzig: Graphische Werkstätten.

Dietrich, Isolde. 2003. *Hammer, Zirkel, Gartenzaun. Die Politik der SED gegenüber Kleingärtnern.* Norderstedt: BoD.

Eagleton, Terry. 1990. *The Ideology of Aesthetics.* Oxford: Blackwell.

Flierl, Bruno. 1993. In *Den Himmel überlassen wir den Engeln und den Spatzen. Neun autobiographische Gespräche*, eds. Otto Fritz Hayner and Michael Peschke. Berlin: Volksbühne am Rosa Luxemburg-Platz.

Foucault, Michel. 1977/1995. *Discipline and Punish: The Birth of the Prison.* New York: Random House.

———. 2008. *The Birth of Biopolitics: Lectures at the College de France, 1978–1979.* New York: Palgrave Macmillan.

Garcelon, Marc. 1997. 'The Shadow of Leviathan: Public and Private in Communist and Post-Communist Society'. In *Public and Private in Thought and Practice. Perspectives on a Grand Dichotomy*, eds. Jeff Weintraub and Krishan Kumar, 303–332. Chicago: University of Chicago Press.

Ghodsee, Kristen Rogheh. 2018. *Why Women Have Better Sex Under Socialism: And Other Arguments for Economic Independence.* New York: Nation Books.

Goonewardena, Kanishka. 2009. 'Urban studies, Critical Theory, Radical Politics. Eight Theses for Peter Marcuse', *City* 13 (2–3): 2008–2018.

Gremler, Claudia. 2007. 'Country Escapes and Designs for Living: Christa Wolf, Sarah Kirsch and Judith Hermann'. In *Women's Writing in Western Europe: Gender, Generation and Legacy*, eds. Adalgisa Giorgio and Julia Waters, 119–131. Newcastle, UK: Cambridge Scholars Publications.

Grotewohl, Marlene. 1952. 'Über die Wohnung der werktätigen Frau', *Planen und Bauen* 6 (5): 98–101.

Habermas, Jürgen. 1962/1990. *Strukturwandel der Öffentlichkeit*. Frankfurt/Main: Suhrkamp.

Hain, Simone. 1993. 'Reise nach Moskau. Erste Betrachtungen zur politischen Struktur des städtebaulichen Leitbildes des Jahres 1950 in der DDR'. Hochschule für Architektur und Bauwesen (Weimar): Wissenschaftliche Zeitschrift / A, 39(2), 5–14.

———. 1996a. *Archäologie und Aneignung. Ideen, Pläne und Stadtfigurationen. Aufsätze zur Ostberliner Stadtentwicklung nach 1945*. Erkner (bei Berlin): Institut für Regionalentwicklung und Strukturplanung, IRS.

———. 1996b. 'Kolonialarchitektur'. In *Karl-Marx-Allee. Magistrale in Berlin*, eds. Helmut Engel and Wolfgang Ribbe, 75–101. Berlin: Akademie-Verlag.

Hannemann, Christine. 1996. *Die Platte. Industrialisierter Wohnungsbau in der DDR*. Braunschweig/Wiesbaden: Vieweg.

———. 2005. *Die Platte. Industrialisierter Wohnungsbau in der DDR*. Berlin: Verlag Hans Schiler.

Harth, Annette. 2010. 'Frauen, Wende(n), Wohnen. Zur Wohnweise ostdeutscher Frauen im Transformationsprozess'. In *Wohnen und Gender. Theoretische, politische, soziale und räumliche Aspekte*, ed. Darja Reuschke, 132–149. Wiesbaden: Verlag für Sozialwissenschaften.

Harvey, David. 2000. *Spaces of Hope*. Berkeley, CA: University of Berkeley Press.

Häußermann, Hartmut, and Walter Siebel. 1996. *Soziologie des Wohnens*. Weinheim, Munich: Juventa.

Henselmann, Hermann. 1991. 'Aus der Werkstatt des Architekten'. In *Zwischen Bauhaus und Stalinallee*, ed. Andreas Schätzke, 156–165. Braunschweig/Wiesbaden: Vieweg & Sohn.

Horkheimer, Max, and Theodor Adorno. 1947/2002. *Dialectic of Enlightenment*. Stanford, CA: Stanford University Press.

Hughes, Thomas P. 1989. *American Genesis: A Century of Invention and Technological Enthusiasm, 1870–1970*. New York: Viking.

Hund, Johanna. 1987. 'Das Recht auf Arbeit und gleichen Lohn'. In *Geschichte der Deutschen Frauenbewegung. Zur gewerkschaftlichen Frauenarbeit in der Bundesrepublik*, ed. Florence Herve, 235–254. Cologne: Pahl-Rugenstein Verlag.

Kahl, Alice. 2003. *Erlebnis Plattenbau. Eine Langzeitstudie.* Opladen: Leske + Budrich.

Kleinschmidt, Christian. 2008. *Konsumgesellschaft.* Göttingen: Vandenhoeck & Ruprecht.

Kohn, Margaret. 2003. *Radical Space. Building the House of the People.* Ithaca, NY: Cornell University Press.

Kopp, Anatole. 1978. *L'Architecture de la Periode Stalinienne.* Grenoble: Presses Universitaires de Grenoble.

Kopstein, Jeffrey. 1997. *Politics of Economic Decline in East Germany. 1945–1989.* Chapel Hill/London: The University of North Carolina Press.

Kosel, Gerhard. 1957. *Produktivkraft Wissenschaft.* Berlin: Verlag der Wirtschaft.

Kropp, Cordula. 2011. 'Gärtner(n) ohne Grenzen: Eine neue Politik des 'Sowohl-als-auch' urbaner Gärten?'. In *Urban Gardening*, ed. Christa Müller, 76–87. Munich: oekom Verlag.

Lefebvre, Henri. 2003. *The Urban Revolution.* Minneapolis: University of Minnesota.

Liebknecht, Kurt. 1954. 'Die Architektur der Wohnung für die Werktätigen unter besonderer Berücksichtigung des Möbels'. In *Besser Leben – Schöner Wohnen: Raum und Möbel*, eds. Deutsche Bauakademie and Ministerium für Leichtindustrie, 7–74. Leipzig: Graphische Werkstätten.

Liebscher, Robert. 2009. *Wohnen für alle. Eine Kulturgeschichte des Plattenbaus.* Berlin: Vergangenheitsverlag.

Maaß, Anita. 2006. *Wohnen in der DDR: Dresden-Prohlis: Wohnungspolitik und Wohnungsbau 1975 bis 1981.* Munich: m press Martin Meidenbauer Verlag.

Marcuse, Peter, and Wolfgang Schumann. 1992. 'Housing in the Colours of the GDR'. In *The Reform of Housing in Eastern Europe and the Soviet Union*, eds. Bengt Turner, Joszef Hegedus, and Ivan Tosics, 74–144. London/New York: Routledge.

Marx, Karl. 1843/1978. 'On the Jewish Question'. In *The Marx-Engels Reader*, ed. Robert C. Tucker, 26–52. New York: Norton.

———. 1875/1978. 'Critique of the Gotha Program'. In *The Marx-Engels Reader*, ed. Robert C. Tucker, 525–541. New York: Norton.

———. 1887. *Capital.* Moscow: Progress Publishers.

Merkel, Ina. 1996. 'Der aufhaltsame Aufbruch in die Konsumgesellschaft'. In *Wunderwirtschaft. DDR-Konsumkultur in den 60er Jahren*, eds. Ina Merkel and Felix Mühlberg, 8–20. Cologne: Böhlau Verlag.

Neues Deutschland. 1951. 'Wäre es schön? Es wäre schön!', 25 November.

Nicolaus, Herbert, and Alexander Obeth. 1997. *Die Stalinallee: Geschichte einer deutschen Straße.* Berlin: Verlag für Bauwesen.

Palmowski, Jan. 2009. *Inventing a Socialist Nation: Heimat and the Politics of Everyday Life in the GDR, 1945 – 1990.* Cambridge: Cambridge University Press.

Schmidt, Heike. 2007. *Frauenpolitik in der DDR. Gestaltungsräume und -grenzen in der Diktatur.* Berlin: Wissenschaftlicher Verlag Berlin.

Schretzenmayr, Martina. 1998. 'Wohnungsbau in der ehemaligen DDR'. disP -The Planning Review, 34:133, 40–48, DOI: 10.1080/02513625.1998.10556676.

Schuster, Franz. 1984. 'Die neue Wohnung und der Hausrat'. In *Neues Bauen, Neues Gestalten: Das Neue Frankfurt/die neue Stadt – Eine Zeitschrift zwischen 1926 und 1933*, ed. Heinz Hirdina, 174–178. Dresden: VEB Verlag der Kunst Dresden.

Sennett, Richard. 2008. *The Craftsman.* New Haven, CT: Yale University Press.

Stadt und Land Wohnbauten-Gesellschaft mbH. Museumswohnung WBS 70. https://www.stadtundland.de/Unternehmen/Museumswohnung.php. Accessed 25 March 2021.

Stalin, Joseph V. 1954. 'Concerning Questions of Leninism'. In *Stalin Works: Vol. VIII*, ed. Joseph V. Stalin, 13–96. Moscow: Foreign Languages Publishing House.

Stam, Mart. 1984. 'Das Mass, das richtige Mass, das Minimum Mass'. In *Neues Bauen, Neues Gestalten: Das Neue Frankfurt/die neue Stadt – Eine Zeitschrift zwischen 1926 und 1933*, ed. Heinz Hirdina, 215–217. Dresden: VEB Verlag der Kunst Dresden.

Topfstedt, Thomas. 1988. *Städtebau in der DDR.* Leipzig: Seemann Verlag.

Ulbricht, Walter. 1951. 'Das nationale Aufbauwerk und die Aufgaben der deutschen Architektur'. Speech on December 8. Berlin: Amt für Information der Regierung der Deutschen Demokratischen Republik.

———. 1991. 'Kunst und Wissenschaft im Plan. Rede vor der Volkskammer'. October 31, 1951. In *Zwischen Bauhaus und Stalinallee. Architekturdiskussionen im östlichen Deutschland. 1945–1949*, ed. Andreas Schätzke, 143–145. Braunschweig/Wiesbaden: Vieweg & Sohn.

Voigt, Wolfgang. 1999. 'Vitruv der Moderne: Ernst Neufert'. In *Ernst Neufert: Normierte Baukultur im 20. Jahrhundert*, ed. Walter Prigge, 20–34. Frankfurt am Main: Campus.

Zizek, Slavoj. 1998/2008. *The Sublime Object of Ideology.* London/New York: Verso.

5 Divided City II: West Berlin and the Reconstruction of Liberalism (1949–1970)

Abstract
In West Germany, the decentralized city landscape was celebrated as the ideal urban form and environment for societal renewal: the unfolding of individuality, the experience of freedom, and the nurturing of 'healthy' families. West Berlin's Hansa Quarter served as a showcase housing project for a liberal, new beginning. Given the decision to rebuild housing and cities by means of industrialization, ultimately West German mass housing looked strikingly similar to East German mass housing. Yet it differed regarding normative content: its core rationale was recommodification. In fact, West German housing policies embody an early and specific manifestation of neoliberalism: ordoliberalism. The latter's underpinning norms were politicized, among others at West Berlin's housing estate, the *Märkische Viertel*, and in West Berlin's most famous commune, the *Kommune 1* – two hotbeds of the counterculture.

Keywords: West Berlin, ordoliberalism, city landscape, mass housing, counterculture, communes

East Germany's adoption of the Sixteen Principles of Urban Design and their materialization in the 'showcase housing project', the *Stalinallee*, brought an abrupt end to the initially *joint* post-WWII experiments in the aesthetics and politics of modernism. Hans Scharoun's vision for Great Berlin, which was based on egalitarian and democratic principles, was to find itself in the dustbin of post-WWII German history before it could grow roots. Certainly, as this chapter will show, in West Berlin in particular and West Germany (the Federal Republic of Germany, FRG) more generally modernism continued to dominate urban planning and architecture. Yet after 1949, modernism was largely stripped of its politically radical thrust, including its questioning of

Haderer, M., *Rebuilding Cities and Citizens: Mass Housing in Red Vienna and Cold War Berlin*. Amsterdam: Amsterdam University Press 2023
DOI: 10.5117/9789463724944_CH05

capitalism. Kanishka Goonewardena's equation – 'modernism – revolution = modernization' (2009) became a reality in West Germany (no less than in East Germany) and West Germany's showcase housing project for the new liberal society to come – the *Hansa Quarter* – bears evidence to this reality (see section 5.1). In fact, West German housing policies embodied an embrace of a specific variant of liberal capitalism – an early, neoliberal version of it. In the FRG, social housing was never meant to remain decommodified for the long term. Instead, it was expected to constitute an intermediary step towards what was then conceived as the 'truly' ideal form of dwelling: the single family home. Whereas the beginning of neoliberalism is usually located in the 1970s, this chapter demonstrates that in West German politics the market was conceived as the primary source of freedom and political legitimacy from as early as the 1950s (see section 5.2). The chapter also shows that the highly standardized, prefabricated concrete slab building was by no means a unique symbol of post-WWII socialism, as is commonly assumed, but also one of post-WWII liberalism. Within the context of the latter, the prefabricated concrete slab building did not, however, primarily signify social equality as was the case in East Germany but an intermediary step towards the privately owned, single family home, a symbol of personal achievement (see section 5.3). Yet also the norms that underpinned the West German approach to housing did not go unchallenged (see section 5.4). In one of West Berlin's largest social housing estate, the *Märkische Viertel*, inhabitants – together with students – mobilized against rising rents and the lack of community facilities, protests that were to usher in a social movement, the extra-parliamentary opposition [APO], that sought to renegotiate not only housing policies but the logics of the West German state and society more generally. Another hotspot of extra parliamentary opposition was the *Kommune 1*, a commune that attracted media attention because of its break with dominant family and gender norms that had underpinned housing policies and dwelling forms. As will be shown, the communards experimented with the dissolution of the nuclear family model, which had shaped (ordo-) liberal housing policies, but also and ironically socialist ones, albeit to varying degrees.

5.1 Interbau 1957: Proclaiming the City of Tomorrow, Exhibiting the City of Yesterday

After a delay of several years – due to the political and economic instability caused by the 1948 currency reform that Western Allies had pushed for and to which East Germany had responded with the Berlin blockade (1948–1949),

5.1 Interbau 1957, Hansaviertel: Display Window of West German Housing Development.

in 1955, also West Germany finally began constructing its 'showcase housing project' in Berlin, the *Hansa Viertel* [Hansa Quarter]. Propagandistically stylized as the West's display window of freedom, the Hansa Quarter was meant to serve as the antidote to *Stalinallee*. Built within the framework of the FRG's most important post-WWII building exhibition, the *Interbau 1957*, the Hansa Quarter was designed as a model housing project located in a model urban form, a city landscape. The purpose of both the Hansa Quarter and the *Interbau 1957* was to showcase West Germany's response to East Germany's reconstruction efforts. The building exhibition itself turned out to be a huge success. Over the course of only three months, it attracted 1.37 million visitors from West as well as East Germany (Wagner-Conzelmann 2007, p. 9) [see Illustration 5.1].

Despite the success of *Interbau 1957*, the actual urban form that emerged in the Hansa Quarter was in fact less a reflection of a clearly delineated and programmatic urban vision than that of an eclectic collection of different architectural forms. Designed by elite figures of modernism, among them Walter Gropius, Max Taut, Egon Eiermann, Oskar Niemeyer, and Alvar Aalto, 1,300 social housing units were constructed on an area of 25 hectares in the middle of the 'half city'. The lack of a clear programmatic vision undergirding the Hansa Quarter that was actually built was due to a tension between two conflicting goals: the Hansa Quarter's reconstruction, which required plans that were 'practicable' and 'realizable' within the given topographic parameters; presenting a *programmatic* vision for West German reconstruction. To counter the Hansa Quarter's lack of an overarching vision for West Germany's approach to urban reconstruction, the organizers of the *Interbau 1957* exhibition decided to shift the programmatic focus away from the actually built form to a special exhibition titled *die stadt von morgen* [the city of tomorrow], an exhibition that was meant to fundamentally challenge the ideal socialist city as formulated by the Sixteen Principles.

Of particular influence on the 'city of tomorrow' exhibition and, more generally, post-WWII reconstruction was – again[1] – the Charter of Athens (1943), the formalized version of the discussions held at the Fourth International Congress for Modern Architecture (CIAM) in 1933. The Charter's most important tenets included the rejection of the nineteenth-century industrial city, an urban form that was equated with 'the ruin of mankind'; the emphasis on decentralization and adaption to local geography and topography; a celebration of organicism, a conception of the city as an organism consisting of 'living cells' that are to be rationally ordered into 'habitation units' or neighborhoods of a predetermined ideal size; and, finally, the stipulation of functionalism, most importantly, the carving up of urban life and space according to the functions of habitation, work, leisure, and traffic (Le Corbusier 1973).

In preparation for the 'city of tomorrow' exhibition, the so called *Bauherren-Gespräche* [Builders' Talks] were held from 1955 to 1956, talks to which the exhibit's organizers, Erich Kühn and Karl Otto, summoned city planners, architects, landscape architects, and designers who shared the organizers' commitment to the decentralized, green city (Otto 1956a, 1956b). Although several of the principles of the Charter of Athens were challenged at these talks, the planning principles presented at the 'city of tomorrow' exhibition in 1957 mirrored rather than critically appropriated the Charter's legacy. First, 'the city of tomorrow' was expected to unite urban density and rural vastness, urban life and rural tranquility. Second, it would render nature instead of industry as the basis of urban planning. Verdant areas and local topography were meant to serve as a structuring skeleton. Third, based on this skeleton, the functions of work, dwelling, recreation, and circulation were to be spatially arranged in a meaningful and economical way. Fourth, the 'city of tomorrow' was to be designed as an agglomeration

1 Also Scharoun's vision for Great Berlin (see chapter 3) was informed by key principles that undergirded the Charter of Athens, such as functional differentation and decentralization.

of manageable urban units, units in which inhabitants would be able to live both in community and in independence. Family cells – considered loci of intimacy and retreat – were to be united and complemented with social facilities to form neighborhoods, the ideal environment for educating people about 'real democracy' and 'responsibility for one's fellow human beings'. Fifth, in contrast to the modern metropolis in which, as was suggested, the family was threatened by moral erosion (not least because women ceased to serve as 'the family's backbone' due to their integration into the labor force), the 'city of tomorrow' would put the family (and with it, traditional gender roles) back into its 'natural place'. Sixth, the 'city of tomorrow' was moreover to be a city that offered meaningful leisure activities. Given the assumption that automation and nuclear energy were about to considerably increase leisure time, the danger that people would waste the time gained in a passive and futile way was to be averted by encouraging people to engage in *pre-industrial* activities such as farming, gardening, and crafts. Seventh, in terms of traffic, the future city would not only separate the different types of traffic but also reduce it by rationally rearranging areas of work, dwelling, and leisure to limit commutes. And finally, the 'city of tomorrow' was to constitute the basis for healthy living – a life that would be in sync with 'biological laws' – by providing ample green space for active use (Interbau GmbH 1957) [see Illustration 5.2].

The purpose of the 'city of tomorrow' exhibition was to inform the public about the future of urban planning and to elicit consent to it. To achieve the latter, visualized and often moralizing opposites were employed. By contrasting symbols of innocence (children) with images of decay and chaos (urban ruins), by promising a city that would nurture instead of deprive future generations, the exhibition's organizers hoped to morally engage the public. Moreover, it was the organizer's plan to actively engage the public with questions of city building and to encourage it to participate in the planning process (Otto 1959). In practice, not much emerged out of the proclaimed democratization of urban planning. In contrast to the democratic dimension that underlay Hans Scharoun's Collective Plan, the actual plans displayed at the 'city of tomorrow' exhibition largely sidestepped participation and operated under the assumption that people would agree to what was being proposed. Accordingly, the planning of West Germany's city of tomorrow was not, as initially and propagandistically promised, radically different from the top-down implementation of the Sixteen Principles of Urban Design in East Germany. 'Tomorrow', as was suggested at the exhibition, 'the city planner has the time, money and power of a *general*! [my emphasis]' (Wagner-Conzelmann 2007, p. 125). As the contrivance of an all-powerful city planner – a specialist

5.2 Ideal(ized) City Landscape

who purportedly had access to the secret of how to produce a new society by producing a new space – West Germany's ideal 'new city', a city that promised democratization, was thus compromised from its inception.

What is revealed by the exhibition's authoritarian underpinnings is the logic of urbanism. As a state-administered, technocratic rationality that was applied to the city, the logic of urbanism was to steer not only East German but also West German reconstruction. As Lefebvre remarks critically, '[l]ike classical philosophy', urbanism 'claims to be a system [that] pretends to embrace, enclose, possess a new totality. It wants to be the modern philosophy of the city, justified by (liberal [or, as I would add, socialist]) humanism while justifying a (technocratic) utopia' (Lefebvre 2003, p. 153). The seeds for West Germany's technocratic utopia were already sown in the discussions at the CIAM in the 1930s. Its outcome, the Charter of Athens, which informed the planning principles of the 'city of tomorrow', suggested that the general 'disregard of the principles of contemporary urbanism' – principles stipulated by 'qualified technical specialists' in the art of building, health, and social organization – would be the main 'cause of the anarchy that prevails in the organization of cities and in the equipment of industries' (Le Corbusier 1973, pp. 94, 104–105). Yet why did the seeds of authoritarian urbanism fall on fertile ground again in post-WWII Germany? The fact that they did is striking in two ways: first, because of the obviously disastrous effects of the National Socialists' pursuit of not only a nationalistic but also a technological utopia (Herf 1984); and second, because of the widespread post-WWII desire for a new, *democratic* beginning, which the *Interbau 1957* promised to give expression to.

Certainly, the various visions, plans, and models of 'building democracy' spatially were part and parcel of the Cold War. Hence, the showcasing of competing visions was often more important than the sincerity of the political promises. The *desire* for a new democratic beginning, however, was not merely showcased but very much present and real in post-WWII German society. Despite this desire, it was once more trumped by an expert-driven, technocratic approach to city building. As Marx already observed, straddling the gap between one's entanglement with the past and one's yearning for a radically different future is a difficult undertaking, as more often than not, the new is lost in the guise of the old during attempts to break with history (Marx 1852/1978, pp. 594–598). This applies to West German urbanism, which prided itself on being innovative and democratic and yet wound up being technocratic in practice. That the poetry of the future is easily eclipsed by the poetry of the past is also revealed by a closer look at post-WWII West German ideals concerning architecture and city building.

Akin to East Germany, where the socialists unearthed past aesthetics of totality, beauty, and national traditions to sanctify the 'new society' by way of a socialist-realist urban *Gesamtkunstwerk* [total work of art], in West Germany, the proclaimed 'city of tomorrow' emanated as an idealized version of the 'city of yesterday'. For one, the exhibition reproposed modernist planning maxims and models that had already been subjected to major criticism by the mid-1950s[2] (Wagner-Conzelmann 2007). Second, the exhibition ironically coupled modernist planning principles with romantic ideals of the distant past to portray a life of order, wholeness, and human scale that was to be replicated by creating manageable neighborhoods with housing based on traditional family models as well as spaces for 'meaningful' leisure activities that were equated with pre-industrial forms of occupation (Wagner-Conzelmann 2007, p. 128). Thus *both* the East German ideal 'socialist city' and the West German ideal 'city of tomorrow' drew their poetry from the past rather than the future. While the former took to national traditions to reinvent its ideal urban form, the latter resuscitated conservative elements of organic city planning.

2 Already by the mid-1950s, a number of the positions of the Charter of Athens such as its idealization of decentralization, its conception of neighborhoods, and its underlying functional division – positions that the 'city of tomorrow' exhibition largely adopted – had already drawn extensive criticism (see, among others, Mitscherlich 1965).

While organicist analogies have a long history in art and design, the particular concepts of nature underpinning them have changed over time. Often, these changes went hand in hand with political changes. The specific 'nature fetishism' in West German planning harked back to biological concepts that emerged in the nineteenth century. These concepts were appropriated by architects and planners affiliated with the garden city movement of the 1920s and carried on by their students into the years of fascism and post-war reconstruction (Durth and Gutschow 1993; Sohn 2007). As is well known, the garden city movement, a movement that originated in Great Britain in the nineteenth century, criticized the industrial city and its 'condition of possibility': unrestrained capitalism. The industrial city was considered responsible for causing dire living conditions for the urban masses. In pursuit of a fundamental reform of life, the movement suggested dissolving the metropolis in favor of decentralized urban forms. This dissolution was expected to serve as the basis for self-sufficient communities of production typically modeled on medieval guilds and their emphasis on craftsmanship. Architecture and planning were seen as the midwives of a society in which city and nature would be rebalanced. Since critique of the modern metropolis was as widespread among the political right as the political left, the idea of the garden city appealed to both (see also chapter 3). Proponents of the *Rassenhygiene* [racial hygiene] considered the garden city to be fertile ground for a new, superior type of man. Proponents of the New Building – that is, left-leaning supporters – deemed the garden city as the ideal urban form for a society in which art, technology, and nature would finally be reconciled (Durth 1989, pp. 222–223, 225).

As Elke Sohn shows in her genealogy of organicist planning in Germany, the concept of nature as a foundation for the garden city ideal was taken from monism. Derived from natural science, monism holds that all existing things are fundamentally composed of one substance and that a universal, unified set of laws underlies nature (Sohn 2007, p. 515). Particularly influential for monism was the work of the biologist Raoul Heinrich Francé (1874–1943), who was widely published and positively received in Germany. Francé suggested conceiving of natural organisms as autonomously active and autonomously regulated 'living things'. Given their autonomy, natural organisms are not to be understood as divine creations but as products of causality and mechanical evolutionary laws, laws that regulate even the smallest units of organic life (Sohn 2007, pp. 516–517). Moreover, according to Francé, intelligence would increase proportionally with an organism's complexity and with a greater division of tasks between its component parts. The biologist himself drew a parallel between the life world of plants and that of citizens, a parallel that planners who were committed to organic city planning would later capitalize on:

> All the plants or animals perceived by our shared experience are communities, associations of cells, groups of citizens joining together to form guilds capable of performing more advanced tasks, as organs, than would be possible for the weak individual; they offer each other mutual aid and experience the same blessing of harmony as those pile-village dwellers who swore mutual peace, supporting each other and organizing themselves into small towns. Both arrived at a multiplication of their qualities. In the cell state, wonderful, advanced capabilities emerged [...]. (Francé 1907, p. 13)

Planners and architects were influenced by this concept of the autonomous cell as well as the idea that every form in nature emerges in response to functional interests that are shaped by absolute economy, the saving of energy, and harmony. From Francé, it was a relatively small step to Jean-Babtiste de Lamarck and environmental determinism: the idea that the conditions under which men live crucially affect the development of their characteristics. Accordingly, healthy food, hygiene, light, and fresh air were believed to have an impact on people's physical health as well as their mental, moral, and civic disposition. The 'healing' of the world, according to organicist planners, required the recognition of natural or cosmological law. Yet to truly prevent humankind from dancing the 'dance of death', recognition alone would not suffice. It had to be followed by implementation – a task that organicist architects and planners took on, conceiving of themselves either as 'creative geniuses' (see Scharoun), 'experts' (see Le Corbusier), or 'generals' (see 'the city of tomorrow' exhibition) who would redeem nature's 'laws' on the urban scale. Given the dependency of architecture and planning on given economic and socio-political conditions, the redemption of natural laws also entailed the mingling with – or adaption to – dominant political worldviews.

Although the norms and ideas undergirding the planning models presented at the 'city of tomorrow' exhibition were similar in form to Scharoun's city landscape, they no longer shared Scharoun's radical democratic and egalitarian political vision. Instead, they were instantiations of political revision. For instance, Hubert Hoffman's planning model was a condensation of the principles that underpinned the book *Die gegliederte und aufgelockerte Stadt* [The Structured and Decentralized City] co-authored by Johannes Göderitz and Roland Rainer. This book, written during WWII and published in 1957, became a must-read for urban planners in the late 1950s. Continuing the Fascist discourse of biologism and Lamarckianism, the book argued that 'town planning' had to carry out a crucially important task. Besides repairing the physical destruction caused by the two world wars, it also had 'to repair destructions of the *Volkskörper* [body of the people]'. Accordingly, 'priority should be given to those solutions that are apt to counteract any heavy loss of the people [*Volk*] through creating a healthy and efficient *Stadtkörper* [urban bodies]' (Göderitz et al. 1957, p. 91). Moreover, as the authors suggested, 'there are good reasons to consider a vivid relation between men and nature, between landscape and soil, and the health and development of vitality'. Referring to statistics from 1939, the authors claimed, for example, that people who owned and cultivated their own land would have a higher birth rate (ibid., pp. 34–35).

The excavation of various roots of the 'city of tomorrow' brings to light a problem that seems to have plagued architecture and city planning: both are bound by political and economic constraints. As noted by Adorno, the fact that visionary architects could often realize only a small fraction of their plans cannot be explained by 'unreasonable contractors and administrators' alone. Instead, this fact

> is conditioned by a social antagonism over which the greatest architecture has no power: the same society which developed human productive energies to unimaginable proportions has changed them to conditions of production, imposed upon them; the people who in reality constitute the productive energies become deformed according to the measure of their working conditions. This fundamental contradiction is most clearly visible in architecture. [...] Because architecture is in fact both autonomous and purpose-oriented, it cannot simply negate men as they are. And yet it must do precisely that if it is to remain autonomous. (1965/1997, p. 16)

On a conceptual level, the organicist city was meant to be independent of social constraints. It represented a universal type that was understood as organic anatomy or as original form. It was up to the architect – the 'creative genius' or 'general' – to bestow upon the city its individual form. In theory, the organic city was only adapted to landscape and local topography. In practice, it was dependent on historical circumstances, socio-economic conditions, and political demands. Often, as it turns out, historical, socio-economic, and political contingencies have informed the actual city to a larger extent than ideals of urban form. Against this backdrop, it is not surprising that organicist planning ideals lent themselves to radically different socio-political appropriations. The city landscape was attractive to the left-leaning modernists of the New Building [*Neues Bauen*] movement, to the reactionary modernists of the Fascist era, to East German socialists (after Stalin) as well as to West German liberals, who were shaped by cultural conservatism and economic liberalism. Albeit similar in form, the normative content underpinning West German city landscapes in general and the mass housing they accommodated in particular was specific. West German city landscapes were 'the home' of decommodified mass housing for a limited term, namely until the expected full recovery of a market economy, which was considered to be *the* key source of freedom in the post-WWII era.

5.2 'Economic Policies Are the Best Social Policies': German-style Neoliberalism

Informed by memories of the poor housing conditions in the 1930s and related social unrest, housing was strictly regulated by rent control, tenant protection and state-administered redistribution in the immediate aftermath of 1945. Whereas East German housing policies maintained and built on key elements of this post-1945 pathway, West Germany diverged from it fundamentally as a brief comparison between the laws underpinning the two approaches illustrates. In East Germany, three major legal mechanisms ushered in the hegemonization of *public* housing, that is, publicly owned housing[3]. First, the First Housing Reconstruction Law of 1950 equipped the state with an extensive right to expropriate and establish public control over urban development. Second, the constitution of 1968 stipulated housing as a right. And third, Honecker's promise to solve the housing question by 1990 led to an encompassing housing construction program to turn the formal right to housing into a substantive one, a program that – as above discussed – prioritized the quantitative provision of housing units over qualitative considerations of city building (Marcuse & Schumann 1992, pp. 61–64). In short, the decommodification of housing, the sidelining of private homeownership and the pursuit of housing equality are key characteristics of the GDR's housing policies. By contrast, the key features

3 It is important to note that in German, there is an important semantic difference between *public* housing and *social* housing, though in everyday discourse, the two terms are used interchangeably. As above explained, in East Germany, public housing was owned and provided by the state. Public housing is, however, also a term used for not-for-profit housing built in the Weimar Republic. Social housing, by contrast and as also above explained, means, at least in the German context, limited-term, state-subsidized housing.

of West German housing policies are recommodification, the fostering of private property and social differentiation as the following closer look at West Germany's, the FRG's, *Erste* and *Zweite Wohnbaugesetz* [First and Second Housing Construction Laws] of 1950 and 1956 will reveal. These laws had shaped housing policies well into the 1970s. They are, more generally, indicative of the specific kind of liberalism that became hegemonic in West Germany: an early and specific form of neoliberalism, ordoliberalism. Yet first, let us take a closer look at the specifics of the FRG's post-WWII housing policies.

The First and Second Housing Construction Laws foresaw the provision of *social* housing as opposed to *public* housing, that is, housing that was publicly subsidized, but transformable into private property once the builder of the housing units had paid back the public loans (§ 3, ¶ 1, I. WoBauGe). By the mid-1950s, the state began to withdraw from providing public loans and decided to subsidize builders for taking up private loans instead (§ 42, II. WoBauG). The central thrust behind both legal interventions was to reestablish the private capital market as the main financial source for housing construction (Hanauske 1995, pp. 55–56). Furthermore, West German housing laws foresaw the replacement of the *Richtsatzmiete* [benchmark rent], a highly regulated form of rent that sought to secure equal access to equal housing, with the *Kostenmiete* [cost-based rent] as early as in the 1950s. Cost-based rent covered current and variable costs, including the costs implied in borrowing public capital. The gradual adaptation of rents to market conditions was the driver behind this legal innovation.

In addition, the First and Second Housing Construction Laws, including amendments to them, fostered social differentiation and the individualization of risk. They did so, among others, by distinguishing between three housing types: publicly funded or subsidized social housing, tax-advantaged housing and freely financed housing. Freely financed housing was purely market-based and, in contrast to the two other housing types, exempt from state regulations. What is important to note is that the social meaning and function of the introduced housing types was not value neutral. Instead, it implied a hierarchy as the housing laws also stipulated the acquisition of private property as a desirable goal and the privately owned single family home as *the* ideal form of dwelling (I. WoBauG, II. WoBauG). In this context, social housing took on a specific meaning and function. In contrast to public housing, which meant long-term, decommodified housing, social housing was conceived of as a stepping stone towards tax-advantaged or freely financed housing in the form of private property and, ideally, a single family home. Paul Lücke, who served as Chancellor Konrad Adenauer's Minister of Housing Development from 1957 to 1961, argued these shifts as follows: the privately owned single family home is the only form of housing that is able to sufficiently 'protect families' and to avoid the dangers of 'massification' [*Vermassung*] and collectivization (Hanauske 1995, p. 48). In addition, it was assumed that the stipulated dwelling ideal was likely to encourage people's 'will to save [*Sparwille*] and to take initiative [*Tatkraft*]' [§ 1, II. WoBauG, my translation].

The active fostering of social differentiation (as opposed to the active fostering of social equality, as was the case in East Germany) also underpinned another major change in post-WWII West German housing laws: the shift from the public support of affordable housing (the subsidization of *objects*) to an individualized, case-by-case support of subjects by means of housing allowance or subsidies (the subsidization of *subjects*) (Häußermann and Siebel 1996, pp. 146–147). This reconfiguration of subsides meant another shift away from the decommodification of housing and towards social differentiation, among others, between those who are in need of public support to secure adequate housing and those who are not. In addition, this legal change also meant the individualization of risk: housing market volatilities *were* buffered by the West German State, but increasingly in an individualized way.

Yet how did West German housing policies and their three main features – the provisional as opposed to permanent character of social housing (the recommodification of housing), the normalization of homeownership (among others, in the form of single family homes) and the related devaluation of others forms of tenure, and the state's decision to subsidize subjects instead of objects and with it, to individualize risk – fit into the larger picture of rebuilding the West German society as a liberal society? To answer this question, it is important to throw into sharper relief the aforementioned strong role that the market economy played in reconstituting West Germany's political sovereignty in particular and vision of a liberal society in general. This reconstitution occurred during the chancellorship of the Christian Democrat Konrad Adenauer (1949- 1967) and ushered in the West German 'economic miracle', of which the 'housing miracle', i.e., the (quantitative) overcoming of the post-WWII housing shortage, was a facet. Adenauer's 'economic miracle' implied the introduction of what his minister of economics, Ludwig Erhard, termed 'social market economy' [*soziale Marktwirtschaft*]. In contrast to what the term may suggest, the FRG's social market economy had less to do with traditional, redistributive welfare policies than with the normalization of economic freedom as freedom *tout court*. For this to be possible, Adenauer and his ordoliberal acolytes and advisers, such as Ludwig Erhard, but also Walter Eucken, an influential economist, conceived of state intervention as key, among others, to secure competition. Akin to neoliberals, ordoliberals *are* committed to the regulative ideal of a free market economy. Yet in contrast to 'classic' neoliberals, such as Friedrich Hayek or Ludwig van Mises, they did not belief in a *self-regulating* free market. Ordoliberals made the case for an interventionist state, yet not to redistribute wealth or to protect the poor against 'market failures' but to secure economic competition (Ptak 2009, Haderer 2018, Slobodian 2018).

What both 'classic' neoliberals and ordoliberals loathed was the controlled economy, as introduced, among others, by the National Socialists, a type of economy they framed as *Zwangswirtschaft* [constrained economy]. According to West German ordoliberals, the edifices of the 'new Germany' were not to be built on the foundations of the 'old Germany' – foundations shaped by a totalitarian state's grip on every nook and cranny of society – but on the foundations of a free market economy whose very principles were expected to not only inform but also *reform* the state and society (Foucault 2008, p. 118). The main concern of the specific 'liberal governmentality',[4] as Foucault put it, that emerged in West Germany after 1945 was no longer the excavation of a free space for the market within an already given and delimiting political society, a major concern of economic liberalism in the nineteenth century, but the projection of the formal principles of a market economy onto the 'general art of government' (ibid., p. 131), the art of regulating society at large.

This chosen course was already prefigured at the 2nd Party Congress of the Christian Democratic Union (CDU) in August 1948:

> With the politico-economic turn from a controlled to a market economy, we took more than economic measures in the narrow sense. Instead, we established *a new basis and beginning for our socio-economic and social life.* We had to renounce intolerance, which led from intellectual bondage to tyranny and from tyranny to totalitarianism. We had to reorient ourselves toward an order which, by means of voluntary commitment and a sense

4 Foucault explained his study of governmentality as follows: 'I would like to try to determine the way in which the domain of the practice of government, with its different objects, general rules, and overall objectives, was established so as to govern in the best possible ways. In short, we could call this the study of the rationalization of governmental practice in the exercise of political sovereignty.' (Foucault, 2008, p. 2)

of responsibility, aspires to unity in a meaningful and organic way. [my translation; emphasis added] (Erhard 1957, p. 23)

This distinctiveness of post-WWII West German liberalism was conditioned in two ways. First, the West German state's legitimacy could not strongly draw on constitutionally anchored, sovereign power because the country was *de facto* occupied and divided. Second, the young state's legitimacy could also not build on history or tradition – historic right – given the country's fascist and totalitarian past (see also Foucault 2008, p. 82). As a result, Ludwig Erhard, the mastermind of the West German *Wirtschaftswunder* [economic miracle], pushed for making the economy itself the basis of a legitimate state and society. As stated in a speech held in Frankfurt in April 1948: 'We must free the economy from state controls [...]. We must avoid both anarchy and the termite state [because] only a state that establishes both the freedom and responsibility of the citizens can legitimately speak in the name of the people' (1948/1981). According to Erhard, competition was the best protection against 'anarchy and the termite state' and the best guarantee for a *freiheitliche Gesellschaftsordnung* [liberal social order] (1957, p. 9).

Why was the remodelling of the West German economy into an ordoliberal one as well as the remodeling of the entire West German society and state according to principles of economic freedom so appealing after 1945? Foucault provides two reasons. First, in contrast to historic right as a source of state legitimacy, the origin of a market economy, including the institutional framework it draws on, is, from a political and social perspective, unimportant. Second, the main function of a market economy is not the exercise of sovereignty, as is often the case with political power, but to guarantee freedom, economic freedom. In post-WWII West Germany, citizens were eager to play the game of freedom. By joining this game, they implicitly gave their consent to any (state) decisions that were made to guarantee and secure freedom understood as economic freedom. In short, in West Germany, the institution of economic freedom itself functioned 'as a siphon, as it were, as a point of attraction for the formation of political sovereignty' (Foucault 2008, pp. 82–83).

Erhard made it clear that the principles of consumption and competition were to become the basis of West German society, that economic freedom, development, and growth was to be the primary concern of public law and, more generally, of *Gesellschaftspolitik* [societal policy]. In *Wohlstand für Alle* [Prosperity for All] (1957), a book in which Erhard summarized his politico-economic outlook, he stated that a citizen's freedom means, first and foremost, 'to consume [...] according to one's individual financial possibilities, personal desires, and beliefs'.

> [Citizens have a] democratic, basic right to consumption [that] must find its logical complement in the freedom of the entrepreneur to produce and sell whatever he deems to be necessary and commercially promising depending on the market's conditions and people's expression of needs... [The] freedom of consumption and the freedom of economic enterprise have to be perceived by each citizen's consciousness as *inviolable basic rights*. [my translation, emphasis added] (1957, p. 14)

The foundation for expanding the 'catalogue of basic human rights' to include the right to free consumption and the right to free production and trade was, according to Erhard, competition. If the latter is compromised, the rights to consumption, production, and trade are compromised as well and so is the possibility of prosperity (ibid., p. 8).

Whereas, as above already mentioned, a traditional welfare economy typically pursues the objective of equal access to consumer goods by means of redistribution, West Germany's social-market economy took a different course – a course rooted in the idea that competition, economic development, and growth were necessary to solve the 'social question'. 'Prosperity through the expansion of the GDP, instead of prosperity through the redistribution of the GDP' (ibid., p. 10) was a leitmotiv of West German liberalism. Essential to Erhard's policies of economic expansion was the limitation of *artfremder Staatsfunktionen*, functions 'foreign to the species of the state', such as the politics of planning, price control, and tax-based public revenues (ibid., p. 12).

To be certain, the phenomenon that the economy produces legitimacy for the political system that is its guarantor is not unique to West German history. Had the highly interventionist Austro-Marxist policies not produced the results they promised – i.e., the creation of a wide-ranging public infrastructure – it is hard to imagine that their legitimacy and widespread public support would have lasted as long as they did. On the other hand, to mention an example of failed legitimacy: because East German economic policies largely failed to produce the economic outcomes the state had promised, the state's legitimacy was severely hampered. Hence, in the case of East Germany, it was not only the regime's authoritarianism that caused public discontent but also the poor standard of living it afforded its citizens. Although economic success and political legitimacy are to a certain extent always linked, Foucault was right in stipulating that there was nonetheless something unique about West German liberalism and its interweaving of the economic and the political. Thus, when Erhard, the architect of the West German 'economic miracle', suggested that '[i]n the middle of the twentieth century [...] the recognition of each government and state is dependent on the success or lack of success of its economic policies' (1957, p. 17), more was at stake than the mere assertion that political success is highly dependent on economic prosperity. What *was* at stake was the beginning of a specific form of neoliberalism, ordoliberalism, shaped by the interlacing of the formal principles of a market economy and the art of government long before the 1970s (Foucault 2008, p. 131, see also Slobodian 2018). Although social housing was the predominant building form well into the 1970s in West Berlin, where economic developments often differed from the developments in West Germany more generally, the federal housing policies passed in the 1950s clearly blazed the trail for the recommodification of housing as a long-term political goal also in the half-city.

Most social housing units built up to the 1970s emerged in prefabricated, suburban, high rise buildings – a planning decision that the West German government, similar to the East German one, deemed to be particularly cost-effective. By the mid-1970s, the post-WWII housing shortage was considered to be remedied. As Hanauske underscored, the West German 'economic miracle' *was* matched by a 'housing miracle'. The number of housing units in 1950 (10 million) was more than doubled by 1975 (23 million) and corresponded with the number of households in need of housing (ibid., pp. 68–70). The rationalization and standardization of dwellings made this possible, yet led – as will be shown next – also to curtailments of (individual) freedom and, relatedly, to discontent.

5.3 Standardized Dwelling, Normalized Living

In post-WWII West Germany, building researchers were entrusted with the task of defining the bottom line for apartment sizes and equipment for mass housing, a bottom line that was likely to be accepted by future inhabitants (Hafner 1993, p. 130). To achieve a certain level of quality of life, the researchers' goal was to use space as efficiently as possible. For this purpose, industrial norms were developed to define and standardize the uses and functions of dwelling spaces. The two norms that shaped West German social housing in an enduring way were the *Deutsche Industrienormen* [German Industrial Norm] DIN 18011 '*Stellflächen für Möbel und Öfen im Sozialen Wohnungsbau*' [Utility Space for Furniture and Furnaces in Social

Housing] (1951) and DIN 18022 *Küche und Bad im Wohnungsbau* [Kitchen and Bathroom in Social Housing] (1957).

The DIN 18011 differentiates between utility space [*Stellflächen*], movement space [*Bewegungsflächen*], and interspace [*Abstandsflächen*] (Deutscher Normenausschuss 1953, pp. 14–16). Its goal was to optimize space by prescribing the use of highly standardized, often in-built furniture and by tailoring it to predetermined functions such as sleeping, eating, hygiene, and dwelling (Hafner 1993, p. 131). Similarly prescriptive was the DIN 18022. It stipulated that the single-household kitchen was to be the functional kitchen, which was assumed to be particularly cost-saving, space-saving, and time-saving given its scientific-managerial setup and its limited functionality confined to meal preparation. A space of approximately six square meters was considered sufficient for cooking for a family of four to six (ibid., p. 135). Using the kitchen for activities other than preparing meals such as eating, dwelling, socializing, or tending to children was made impossible. As mentioned in the context of the *Platte*, although the functional kitchen was meant to contribute to the emancipation of women by rendering the kitchen as efficient as possible, it contributed to their isolation and 'naturalization' as caretakers. For one, rationalizing the household increased isolation because it sidestepped the socialization of reproductive labor (Beer 1994, pp. 102–106, 113–119). Second, it reentrenched a gendered division of labor, not least because the measurements of the kitchen's furniture were tailored to none other than the average *female* body (Dörhofer 1999) [see Illustration 5.3].

For a builder to be eligible for public funds for social housing, the prescribed German Industrial Norms had to be implemented. Thus, although the West German liberal state left the actual construction of social housing to the private and not-for-profit sector, it nonetheless heavily intervened in the social signification of space and dwelling. Certainly, one of the main purposes of the industrial norms in the immediate aftermath of WWII – norms that were passed in conjunction with the Housing Construction Laws – was to secure a minimal standard of living.[5] Yet both the lingering importance of the norms even in times of economic prosperity and the fact that these norms were applied to social housing in particular bear testimony

5 The First Housing Construction Law stipulated that apartments should not be smaller than 32 square meters and not bigger than 65 square meters (§ 17, ¶1, I. WoBauG). The Second Housing Construction Law stipulated that 85 square meters was the maximum for publicly supported rental units (§ 39, II. WoBauG). The latter also determined a minimum standard for the apartment's facilities: a hallway, storage space, outlets for appliances, etc. (§ 40, II. WoBauG).

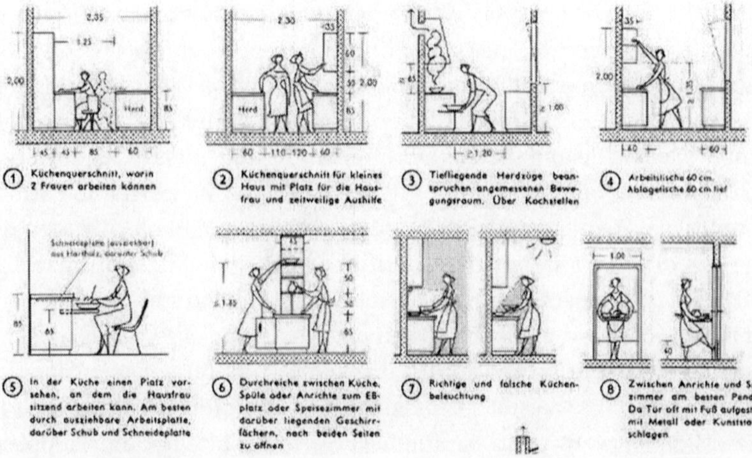

5.3 Industrial Norms and their Gender © Neufert Stiftung, Weimar (e-book) & SNCSC (print)

to the fact that, ultimately, the minimum was normalized *only* for those who could not afford housing on the free market. The functional three-room apartment – two bedrooms, one living room, and a kitchen – emerged as the 'normal dwelling' for the 'normal nuclear family' and would shape mass housing in particular – and West German dwelling culture in general – well into the second half of the twentieth century (Hafner 1993, p. 128).

To be sure, since the inception of rationalization, increasing cost-effectiveness was one of the motivations for carving up space according to norms and functions. Yet, as was already known since the New Building's push for standardized mass housing in the 1920s, rationalization did not in fact always lower housing construction costs, as proclaimed by its proponents (Kähler 1988, p. 553; Beer 1994, p. 122). Often the reverse was true. Due to the high costs involved in both major restructurings of industry (e.g., from small to large scale) and the development of peripheral land, housing costs were often driven up instead of down. In the context of West Germany, as Hafner explains, the main significance of rationalization and industrialization was the increased quantitative output of housing units and the relative improvement in the quality of life in comparison to pre-WWII housing conditions *despite* continuously increasing production costs (Hafner 1993, p. 273).

If standardization and rationalization did not necessarily guarantee cost-effectiveness, why were they nonetheless employed in both West German social housing and East German public housing? As mentioned in the context of East Germany's *Plattenbauten*, the answer lies in the increasingly hegemonic equation of modernization with Taylor's rationalization based on a quasi-scientific analysis of activities and processes along the vectors of time and motion, and Ford's coupling of rationalized mass production with redistribution in the form of mass consumption. This equation left its mark not only on the reproduction of labor but also on the reproduction of everyday life and society more generally *regardless of* the society's specific political outlook. In other words, although Taylorist and Fordist rationalities were ultimately accepted as pinnacles of modernization on both sides of the Wall, these rationalities were utilized to legitimize different political projects. The West German (ordo-)liberal state drew on and normalized economic parameters for the reproduction of society shaped by Taylorist rationalization and Fordist mass consumption, yet entrusted the market – instead of the state – to redeem the two rationalities' promises of material plenty. By contrast, the East German state not only adopted rationalization and mass consumption for its economic framework but also made itself the framework's redeemer by socializing and centralizing the construction industry, for instance. As mentioned in the previous chapter, both political models pursued the dream of a conflict-free society, and both considered Taylorism and Fordism essential for the realization of that dream. Ford's vision of a 'spiral of prosperity' was attractive to (ordo-)liberals no less than to socialists. The components of this spiral were, as Fehl puts it in the form of a litany: 'standardization – mass-production – increased productivity – decreased unit and product cost – increased wages – increased consuming power – increased leisure – increased demand – expansion of mass production' (1995, p. 20).

Given the hegemonic conception of modernization as equal to rationalization and mass consumption, Taylorist and Fordist ideas spilled over into fields that were not directly related to the consumer goods industry, such as architecture and planning. This spillover happened even before the onset of the Cold War. The industrial norms and floor plans implemented in West Germany were largely a continuation of the industrial norms and floor plans that the National Socialists, especially the German Labor Front spearheaded by Robert Ley, had developed. Ley's work as well as Gustav Wolf and Karl Ludwig's book, *Vom Grundriss der Volkswohnung*, prepared during the war and published in the 1950s, were key references for the layout and design of West German social housing (Hafner 1993, p. 131). To be certain, the rationalization undergirding the National Socialists' vision of *Volkswohnungen* itself drew on a precedent. It harked back, of course, to the work of the modernists of the 1920s who embraced rationalization not for *völkische* [nationalistic] aspirations but for social-emancipatory goals (Mumford 2000, pp. 27–43, 104–116).

Taylor's rationalization of industry and Ford's mass production for mass consumption found its way into the planning, production, and architecture of housing *by analogy*. Human needs were assumed to be similar and to be satisfied by technological means. In the realm of planning and architecture, this assumption typically resulted in uniform and schematic built environments. The 'dwelling ration' was to be distributed according to pseudo-scientifically determined human needs (Kähler 1988). '[F]loor plans and, more generally, town planning were to be scientifically developed and devised in such a way as to best possibly maximize the "leisure ration" to secure reproduction and to discipline workers' conduct for the sake of enhanced productivity' [my translation] (Fehl 1995, p. 24). This was the case on both sides of the Wall: at the level of urban form and at the level of dwelling. On the urban scale, the 'dwelling cell' or 'neighborhood' was to secure social reproduction in West Germany. In East Germany, this task was attributed to the 'socialist dwelling complex'. The dwelling cell emphasized individuation; the socialist dwelling complex stressed socialization. Despite differing conceptions of social reproduction, the two urban forms were both infused by the functional and spatial separation of needs and activities. Whereas in Red Vienna, childcare, swimming pools, shops, restaurants, poly clinics, party locals, and laundry facilities were integrated into the social housing unit, in West and East German mass housing alike, such social and communal facilities were spatially separated from the housing units. In terms of the dwelling, the degree of standardization was certainly considerably higher in East German public housing than in West German social housing, as mentioned in the context of East Germany's *Platte*. The West German state prescribed industrial norms for building parts and floor plans yet refrained from prescribing apartment and building types, as was the case in East Germany (Geist and Kürvers 1980, 3: pp. 469–487, 510–516). Furthermore, because West Germany put the market rather than the state in charge of developing housing, the building forms and floor plans were not as uniform as they were in East Germany.

Despite these differences, West German mass housing shared important features with East German mass housing. First, both regimes sought to secure social cohesion by expanding people's share in scientific-technological progress. Key to this pursuit was the provision of 'healthy' and 'hygienic' dwellings for the masses (however minimal the equipment of these dwellings might have been) as well as access to a certain dwelling culture through consumption (which worked better in West Germany than in East Germany). Second, both states entrenched the nuclear family as the 'normal family' and therefore tailored the standard dwelling in mass housing to the 'smallest cell of society'. By doing so, the legacy of a key element of bourgeois dwelling culture, the gender divide, was perpetuated. Although the roles attributed to the family in general and women in particular were clearly different in West and East Germany – West Germany normalized the role of women as housewives whereas East Germany pursued the integration of women into the labor force – neither state fundamentally challenged inherited spatialized gender norms, such as the tailoring of the kitchen to the average female body. Whereas the logic of the modern factory was expanded into the domestic space in the form of, for instance, the functional kitchen, the thrust of modernization stopped short of questioning who would work in the kitchen. In other words, at the rationalized factory, history was overhauled; by contrast, in the rationalized dwelling, history remained the same: the space of reproductive labor was to be preserved as a 'female space' (Hannemann 1999, pp. 424–425).

Since the guarantee of individuality and freedom was essential to the West German political project, why did it rarely translate into the realm of dwelling? As Christine Hannemann puts it, in contrast to other social spheres, modernization in mass housing did not lead to an increased differentiation of the 'ways of life' but instead to their standardization. A 'reduced modernity' was the result (Hannemann 1999, p. 425). However, alternatives to a 'reduced modernity' existed. Already in the 1920s, modernist architects such as Mies van der Rohe and Hans Scharoun experimented with floor plans that gave ample space to individual appropriation, experiments that were motivated by the idea of redeeming the modern promise of freedom and autonomy (Kähler 1988, p. 553). Even at the *Interbau 1957*, 'free floor plans' were introduced, i.e., floor plans that were not carved up along predetermined functions and measurements (Deutscher Werkbund Berlin 1958, pp. 64–65). Although leaving it up to inhabitants to decide on how to appropriate space was not necessarily more expensive, the fact that free floor plans did not become hegemonic had less to do with cost effectiveness than with the prevalence of Taylorist and Fordist rationalities and their equation with modernization and progress *tout court* (Kähler 1988, pp. 553–554). Historically, the appropriation of space for the unfolding of individuality and the exercise of autonomy was a prerogative of the bourgeoisie. East Germany sought to undermine the desirability of this prerogative by providing access to housing to the masses and by guaranteeing relative equality. By contrast, in West Germany, the prerogative remained prominent and realizable only by those who were not economically dependent on social housing. Yet as will be shown in the next section, this social constellation did not go unchallenged.

5.4 Spanners in the Works of Dwelling Machines: Two Experiments in Counter-Culture

5.4.1 The Märkische Viertel: Contesting Abstract Space

One example of a highly standardized living environment is the *Märkische Viertel*, a social housing estate of about 17,000 apartments located in 18-storey high rises built from 1964 to 1974 by the GeSoBau, the *Gesellschaft für sozialen Wohnungsbau* [Society for the Construction of Social Housing]. The *Märkische Viertel* by far exceeded the scale of the *Hansa Quarter* or, more generally, the scale of mass housing in the 1950s. Whereas the city landscapes of the 1950s were typically planned as an agglomeration of neighborhoods of no more than 5,000 inhabitants, the *Märkische Viertel* was built for 50,000 tenants. When viewed from above, the residential development mirrors an organic physiognomy consisting of individually designed building forms (Wilde 1990b, p. 73). Yet what presents itself as harmonious organicism 'from above', from the perspective of the modern plane, was not forcibly experienced as such 'from below'. Despite a certain degree of architectonic plurality, the carving up of urban and private space according to predetermined functions dominated everyday life in the *Märkische Viertel*. As Wilde put it, the exemplary modernist suburb can be seen as an expression of an 'ideology of growth and progress' that brought predictability to center stage and that considered 'any increase in effectiveness and rationalization as contributive to the future's salvation' (ibid., p. 44) [see Illustration 5.4].

The *Märkische Viertel* is a concrete example of the fact that progress was narrowed down to a techno-scientific notion not only in East Germany but also in West Germany. However, the hegemonization of techno-scientific modernization did not go unchallenged. In East Berlin, allotment gardens were an expression of how people appropriated space for their own purposes, purposes that were often radically different from the ones inscribed into the state-created urban and domestic spaces. In West Berlin, the logic inherent to mass housing was challenged in the form of grassroots democratic initiatives. As a matter of fact, the *Märkische Viertel* was a hotbed for West Germany's government-critical, social movements – the extra-parliamentary opposition [*Außerparlamentarische Opposition, APO*] – which emerged in the late 1960s. Although public officials celebrated the suburban development as an epitome of modern living, it increasingly became a fermenting ground for political unrest. The APO organized self-help initiatives and forms of protest on issues such as rent increases, the lack of community

5.4 West Berlin's "Plattenbauten": Märkisches Viertel. © Landesarchiv Berlin

facilities and social spaces (daycares, schools, children and youth centers), the lack of democratic accountability of the housing corporations, and the (sometimes forced) relocation of socially vulnerable people from inner city housing to suburban mass housing – relocations that were the result of urban renewal.

Built on the premises of a former wild settlement that prior to its clearing was decried as a 'green slum', the West German construction of new suburban neighborhoods was driven by three factors: labor drain, the increase in inner city rents, and urban renewal. The political and economic isolation of West Berlin in 1961 had a severe negative impact on the availability of labor. Since many worked in the Western parts of the city but lived in the Eastern districts, the sealing off of West Berlin ushered in a labor shortage. To counteract the shortage, West Berlin's senate decided to provide mass housing quickly to settle workers in the West (Autorengruppe 'Märkische Viertel Zeitung' 1974, p. 27). Moreover, the construction of large-scale social housing projects was made necessary because of the expansion of the so-called 'white circles', that is, urban areas where rent control was abolished which brought an end to political intervention in the supply and demand of housing. The latter was the result of the *Lücke Plan*, a plan that, similar to the First and Second Housing Construction Law, aimed to deregulate the housing market (Häußermann and Siebel 1996, p. 158). The *Lücke Plan* was not nearly as successful in West Berlin as elsewhere in West

Germany, where rents were largely subject to the free market by the end of the 1960s. Nonetheless, also in West Berlin, the plan led to a rent increase and, subsequently, to a heightened demand for social housing. Apart from measures to attract labor and to deregulate the housing market, inner city urban renewal stepped up the need for affordable housing. In West Berlin, urban renewal was not primarily driven by capital investment, as was the case in other West German cities, but by concerns for housing quality. There was a post-WWII consensus that the historically grown industrial city had spawned social disorder and decay, and this fed the momentum for inner city clear cutting in the 1960s. Sun, light, and air were to be brought to 'Old Berlin' by reducing density and mixed use. The hope was that this would also improve the socio-economic make-up of working class areas. A study commissioned by the senate in 1961 found 430,000 apartments built before WWI to be either condemned or in need of rehabilitation (Bodenschatz 1987, p. 30). Although renovation would have been an option in many cases, the city's First Urban Renewal Program (1961) stipulated clear cutting as the most effective strategy. The reduction of inner city housing was then matched by an expansion of suburban mass housing. The city's decision for clear cutting had advantages mainly for the construction industry. First, it allowed the industry to implement its rationalized prefabrication methods. Second, it created a steady and secure market for the housing industry, since the destruction of inner city housing was matched by the construction of suburban mass housing. One effect of the housing corporations' relatively secure financial status was that they acted in the interest of profit rather than in the interest of the tenants' needs (Bodenschatz 1987, pp. 31–32). The housing corporations' lack of democratic accountability, the brutalist architecture of suburban mass housing, the arbitrary mix of inhabitants from different neighborhoods, the relatively high cost of living in social housing, and the lack of social infrastructure in suburban settlements were some of the grounds on which forms of protest emerged in Berlin's *Märkische Viertel*.

One of the first explicit critiques of post-WWII mass housing was expressed by the '*Diagnose*' exhibition in 1968. Organized by affiliates of the Technical University Berlin, the exhibit compared the intentions of the architects and builders of the *Märkische Viertel* with the inhabitants' actual experience of the built environment. The exhibition showed a clear disconnect between ideational intentions and the reality of everyday life. Whereas the builders and architects thought they could accommodate people's needs by building according to the latest standards of hygiene and by implementing a plurality of housing types, many inhabitants considered existing housing to be like a prison and complained about the urban environment's monotony, the high cost of living, and the stigmatization due to individualized housing subsidies (Beck et al. 1975, pp. 32–37). The exhibit was followed by numerous protests and self-help initiatives. Many of them were initiated by students who thought of the *Märkische Viertel* and its housing conditions as paradigmatic of liberal capitalism's shortcomings. In response to leafleting, a first major assembly of about 300 to 400 inhabitants took place in July 1968. Planners, architects, and politicians were also invited and subsequently pressured to account for the lack of social infrastructure (Wilde 1990b, pp. 38–39). Furthermore, a local district newspaper was started, the *MV-Zeitung*, whose declared goals were to serve as a platform for inhabitants, mainly working class inhabitants, to educate themselves on and organize themselves around housing and rent issues as well as to foster and reestablish social networks that were destroyed by urban renewal and people's relocation to the suburbs. To counter the lack of social infrastructure, a makeshift self-help infrastructure emerged. Adventure playgrounds were established, playgrounds consisting of objects whose use and function was not predetermined but left open to children's creative appropriation. Parent-child groups were founded in response to the lack of daycares, self-help initiatives that allowed women to reintegrate themselves into the labor market. Often to the dismay of working class parents, the parent-child groups also experimented with anti-authoritarian education. Empty spaces were illegally appropriated, such as a factory building that squatters intended to transform into a center for children and youth. Working groups on rent and housing emerged, and so did forms of protests against evictions and rent increases, such as the *Handtuch-Aktion* [towel action]. In the case of the *Handtuch-Aktion*, 3,000 inhabitants expressed their frustration about one of the housing corporations' 20 percent rent hike by hanging their towels and linens outside of their windows and balconies despite the corporations' attempts to intimidate tenants by registering those who joined the action (Beck et al. 1975, pp. 160–161) [see Illustration 5.5].

The grassroots democratic initiatives in the *Märkische Viertel* undoubtedly highlighted key shortcomings of post-WWII West German housing policies and their materialization in the form of social housing: mass housing's rigid design and architecture, including its disregard for tenants' needs and desires; the undemocratic structure of the housing corporations; the recommodification of housing; and the individualization of the housing problem that was a result of a subsidy system that supported subjects (tenants in need) instead of objects (affordable housing). The initiatives also brought to light the fact that tenants – including economically disadvantaged tenants – were not merely passive subjects but agents who readily challenged the norms

5.5 Protest Against Rent Hikes, Märkisches Viertel, West Berlin, 1971. © ullstein bild

implicit in spatial arrangements to make a home for themselves. What the initiatives also revealed, however, was a certain disconnect between the goal of the mainly student-led APO, i.e., the overhaul of capitalism, and the goal of the majority of tenants, i.e., the improvement of immediate living conditions. The assumption of Ulrike Meinhof, one of the APO's leading figures, that once the proletariat were impoverished enough, they would radicalize and join the students in Berlin's unfolding class wars – proved to be faulty (1990). In fact, financially destitute and socially marginalized tenants engaged in anarchic acts of destruction of the built environment and violence against students rather than in acts of solidarity (Wilde 1990b, 114–115, 120–121). The APO's attempts to politicize and mobilize the *Märkische Viertel's* tenants were welcome only insofar as they helped tenants to self-organize. What most tenants did not approve of was the students' – and, more generally, the APO's – endeavor to implant a specific worldview, not least because this often implied that tenants were again being treated as immature objects of transformation rather than as autonomous subjects capable of self-help and change. As one of the inhabitants put it:

> Workers know that students are being educated to ultimately be part of the apparatus of oppression that workers are exposed to on an everyday

> basis. Therefore, workers have developed distrust toward intellectuals, because they believe and feel that they are being studied only to then be better exploited. [my translation] (Wilde 1990a, p. 119)

Similarly, tenant members of the working group 'Renting and Dwelling' complained that by assuming the role of translator between inhabitants and bureaucrats, students de-emotionalized the tenants' language, rendered it more objective and reasonable, and thereby adjusted it to the language of the bureaucrats that many tenants had experienced as objectifying and alienating (ibid., p. 124)

On a more theoretical plane, it could be argued that despite the APO's pursuit of the goal of emancipation, such a pursuit effectively exposed tenants' 'stultification', in a manner similar to how the tenants of municipal housing in Red Vienna were treated. Stultification, according to Jacques Rancière, is based on the order of explication, the 'myth of pedagogy' that divides the world into 'knowing minds and ignorant ones, ripe minds and immature ones, the capable and the incapable, the intelligent and the stupid' (1991, p. 6). While an explicator's concern and intention might be noble and well-meaning, such as to enlighten and politically educate the ignorant, it nonetheless defeats the purpose of emancipation. It demonstrates to the ignorant that they cannot understand certain things by themselves, which only perpetuates rather than remedies inequality. As Rancière puts it:

> [Explication] brings halt to the movement of reason and destroys its confidence in itself because it breaks the world of intelligence into two – the groping animal and the learned little man/common sense and science. Perfections of the ways of making things understood, the great preoccupation of men of methods and progressives, is progress toward stultification. What is being incorporated/acquired: a 'new type of intelligence', namely that of the master's explications. (ibid., p. 8)

Inhabitants were frustrated with the APO's approach to emancipation and with their framing of the self-help initiatives in the master narrative of socialism, a narrative most tenants were not interested in and conceived of as yet another subjection to predetermined social or political goals that had little to do with their specific needs and desires. These frustrations manifested themselves, among others, in the municipal elections in March 1971. Given the high degree of activism, it was expected that the Socialist Unity Party of West Berlin (SEW), a party closely affiliated with the East German SED, would achieve considerable gains, especially in the *Märkische Viertel*. Against all expectations, the SEW secured only three percent of the votes in this neighborhood, whereas 95 percent of the votes went to the parties that distanced themselves from Marxist-Leninist teachings (Wilde 1990b, p. 124).

5.4.2 Kommune 1: From Minimum to Maximum Existence

The forms of protest and numerous self-help initiatives in the *Märkische Viertel* are examples of how people questioned the norms implicit in the built environment of West German mass housing. These experiments in grassroots democracy on the urban scale have their corollary in the personal and private realm. In 1967, West Germany's most famous (or one might say infamous) commune was founded in an apartment in inner city West Berlin by members who had close ties to the *Sozialistischer Deutscher Studentenbund* [SDS], a student organization that played a key role in West Germany's extra-parliamentary opposition. The declared goal of *Kommune 1* (K1) was nothing less than the 'revolutionizing of everyday life', the breaking free of the narrow constraints of the so-called bourgeois society. Among the strategies to achieve this goal were the disregard of state order, the abolition of the private sphere by abolishing private property and by introducing 'general sexuality' in defiance of the institution of marriage, and the tackling of the housing problem and problems of subsistence by illegally appropriating uninhabited housing and consumer goods (Langhans and Teufel 1968/1977). A praxis in the form of experiments with alternative forms of dwelling and subversive political action was part and parcel of life in the commune. As the commune's founder, Dieter Kunzelmann, put it in his essay titled *Notizen zur Gründung revolutionärer Kommunen in den Metropolen* [Notes on the Founding of Revolutionary Communes in Metropolises]: 'In order to go beyond the complacent closure of the seemingly natural belief in progress, a belief that only helps to consolidate the momentary violence, radical utopia and radical praxis are necessary. The commune is a call for action [...]' [my translation] (Kunzelmann 1968/1977).

The implemented forms of action, actions that sought to bring about 'the man of the 21st century' (Kunzelmann 1968/1977), affected the personal and political level and sought to overcome the dichotomy between the two. Aiming to revolutionize themselves, the members of the commune created a living arrangement in which private property and traditional relationships were annulled. Critical of the hegemonic nuclear family model and the gendered roles that were ascribed to them spatially in the private sphere, the communards shared rooms, raised children conjointly, and transformed parts of their apartment into community spaces. As Christa

Ritter, one of the commune's members, explained retrospectively about living in the commune: 'The mechanisms, the reflexes which thereby surfaced, seemed to be a cage that conflicted with real life' (Langhans and Ritter 2008, p. 8). Throughout its existence, the K1's living arrangements and philosophy attracted much media attention, particularly West Germany's boulevard press, including the *Spiegel* and the *Stern*. Much of the media's focus was given to the communards' 'subversive political actions', such as the distribution of leaflets that celebrated the arson of shopping centers or the so-called 'pudding assassinations' of high ranking political officials (see Langhans and Teufel 1968/1977; Langhans and Ritter 2008).

In search of 'real life', the communards sought to defy traditional 'everydayness' and forms of objectification. Inspired by Herbert Marcuse, they claimed a 'natural right' to resistance, the right to employ extra-legal means to break free from the perceived repressiveness of a society of 'total administration' (Langhans and Teufel 1968/1977). Their actions were informed by the Situationists International (SI), a revolutionary organization of avant-garde artists, intellectuals, and political theorists that was active from the 1950s to the 1970s. The founder of the K1, Dieter Kunzelmann, had ties to the organization due to his previous involvement with the *Gruppe Spur*, a group of German avant-garde artists affiliated with the SI. For the Situationists,

> [a] revolutionary action within culture cannot have as its aim to be the expression or analysis of life, but its expansion. [...] Revolution does not only lie in the question of knowing what level of production heavy industry is attaining and who will be its master. Along with the exploitation of man, the passions, compensations, and habits that were its products must also wither away. Now, we must define desires appropriate to today's potentialities. Even at the height of struggle between present-day society and the forces that will destroy it, we must already find the initial components of a higher construction of the environment and of new conditions of behavior – the latter through experimentation and propaganda. All the rest belongs to the past and is its servant. (Debord 1957/2004, p. 42)

It was also the communards' goal to construct elements of a new society by creating new environments and behaviors from existing ones. Experimentation was utilized in the pursuit of this goal, as was propaganda. The implemented alternative forms of living and the conjoint 'political happenings' were meant to be ostentatiously and sensationally displayed in order to shock the predominantly conservative West German society.

5.6 "Kommune 1" Imitating a Police Raid (1967). © SZ Photo

And, in light of the media coverage, shock they did [see Illustration 5.6]. The Situationists called for resisting the passivity, divisiveness, and alienation instilled by late capitalism's 'society of spectacle' by means of frightening 'terrorist' passion (Anonymous 1966/1976, p. 17). It is this call to resistance that Berlin's communards were responding to. However, the Situationists also stipulated that whenever interventions are developed, attention needs to be paid to the 'material setting of life' as much as to the behaviors that this setting conditions (Debord 1957/2004, p. 44). Concerning the situationist Guy Debord's specification of radical interventions, it can be argued that the *Kommune 1* was more focused on ostentatiously displaying radical behavior than on consistently reflecting on their behavior's entanglement with actual material conditions.

The K1's perhaps most important intervention in post-WWII West German history was its radical questioning of the public-private divide. By explicitly and implicitly politicizing and redefining the intimate, the commune called into question what post-WWII policies, including housing policies, sought to normalize: heterosexuality, monogamy, the nuclear family, the demarcation of a woman's sphere (i.e., the household), and the ascription of reproductive labor to this sphere. The K1 politicized the private and its spatial dimension, the dwelling. In contrast to the logic of Fordism, the communards appropriated the dwelling in such a way that it would no longer serve the functions of reproducing docile labor and consumption but that it would constitute a place for personal exploration, experimentation, and political agitation. The communards understood their form of living as a micro-laboratory for a different society, a micro-laboratory in which dwelling itself was to become a field of cultural-revolutionary intervention. Whereas post-WWII mass housing was oriented along the lines of a 'minimum existence' [*Existenzminimum*], the communards sought to experiment with and to explore the possibilities of the opposite: a spatialized 'maximum existence' [*Existenzmaximum*].

The K1 experiment in communal living was short-lived. It came to an end in 1969, not least because of internal quarrels and challenges, such as drug use. K1 inspired numerous other communes. Its most important legacy is, however, that it managed to ignite a public debate on the conservative family norms and inegalitarian gender relations that had shaped West German society in general and housing policies in particular. Whereas the protests in West Berlin's *Märkische Viertel* prominently reframed the housing question in West Germany as a lingering and pressing social question, the *Kommune 1* brought to public attention that the housing question is not only a question of class relations, but also a question of gender relations – a broadening of perspectives on the very meaning of 'the social' that clearly outlived the experiment itself.

References

Adorno, Theodor. 1950. Spengler nach dem Untergang. *Der Monat* (20): 115–128.

———. 1965/1997. 'Functionalism Today'. In *Rethinking Architecture*, ed. Neil Leach, 6–19. New York: Routledge.

Autorengruppe 'Märkische Viertel Zeitung' (ed.). 1974. *Stadtteilzeitung*. Reinbeck bei Hamburg: Rowohlt.

Bauman, Zygmunt. 2017. *Retrotopia*. Oxford: Polity Press.

Beck, Johannes, Heiner Böhncke, and Gerhard Vinnai (eds.). 1975. *Wohnste sozial, haste die Qual*. Reinbeck bei Hamburg: Rowohlt Taschenbuch Verlag.

Beer, Ingeborg. 1994. *Architektur für den Alltag*. Berlin: Schelzky & Jeep.

Beier, Gerhard, and Bruno Köbele. 1993. *Wir wollen freie Menschen sein: Der 17. Juni 1953: Bauleute gingen voran.* Cologne: Bund Verlag.

Benjamin, Walter. 2002. *The Arcades Project.* Cambridge, MA: Harvard University Press.

Berman, Marshall. 1988. *All That Is Solid Melts Into Air. The Experience of Modernity.* New York: Penguin Books.

Bodenschatz, Harald. 1987. *Platz frei für das neue Berlin.* Berlin: Transit Buchverlag.

Bolz, Lothar (ed.). 1951. *Von deutschem Bauen. Reden und Aufsätze.* Berlin East: Verlag der Nation.

Buck, Hannsjörg. 2004. *Mit hohem Anspruch gescheitert. Wohnungspolitik der DDR.* Münster: Lit Verlag.

Buck-Morss, Susan. 1992. 'Aesthetics and Anaesthetics', *October* 62 (8): 3–41.

———. 2002. *Dreamworld and Catastrophe.* Cambridge, MA: MIT Press.

Chruschtschow, Nikita. 1955. *Besser, billiger und schneller bauen. Rede auf der Unionskonferenz der Baufachleute der UdSSR in Moskau am 7. Dezember 1954.* Berlin: Dietz Verlag.

Debord, Guy. 1957/2004. 'Report on the Construction of Situations and on the Terms of Organization and Action of the International Situationist Tendency'. In *Guy Debord and the Situationist International*, 29–50. Cambridge, MA: MIT Press.

Deutsche Bauakademie, and Ministerium für Leichtindustrie. 1954. *Besser Leben – Schöner Wohnen: Raum und Möbel.* Leipzig: Graphische Werkstätten.

Deutscher Normenausschuss. 1953. *Pflichtnormen für den sozialen Wohnungsbau und das öffentliche Bauwesen. Erste, zweite und dritte Zusammenstellung.* Berlin West: Beuth-Vertrieb GmbH.

Deutscher Werkbund Berlin (ed.). 1958. *Wohnen in unserer Zeit. Wohnungsgestaltung der Interbau.* Darmstadt: Das Beispiel.

Dietrich, Isolde. 2003. *Hammer, Zirkel, Gartenzaun. Die Politik der SED gegenüber Kleingärtnern.* Norderstedt: BoD.

Dörhofer, Kerstin. 1999. 'Der "Männliche Blick" in der Bauentwurfslehre'. In *Ernst Neufert: Normierte Baukultur im 20. Jahrhundert*, ed. Walter Prigge, 159–167. Frankfurt am Main: Campus.

Durth, Werner. 1989. 'Utopia im Niemands-Land'. In *So viel Anfang war nie. Deutsche Städte 1945–1949*, ed. Hermann Glaser, 214–225. Berlin: Siedler Verlag.

Durth, Werner, and Niels Gutschow. 1993. *Träume in Trümmern.* Munich: Deutscher Taschenbuchverlag.

Eagleton, Terry. 1990. *The Ideology of Aesthetics.* Oxford: Blackwell.

Erhard, Ludwig. 1948/1981. 'Rede vor der 14. Vollversammlung des Wirtschaftsrates des Vereinigten Wirtschaftsgebietes am 21. April 1948, Frankfurt am Main'. In *Grundtexte zur sozialen Marktwirtschaft. Zeugnisse aus zwei Jahren ordnungspolitischer Diskussion*, ed. W. Stützel, 39–42. Bonn/Stuttgart/New York: Ludwig-Erhard-Stiftung.

———. 1957. *Wohlstand für Alle.* Düsseldorf: Econ-Verlag.

Fainstein, Susan. 2010. *The Just City.* Ithaca/London: Cornell University Press.

Fehl, Gerhard. 1995. 'Welcher Fordismus eigentlich?'. In *Zukunft aus Amerika*, ed. Stiftung Bauhaus Dessau, 18–37. Dessau: Stiftung Bauhaus.

Flierl, Bruno. 1993. *Den Himmel überlassen wir den Engeln und den Spatzen. Neun autobiographische Gespräche*, eds. Otto Fritz Hayner and Michael Peschke. Berlin: Volksbühne am Rosa Luxemburg-Platz.

Foucault, Michel. 1977/1995. *Discipline and Punish: The Birth of the Prison.* New York: Random House.

——— (ed.). 1980. *Power/Knowledge.* New York: Pantheon Book.

———. 2003 *Society Must be Defended: Lectures at the Collège de France, 1975–1976.* New York: Picador.

———. 2008. *The Birth of Biopolitics: Lectures at the College de France, 1978–1979.* New York: Palgrave Macmillan.

Francé, Raoul H. 1907. *Streifzüge im Wassertropfen.* Stuttgart: Kosmos.

Frisch, Max. 1965. *Tagebuch 1946–1949.* Munich: Knaur Verlag.

Garcelon, Marc. 1997. 'The Shadow of Leviathan: Public and Private in Communist and Post-Communist Society'. In *Public and Private in Thought and Practice. Perspectives on a Grand Dichotomy*, eds. Jeff Weintraub and Krishan Kumar, 303–332. Chicago: University of Chicago Press.

Geist, Johann Friedrich, and Klaus Kürvers. 1980. *Das Berliner Mietshaus.* Vol. 1-3. Munich: Prestel.

Ghodsee, Kristen Rogheh. 2018. *Why Women Have Better Sex Under Socialism: And Other Arguments for Economic Independence.* New York: Nation Books.

Glaser, Hermann (ed.). 1989. *So viel Anfang war nie.* Berlin: Sieder Verlag.

Göderitz, Johannes, Roland Rainer, and Hubert Hoffmann. 1957. *Die gegliederte und aufgelockerte Stadt.* Tübingen: Wasmut.

Goonewardena, Kanishka. 2009. 'Urban studies, Critical Theory, Radical Politics. Eight Theses for Peter Marcuse', *City* 13 (2–3): 2008–2018.

Gremler, Claudia. 2007. 'Country Escapes and Designs for Living: Christa Wolf, Sarah Kirsch and Judith Hermann'. In *Women's Writing in Western Europe: Gender, Generation and Legacy*, eds. Adalgisa Giorgio and Julia Waters, 119–131. Newcastle, UK: Cambridge Scholars Publications.

Grotewohl, Marlene. 1952. 'Über die Wohnung der werktätigen Frau', *Planen und Bauen* 6 (5): 98–101.

Habermas, Jürgen. 1962/1990. *Strukturwandel der Öffentlichkeit.* Frankfurt am Main: Suhrkamp.

Haderer, Margaret. 2018. '"Economic Policies Are the Best Social Policies": West German Neoliberalism and the Housing Question After 1945', *American Journal of Economics and Sociology* 77 (1): 149–167. DOI: 10.1111/ajes.12220.

Hafner, Thomas. 1993. *Vom Montagehaus zur Wohnscheibe: Entwicklungslinien im deutschen Wohnungsbau; 1945–1970*. Basel: Birkhäuser.

Hain, Simone. 1996a. *Archäologie und Aneignung. Ideen, Pläne und Stadtfigurationen. Aufsätze zur Ostberliner Stadtentwicklung nach 1945*. Erkner (bei Berlin): Institut für Regionalentwicklung und Strukturplanung, IRS.

———. 1996b. 'Kolonialarchitektur', In *Karl-Marx-Allee. Magistrale in Berlin*, eds. Helmut Engel and Wolfgang Ribbe, 75–101. Berlin: Akademie-Verlag.

Hanauske, Dieter. 1995. *'Bauen, bauen, bauen…!' Die Wohnungspolitik in Berlin (West), 1945–1961*. Berlin: Akademie Verlag.

Hannemann, Christine. 1996. *Die Platte. Industrialisierter Wohnungsbau in der DDR*. Braunschweig/Wiesbaden: Vieweg.

———. 1999. 'Normiertes Glück Ost und West'. In *Ernst Neufert: normierte Baukultur im 20. Jahrhundert 1999*, ed. Walter Prigge, 405–429. Frankfurt: Campus.

———. 2005. *Die Platte. Industrialisierter Wohnungsbau in der DDR*. Berlin: Verlag Hans Schiler.

Harlander, Tilman. 1992. 'Kleinsiedlung und Selbsthilfe im Wiederaufbau'. In *Siedeln tut not: Wohnungsbau und Selbsthilfe im Wiederaufbau. Aachen*, eds. Hermann Gödde, Tilman Harlander, and Katrin Hater, 19–37. Aachen: Einhard.

Harth, Annette. 2010. 'Frauen, Wende(n), Wohnen. Zur Wohnweise ostdeutscher Frauen im Transformationsprozess'. In *Wohnen und Gender. Theoretische, politische, soziale und räumliche Aspekte*, ed. Darja Reuschke, 132–149. Wiesbaden: Verlag für Sozialwissenschaften.

Harvey, David. 2000. *Spaces of Hope*. Berkeley, CA: University of Berkeley Press.

Häußermann, Hartmut, and Walter Siebel. 1996. *Soziologie des Wohnens*. Weinheim/Munich: Juventa.

Henselmann, Hermann. 1991. 'Aus der Werkstatt des Architekten'. In *Zwischen Bauhaus und Stalinallee*, ed. Andreas Schätzke, 156–165. Braunschweig/Wiesbaden: Vieweg & Sohn.

Herf, Jeffrey. 1984. *Reactionary Modernism: Technology, Culture, and Politics in Weimar and the Third Reich*. Cambridge: Cambridge University Press.

Horkheimer, Max, and Theodor Adorno. 1947/2002. *Dialectic of Enlightenment*. Stanford, CA: Stanford University Press.

Hoscislawski, Thomas. 1991. *Bauen zwischen Macht und Ohnmacht: Architektur und Städtebau in der DDR*. Berlin: Verlag für Bauwesen.

Hughes, Thomas P. 1989. *American Genesis: A Century of Invention and Technological Enthusiasm, 1870–1970*. New York: Viking.

Hund, Johanna. 1987. 'Das Recht auf Arbeit und gleichen Lohn'. In *Geschichte der Deutschen Frauenbewegung. Zur gewerkschaftlichen Frauenarbeit in der Bundesrepublik*, ed. Florence Herve, 235–254. Cologne: Pahl-Rugenstein Verlag.

Interbau GmbH (ed.). 1957. *Die Stadt von Morgen.* Berlin: Interbau GmbH.

Kahl, Alice. 2003. *Erlebnis Plattenbau. Eine Langzeitstudie.* Opladen: Leske + Budrich.

Kähler, Gert. 1988. 'Von der "Raumzelle" zum "Freien Grundriss" – und zurück'. In *Massenwohnung und Eigenheim*, eds. Axel Schildt and Arnold Sywottek, 537–568. Frankfurt am Main/New York: Campus Verlag.

Katholischer Siedlungsdienst e.V. 1956. *Heim und Familie. Zehn Jahre katholische Siedlungsarbeit.* Cologne: Katholischer Siedlungsdienst e.V.

Kirschenmann, Jörg C., and Eberhard Syring (eds.). 1993. *Hans Scharoun: die Forderung des Unvollendeten.* Stuttgart: Deutsche Verlags-Anstalt.

Kleinschmidt, Christian. 2008. *Konsumgesellschaft.* Göttingen: Vandenhoeck & Ruprecht.

Kohn, Margaret. 2003. *Radical Space. Building the House of the People.* Ithaca, NY: Cornell University Press.

Kopp, Anatole. 1978. *L'Architecture de la Periode Stalinienne.* Grenoble: Presses Universitaires de Grenoble.

Kopstein, Jeffrey. 1997. *Politics of Economic Decline in East Germany. 1945–1989.* Chapel Hill/London: The University of North Carolina Press.

Kosel, Gerhard. 1957. *Produktivkraft Wissenschaft.* Berlin: Verlag der Wirtschaft.

Kropp, Cordula. 2011. 'Gärtner(n) ohne Grenzen: Eine neue Politik des "Sowohl-als-auch" urbaner Gärten?' In *Urban Gardening*, ed. Christa Müller, 76–87. Munich: oekom Verlag.

Kunzelmann, Dieter. 1968/1977. 'Notizen zur Gründung revolutionärer Kommunen in den Metropolen'. In *Klau mich*, eds. Rainer Langhans and Fritz Teufel. Munich: Trikont.

Langhans, Rainer, and Christa Ritter. 2008. *K1. Das Bilderbuch der Kommune.* Munich: Blumenbar Verlag.

Langhans, Rainer, and Fritz Teufel (eds.). 1968/1977. *Klau mich.* Munich: Trikont.

Le Corbusier. 1973. *Athens Charter* New York: Grossman Publishers.

Lefebvre, Henri. 2003. *The Urban Revolution.* Minneapolis: University of Minnesota.

Liebknecht, Kurt. 1954. 'Die Architektur der Wohnung für die Werktätigen unter besonderer Berücksichtigung des Möbels'. In *Besser Leben – Schöner Wohnen: Raum und Möbel*, ed. Deutsche Bauakademie and Ministerium für Leichtindustrie, 7–74. Leipzig: Graphische Werkstätten.

Liebscher, Robert. 2009. *Wohnen für alle. Eine Kulturgeschichte des Plattenbaus.* Berlin: Vergangenheitsverlag.

Maaß, Anita. 2006. *Wohnen in der DDR: Dresden-Prohlis: Wohnungspolitik und Wohnungsbau 1975 bis 1981.* Munich: m press Martin Meidenbauer Verlag.

Marcuse, Peter, and Wolfgang Schumann. 1992. 'Housing in the Colours of the GDR'. In *The Reform of Housing in Eastern Europe and the Soviet Union*, eds. Bengt Turner, Joszef Hegedus, and Ivan Tosics, 74–144. London/New York: Routledge.

Marx, Karl. 1843/1978. 'On the Jewish Question'. In *The Marx-Engels Reader*, ed. Robert C. Tucker, 26–52. New York: Norton.

———. 1852/1978. 'The Eighteenth Brumaire of Louis Bonaparte'. In *The Marx-Engels Reader*, ed. Robert Tucker, 594–617. New York/London: Norton & Company.

———. 1875/1978. 'Critique of the Gotha Program'. In *The Marx-Engels Reader*, ed. Robert C. Tucker, 525–541. New York: Norton.

———. 1887. *Capital.* Moscow: Progress Publishers.

Meinhof, Ulrike. 1990. 'Vorläufiges Strategiepapier MV'. In *Das Märkische Viertel*, ed. Alexander Wilde, 120–121. Berlin: Nicolaische Verlagsbuchhandlung.

Merkel, Ina. 1996. 'Der aufhaltsame Aufbruch in die Konsumgesellschaft'. In *Wunderwirtschaft. DDR-Konsumkultur in den 60er Jahren*, eds. Ina Merkel and Felix Mühlberg, 8–20. Cologne: Böhlau Verlag.

Mumford, Eric. 2000. *The CIAM Discourse on Urbanism: 1928–1960.* Cambridge, MA: MIT Press.

Neues Deutschland. 1951. 'Wäre es schön? Es wäre schön!', 25 November.

Nicolaus, Herbert, and Alexander Obeth. 1997. *Die Stalinallee: Geschichte einer deutschen Straße.* Berlin: Verlag für Bauwesen.

Otto, Karl (ed.). 1959. *die stadt von morgen: gegenwartsprobleme für alle.* Berlin: Mann.

Palmowski, Jan. 2009. *Inventing a Socialist Nation: Heimat and the Politics of Everyday Life in the GDR, 1945 – 1990.* Cambridge: Cambridge University Press.

Ptak, Ralf (2009). "3. Neoliberalism in Germany: Revisiting the Ordoliberal Foundations of the Social Market Economy". In *The Road from Mont Pèlerin: The Making of the Neoliberal Thought Collective*, eds.Philip Mirowski and Dieter Plehwe, 98-138. Cambridge, MA and London, England: Harvard University Press. DOI: 10.4159/9780674054264-004

Rancière, Jacques. 1991. *The Ignorant Schoolmaster.* Stanford, CA: Stanford University Press.

Reiche, Jürgen. 1989. 'Zukunft nach dem Ende'. In *So viel Anfang war nie*, ed. Hermann Glaser, 36–49. Berlin: Sieder Verlag.

Ronneberger, Klaus. 1999. 'Bio-Macht und Hygiene. Disziplinierung und Normalisierung im Fordistischen Wohnungsbau'. In *Ernst Neufert: normierte Baukultur im 20. Jahrhundert 1999*, ed. Walter Prigge, 432–464. Frankfurt am Main: Campus.

Scharoun, Hans. 1946/1974. 'Vortrag anlässlich der Ausstellung 'Berlin plant-erster Bericht', September 5'. In *Hans Scharoun. Bauten, Entwürfe, Texte*, ed. Peter Pfankuch, 156–168. Berlin: Gebr. Mann Verlag.

———. 1946. Vortrag Scharoun, April 4: Protokoll der 9. Sitzung des BWA. Berlin: Archiv der Akademie der Künste/ SB Nachlass Scharoun (Mag I/2).
———. 1949/1974. 'Zur Wohnzelle Friedrichshain'. In *Bauten, Entwürfe, Texte*, ed. Peter Pfankuch, 184–188. Berlin: Gebr. Mann Verlag.
———. 1954/1974. 'Vom Stadt-Wesen und Architekt-Sein'. In *Hans Scharoun. Bauten, Entwürfe, Texte*, ed. Peter Pfankuch, 228–232. Berlin: Gebr. Mann Verlag.
Scheffler, Karl. 1947. Phantom Großstadt. *Baumeister,* Vol. 44., Issue 1–12 Munich: Verlag Herrmann Rinn.
Slobodian, Quinn. 2018. *The Globalists. The End of Empire and the Birth of Neoliberalism.* Cambridge, MA: Harvard University Press.
Schmidt, Heike. 2007. *Frauenpolitik in der DDR. Gestaltungsräume und -grenzen in der Diktatur.* Berlin: Wissenschaftlicher Verlag Berlin.
Schuster, Franz. 1984. 'Die neue Wohnung und der Hausrat'. In *Neues Bauen, Neues Gestalten: Das Neue Frankfurt/die neue Stadt – Eine Zeitschrift zwischen 1926 und 1933*, ed. Heinz Hirdina, 174–178. Dresden: VEB Verlag der Kunst Dresden.
Sedlmayr, Hans. 1951. *Verlust der Mitte: die bildende Kunst des 19. und 20. Jahrhunderts als Symptom und Symbol der Zeit.* Salzburg: Otto Müller.
Sennett, Richard. 2008. *The Craftsman.* New Haven: Yale University Press.
Sohn, Elke. 2007. 'Organicist Concepts of the City Landscape in German Planning after the Second World War', *Landscape Research* 32 (4): 499–523.
Spengler, Oswald. 1928. *The Decline of the West. Perspectives on World History.* New York: Alfred A. Knopf Incorporated.
Stadt und Land Wohnbauten-Gesellschaft mbH. Museumswohnung WBS 70. https://www.stadtundland.de/Unternehmen/Museumswohnung.php. Accessed 25 March 2021.
Stalin, Joseph V. 1954. 'Concerning Questions of Leninism'. In *Stalin Works: Vol. VIII*, ed. Joseph V. Stalin, 13–96. Moscow: Foreign Languages Publishing House.
Stam, Mart. 1984. 'Das Mass, das richtige Mass, das Minimum Mass'. In *Neues Bauen, Neues Gestalten: Das Neue Frankfurt/die neue Stadt – Eine Zeitschrift zwischen 1926 und 1933*, ed. Heinz Hirdina, 215–217. Dresden: VEB Verlag der Kunst Dresden.
Topfstedt, Thomas. 1988. *Städtebau in der DDR.* Leipzig: Seemann Verlag.
Ulbricht, Walter. 1991. Kunst und Wissenschaft im Plan. Rede vor der Volkskammer. 31.10.1951. In *Zwischen Bauhaus und Stalinallee. Architekturdiskussionen im östlichen Deutschland. 1945–1949*, ed. Andreas Schätzke, 143–145. Braunschweig/ Wiesbaden: Vieweg & Sohn.
Voigt, Wolfgang. 1999. 'Vitruv der Moderne: Ernst Neufert'. In *Ernst Neufert: Normierte Baukultur im 20. Jahrhundert*, ed. Walter Prigge, 20–34. Frankfurt am Main: Campus.
Anonymous (1966/1976). Vorbereitende Probleme zur Konstruktion einer Situation. In *Situationistische Internationale 1958–1969. Gesammelte Ausgaben des Organs*

der Situationistischen Internationale, eds. P. Gallissaires and H. Mittelstädt, 16–18. Hamburg: MAD Verlag.

Wagner-Conzelmann, Sandra. 2007. *Die Interbau 1957 in Berlin*. Petersberg: Michael Imhof Verlag.

Wilde, Alexander (ed.). 1990a. *Das Märkische Viertel*. Berlin: Nicolaische Verlagsbuchhandlung.

———. 1990b. *Das Märkische Viertel*. Berlin: Nicolaische Verlagsbuchhandlung Beuermann GMBH.

Zizek, Slavoj. 1998/2008. *The Sublime Object of Ideology*. London, New York: Verso.

6 Conclusion and Postcards from the Past

Abstract
The conclusion summarizes the main findings and establishes a relationship with the present, in which the housing question as a key social question makes a prominent return – especially in Berlin, but also in Vienna. Instead of concluding with 'lessons' from history, which the author doubts that the past provides, the book concludes with Benjamin-inspired, postcard-like messages from the past whose purpose is to trigger reflection on the present. What are the scopes and limits of state and market-based approaches to housing? How private is the unbroken dream of the privately owned, single family home? How emancipatory is community-driven self-provision of housing? How can we account for the unbroken relevance of what a non-sexist city and dwelling may be like?

Keywords: return of the housing question, state- and market-based approaches to housing, community-based self-provision, non-sexist city

The relationship between political ideologies and the production of space was the key focus of this book. It involved taking a closer look at competing promises of a new society to come – socialist and liberal ones – and their actualization, contestation, and subversion through the 'politics of dwelling'. 'The residential is political' argue Madden and Marcuse in (2016, p. 1) – a way of thinking about a key everyday space that this book not only endorses but refines: the residential is a key site for making and remaking (sets of) political beliefs and thus a battleground for political ideas that is as useful in understanding the history of ideas as the more commonly studied 'great books' of 'great thinkers' (Freeden 2006, p. 8–9). Whereas the history of ideas traces and reconstructs concepts by the study of texts, the socio-material history of ideas that was pursued in this book looks at what becomes of ideas when they 'hit' space and what becomes of spaces when they are 'hit' by political beliefs.

Haderer, M., *Rebuilding Cities and Citizens: Mass Housing in Red Vienna and Cold War Berlin*. Amsterdam: Amsterdam University Press 2023
DOI: 10.5117/9789463724944_CH06

Political ideologies, as one core message of this book suggests, are never simply inscribed into space but are instead made and remade, negotiated, and subverted in space. The second core message of this book is that the residential was and continues to be a profoundly political question that involves norms and ideals of citizenship, property relations, gender, and family life, as well as norms and ideals of democracy, freedom, and equality. The main 'regimes of truth' (Foucault 1980, p. 131) investigated in this book were Red Vienna's municipal socialism (1919–1934), East German socialism (1949–1970), and West German liberalism (1949–1970). All three political projects viewed urban reconstruction and the provision of mass housing not only as a dire necessity but also as a propitious lever for anchoring their respective vision of a socialist or liberal society to come. Relatedly, all three political projects were infused by the belief in the very possibility of transforming humans by transforming their environment, in bringing about new forms of social life by altering spaces of everyday life such as the city, the neighborhood, and dwellings.

'New men and women' were expected to flourish in the appropriated and rebuilt cities and dwellings. The two socialist projects that this book has shed light on – municipal socialism in Red Vienna and state socialism in East Germany – were informed by a strong belief in the possibility of building an alternative to liberal capitalism. Both operated under the assumption that, sooner or later, an allegedly superior form of social organization – socialism – would find popular acceptance. The decommodification of housing and the reorganization of the latter along more egalitarian and communitarian lines were deemed to be key stepping stones toward a new, socialist humanism. By contrast, the West German regime refrained from basing the 'new society' on appeals to humanism, not least because of Germany's history of fascism and the latter's fatal appropriation of the truly 'human'. Instead of humanism, West Germany took recourse to a seemingly more neutral ground on which they aimed to build a new, legitimate society: economic freedom. As has been shown, West German housing policies are an instantiation of the hegemonization of a market society, more specifically of a 'neo-liberal governmentality' that concerns itself with projecting the formal principles of a market economy onto the art of regulating society at large (Foucault 2008, pp. 131, 146; Haderer 2018). This projection did not begin in the late twentieth century, as is commonly assumed, but as early as in the 1950s.

Radical new beginnings were promised in Vienna after WWI and Berlin after WWII and, in some respects, also delivered. In 1923, the SDAP launched its first housing program financed by a highly progressive tax system, the Breitner housing construction tax, which broke with the legacy of nineteenth-century economic liberalism, a laissez-faire form of liberalism. By the end of the Red Vienna period in 1934, 400 municipal housing blocks had been built, equipped with a wide range of communal, cultural, political, and medical facilities. In the winter of 1951, East Germany embarked on the construction of its showcase housing project, Berlin's *Stalinallee*. In place of the heavily destroyed nineteenth-century industrial city, a socialist city was to emerge. One of the core components of the ideal socialist city was dwelling complexes, i.e., mass housing in the form of 'workers' palaces' that were to be complemented with a rich communal infrastructure to ensure the urban dwellers' politically adequate socialization. Similarly, in 1957, West Germany spatialized its commitment to liberalism in the form of a showcase housing project, the Hansa Quarter. Located in the middle of West Berlin, the Hansa Quarter was designed as a modernist, functionally differentiated, decentralized city landscape in which high rises with different apartment types were as present as single family homes, providing inhabitants with choice and space for individualization.

Ultimately and ironically, however, in post-WWII Germany the urban form and building types for mass housing turned out to be strikingly similar on *both* sides of the Wall *despite* the Cold War. The imperative of economic efficiency and its underpinnings – rationalization, standardization, and industrial prefabrication – supplanted the search for uniquely socialist and uniquely liberal architectural and planning semantics. While similar in form, namely *Plattenbauten* [concrete slab buildings], the socio-political, normative 'content' of East and West German mass housing was decidedly different. In East Germany, mass housing was informed by the ideal of providing equal housing for equal people. In West Germany, social housing increasingly turned into the accommodation of those who could not afford market prices and for whom the 'true' ideal form of dwelling – the privately owned, single family home – remained out of reach. That said, on both sides of the Wall, the housing question as a key social question was 'solved' (albeit only temporarily) by the 1970s.

Some new beginnings *did* emerge in post-WWI Vienna and post-WWII Berlin. In other respects, the promised new beginnings remained proclamatory or were undercut by the 'poetry of the past' and considerations of economy efficiency (Marx 1852/1978, p. 597). In Red Vienna, the Austro-Marxists proclaimed the emergence of a *new* dwelling culture. Yet they abstained from defining it, which meant the renormalization of already established architectural practices and bourgeois dwelling ideals. In East Germany, the promised political new beginning ironically went hand in hand with the excavation or reinvention of national traditions. This was the case until Stalin's death in 1953, which signified the rehabilitation of an initially much-loathed 'imperialist capitalist' practice: Taylorist rationalization, standardization, and prefabrication. Taylorism, more so than Marxism, would continue to shape East German building practices until the late twentieth century. West German architectural and city building practices harked back to the Weimar legacy of modernism. Yet in contrast to the modernism of the 1920s, modernism after 1945 was largely deprived of the movement's initial radical aspirations: to make human beings the subjects instead of objects of science, technology, and the economy by appropriating new technologies and their potentialities for human flourishing instead of, more narrowly, techno-scientific progress. Economic considerations – first and foremost considerations of economic efficiency – became decisive when it came to building practice. Thus, taking into account specific human needs, desires, and differences turned out to be secondary to rapid and efficient industrial production. This applied to post-Stalinist East Germany no less than to West Germany. As a result, ideals of socialist humanism as well as the liberal principle of individuality were undercut. On both sides of the Wall, mass housing was standardized to such an extent that non-standardized and unforeseen spatial appropriations were hardly possible.

The Austro-Marxists, no less than East German socialists and West German liberals, promised to create 'new men'. Whereas the proclamation was meant to comprise women no less than men, in many respects the provided spaces and the policies underpinning them retapped and normalized bourgeois family norms and gender relations. This applies to the West German politics of dwelling in particular but also to a lesser extent the socialist politics of dwelling, particularly the Austro-Marxist variant of socialism.

In West Germany, the politically dominant conservatives, redefined the nuclear family as society's most important 'cell' in line with inherited Catholic Social teachings and accommodated it accordingly. The single family home was stipulated as the family's ideal home. Social housing was conceived of as an intermediary accommodation for people who were expected to pursue the dream of the privately owned home, a pursuit that commonly implied breadwinning husbands and homemaking wives.

Yet not only West Germany's liberal approach but also Red Vienna and East Germany's socialist new beginnings left no doubt about the nuclear family being the ideal family form and certain spaces being female spaces. Evidence for the latter is the allocation policies that gave preference to the two-generational nuclear family as well as to young married couples. The spatialization of bourgeois family and gender norms can also be observed in the floor plans of the mass housing, which allocated space to the functions of eating, sleeping, hygiene, and living for the nuclear family of ideally four people and declared one space as a decidedly female space: the kitchen. Even though socialist experiments in socializing reproductive labor *did* exist and even though workers had a clear preference for kitchens that also served as a *social* space, such as live-in kitchens, the kitchen was to become an efficient, labor saving, functional workspace to be operated by women of 'average size', as a closer look at the building norms reveals. Whereas the industrialization of *productive* labor also implied socialization – workers no longer produced things in the semi-privacy of the home but in the social setting of a factory – the industrialization of *reproductive* labor, at least regarding the kitchen, ushered in isolation and the spatialization of bourgeois gender norms and roles. To be fair, especially in East Germany, bourgeois gender norms and roles were not only replicated but also broken with – most importantly by the integration of women into the labor market and the socialization of childcare. Although reproductive labor (even if socialized) was to remain in female hands economically speaking, East German women were considerably more autonomous than West German ones.

The poetry of the past shaped the studied dwelling cultures with a view to gender roles. It also shaped the educational and emancipatory aspirations related to the respective 'politics of dwelling'. Red Vienna and West Germany held on tight to the ideal of democracy: the former with a strong emphasis on social equality and the latter with a focus on individuality. Yet regarding housing, a key realm of everyday life, these ideals were often compromised rather than implemented. In the case of Red Vienna's politics of dwelling, radical democratic practices such as self-help movements were overridden by expert-driven pedagogy. Workers were deemed to be too immature for taking matters into their own hands. Although the *Gemeindebauten* fundamentally challenged the bourgeoisie's dominance concerning urban space, Red Vienna's educational strategies adopted in the realm of dwelling continued rather than overhauled the widespread 'episteme of bourgeois suspicion' (Maderthaner and Musner 2008, p. 60) with regard to the working class. In West Germany, it was not an episteme of bourgeois suspicion that undermined the regime's public aspirations but the logic of urbanism: a state-administered, technocratic rationality applied to the city that 'claims to be a system' and professes to be putting man first while actually justifying a (technocratic) utopia (Lefebvre 2003, p. 153). Despite West Germany's commitment to liberal democracy and individual freedom, this commitment was seldom reflected in its large social housing estates, which were – similar to the public housing estates in East Germany – shaped by the logics of industrialization and non-participatory administration. In West Germany, asserting one's individuality and freedom through housing remained the prerogative of the wealthy. This was the case even though 'free floor plans' that gave space to individual appropriation would not have been more costly than highly standardized ones. Additionally, some of the providers of mass housing, the cooperatives, had a history of encouraging the inhabitants' active engagement with their living environment, something the West German state deliberately discouraged.

To map the relationship between twentieth-century ideologies and housing was the central goal of this book. This undertaking included accounting for the contestations and appropriations of the actually built environment and the norms underpinning it – contestations that often ushered in alternative visions of social relations and modes of living. In all three cases, such appropriations and contestations 'from below' *did* take place, which may be regarded as concrete manifestations of a philosophical claim made by Zizek that there is always a 'surplus of the Real' with a view to a given ideological 'symbolization' (Zizek 1998/2008, p. vvx) – a given 'production of space' (Lefebvre 1991).

In Red Vienna, the counter-space to the municipal housing built by the city was the initially wild and later recognized settlements: a democratic, co-operative self-help movement that pursued a version of 'revolutionary practice' (Marx 1845/1978, p. 144) in which workers experienced themselves as capable of finding solutions to their specific challenges. The notion of emancipation that undergirded the Viennese settlement movement in the 1920s was radically different from the notion of emancipation that underpinned Red Vienna's politics of dwelling. In the case of the former, the workers experienced themselves as agents capable of bringing about (social) change; in the case of the latter, the workers were recipients of housing and subject to education by experts. The 'myth of pedagogy', Rancière argues, divides 'knowing minds and ignorant ones, ripe minds and immature ones, the capable and the incapable, the intelligent and the stupid' (1991, p. 6). The myth of pedagogy was perpetuated through municipal housing, which was in many respects emancipatory but still challenged in the settlements.

In East Germany as well, settlements were an antidote to the dominant form of social housing, the *Plattenbau*. In contrast to the Viennese settlements, the East German ones were less driven by revolutionary praxis than a desire for fresh fruit and vegetables in an economy of shortage and a yearning for a bucolic utopia that while not radically challenging state space, such as the functional and highly standardized *Plattenbau*, provided a break from the latter. In the garden colonies, as was argued, people could engage in practices that the state in its emphasis on industrial modernization had rendered secondary, such as subsistence gardening and manual skills needed to build and maintain the cottages and the garden colonies' communal facilities.

Finally, also in West Germany, mass housing and the norms underpinning it were challenged. The extra-parliamentary opposition, the APO, repoliticized the housing question as a key social question in light of steep rent increases, the absence or low quality of communal facilities in large social housing estates, the housing corporation's lack of democratic accountability, and the politics of relocating socially vulnerable tenants from inner city districts to the suburbs in the context of urban renewal. In addition, alternative forms of co-habitation were experimented with, such as communes that questioned dominant property relations, family ideals, gender roles, and approaches to child rearing. Thus, whereas in East German allotment gardens the dream of privacy was dreamt, in West Germany the private was repoliticized.

So What? Postcards from the Past

In her outstanding book on the Paris Commune, the historian Kristin Ross stated that her engagement with the past is not driven by a belief of the past being able to 'actually *give* lessons' for the present. Following Walter Benjamin, she does, however, believe that there are moments when particular past political events, debates, and struggles over the signification and meaning of the social may make 'the figurability' of the present visible and may sometimes even enter it vividly (2016). The belief that the past holds neither lessons nor solutions for the present but can provide a different lens through which the present can be perceived is shared by the author of this book. Past responses to the housing question, even if one may deem them as desirable for the present, are hardly ever replicable in the present. Yet the past may denaturalize the present, unveil its becoming and contingency, and challenge and enrich current dominant perspectives. The legacy of the past and its artefacts, such as mass housing, may exceed path dependencies. It may also consist of a questioning or opening up of the present.

As is well known, Walter Benjamin was an avid collector of postcards. Based on these objects of print and popular culture that were highly popular in the early twentieth century, he offered stirring reflections on society and modernity at large, expounding on their promises and pitfalls. Inspired by Benjamin's appropriation of artefacts for reflections on present society and modernity at large, I will conclude with reflections driven by my engagement with artefacts from the past, spaces built in Red Vienna and Cold War Berlin, as if they were postcards from the past with short messages that may intervene in the present. It is in this sense that this book appeals to legacies.

Postcard #1: The Return of the Housing Question as an Affordability Question

Red Vienna and East Germany pursued the path of decommodification. West Germany pursued the path of gradual recommodification. As a matter of fact, the housing question, which *was* the key social question in Vienna after WWI and Berlin after WWII, was largely solved in all three contexts: in Vienna by the 1930s, and in West and East Berlin by the 1970s. In reunified Berlin, however, the housing question has returned prominently. The main factors behind the return of the housing question as a key social question are the active selling out of public housing, the planned reprivatization of social housing after state loans were paid back, the loosening of rent control, and demographic growth (Holm 2014; Vollmer and Kadi 2018; Miraß). Although in contrast to Berlin, Vienna has consciously abstained from privatizing municipal housing and although Vienna continues to brand itself as a model *social* city, the latter has discontinued the building of municipal housing *despite* a continuously growing demand for affordable housing. In addition, housing affordability has also been affected by the national government's loosening of rent control (Kadi 2015; Bärnthaler et al. 2020; Grinzinger et al. 2021).

The East German approach to housing politics is commonly depicted as a failure (which is, in many respects, undoubtedly true). It embodied an extreme: the state as *the* provider for a basic need. On the other spectrum of the scale is neoliberalism. Hayek's warnings from the 1930s against state intervention in the housing market via rent regulation *did* gradually translate into policies (Hayek 1930/2001). Yet one could say that his promise that the market would ultimately be the best and most efficient provider for a basic social need was, in light of the housing question returning as a key social question (Marcuse and Schumann 1992; Smith 2015; Vollmer and Kadi 2018), as utopian as socialism is commonly depicted. Against this backdrop, one question clearly lingers: is housing a commodity among many to be provided by the market, or does it constitute a basic need whose satisfaction is a key public task? The answer to this question might imply the need for public provision, as it did historically during periods in which there was an *absolute* shortage of housing. Yet it may also imply the regulation of existing housing stock in places where there is not an absolute but a relative shortage of housing, i.e., a shortage of affordable housing.

Postcard #2: The Emancipatory Scope and Limits of Cohousing

Municipal housing in Red Vienna was clearly both a site of emancipation from squalor and a site of subjection to expert knowledge and social control. The alternative to municipal housing, Vienna's settlement movement – a predecessor, one may argue, of contemporary cohousing – achieved both emancipation from squalor and emancipation through the experience of self-efficacy. The Viennese settlement movement implied not only the appropriation of space but also the appropriation of skills: the skill to provide for one's basic needs in close cooperation with others. Today, the desire to not be too dependent on either the state or the private market for housing has led to a boom in cohousing initiatives, that is, citizen-driven, co-operative forms of building, owning, and living together (McCamant and Durrett 2011; Tummers 2016). It is often assumed that cohousing may embody a solution to the return of the housing question as a social question. Yet is it?

Red Vienna's settlers were clear that their settlements were *not* an alternative to the municipal housing program. Whereas the Viennese settlement movement was clearly the more radical political experiment, Vienna's municipal housing program embodied a politics of scale that the settlement movement could never have reached. Red Vienna's superblocks stand for the emancipation of the masses from the housing misery. The Viennese settlement movement had no illusions about its inability to deliver housing for the masses, a clarity regarding its limits that is not always shared by contemporary cohousing initiatives (Tummers 2016). This raises the question of what should be the appropriate lever for a politics of dwelling that protects people against precarious housing conditions while at the same time equipping them with the ability to co-shape the environment they inhabit: should it be civil society or the state (local or national), or a mixture of both?

Postcard #3: The Private Home and its Dependency on Public Infrastructure

West German housing policies provided social housing while stipulating the privately owned, single family home as the ideal home – an ideal that has not only outlived the Cold War in Germany but has been prominent throughout Western societies (Ronald 2008). In the West German context, the single family home has been associated with the male breadwinner model as a sign of taking responsibility for and being determined to care and provide for oneself and one's family. It has also been closely linked to the idea of upward social mobility to which social housing served as a stepping stone, and it has been seen as the ideal dwelling form for raising children. In some respects, these norms and ideals continue to be associated, for good or for worse, with the single family home, which is still considered a personal achievement. Yet to what extent is the single family home a personal achievement and to what extent is this type of dwelling dependent on public infrastructure? When Vienna's city officials debated in the 1920s on whether to invest in multi-level, inner city superblocks or garden cities consisting of single family homes of about 200 square meters for 25,000 people (the number of people in need of housing), the following arguments were launched against the garden city model:

> Imagine the gigantic cost of development [...]! A main drainage system, main pipes for water supply, connections for laying on gas and electricity, a network of streets for communications and residences, would have had to be created. Such a great building area would of course have needed also a first-class quick railway connection with the heart of the city, the cost of which would have been excessively high [...] one-third of the city's total investment in housing from 1923 to 1933], since for this purpose only an overhead or an underground railway could be contemplated. (Honay 1926, p. 14)

In Vienna in the 1920s, a deliberate decision was made in favor of dense urban high rises as opposed to decentral suburban low rises in order to keep *public* expenditures low. What this quote reveals is that it requires major public investments to make seemingly private dreams become real, something one may not think of when driving home to one's suburban house (most likely on public streets); when flushing the toilet (using canalization systems), or when switching on the light (using the electric grid) – infrastructures of everyday life that the Foundational Economy collective has shed a new light on (2018). In Vienna in the 1920s, the city opted against de-centralized housing and for superblocks given the former's high development costs. What the debates at that time underscore is that, for one, housing forms and ideals that are commonly related to privacy and personal achievement hinge considerably on public provisions – a dependency that is usually only (and often negatively) connoted with social housing. In the 1920s, development costs stood in the way of the garden city model. Today, environmental costs have also come to play a prominent role.

Postcard #4: The Return of the Housing Question as a Socio-Ecological Question

The goal of liberating large parts of the urban population from housing misery was what drove the municipal housing program in post-WWI Vienna and the reconstruction of post-WWII Berlin. The provision of a basic need – shelter – stood at the forefront in both contexts. Key to this undertaking was the defining of basic needs and the scope and limits of the ways in which the need for shelter could possibly be satisfied against the backdrop of socio-ecological crises such as climate change (Kallis 2019). In contemporary contexts, limits are readily associated with illegitimate encroachments on individual freedom, which prompt some environmental scholars to argue that there is an inherent tension between the need for limits from an environmental perspective and a culture of transgression from a societal perspective (Blühdorn 2022). When looking at housing history, limits stipulated by the state have been contested (e.g., if they decapacitated the inhabitants' influence on their immediate local environment), but they have also been accepted, especially when they resulted in social security, relative equality, or the building of communal facilities (public parks, pools, libraries, or childcare facilities). As mentioned above, the East German *Platte* embodies a standardization of human needs that has evoked protest because it served considerations of efficiency at the expense of desires. At the same time, however, overall satisfaction with dwelling conditions was relatively high because these conditions meant not only the abstraction from desires but also social security and relative social equality.

The point to be made here is not a defense of the East German approach to the housing question nor a depiction of this approach as an ecologically sound one. The point is the following: the acceptance of limits very much hinges on the implications of those limits. In the context of housing, limits have a track record of acceptance if they are paired with social security and relative social equality. They also tend to be accepted when coupled with 'communal luxury' (Ross 2016) such as public parks, swimming pools, theaters, or clubs – as the history of Viennese housing shows. In light of these histories, limits and freedom may not only boil down to a zero-sum game but also to a differentiated understanding of needs and potential solutions.

Postcard #5: The Stickiness of Gendered Space

It was more than 40 years ago that the architectural historian Dolores Hayden wrote her seminal essay 'What Would a Non-Sexist City Be Like?' (1980) in which she stated that the latter would hinge on a legally binding, more egalitarian division of reproductive labor but also on radically different housing and urban design that would imply the socialization of domestic labor such as cooking by 'service houses' or 'communal kitchens'. The conventional home serves the employed woman and her family badly, as Hayden underlines:

> Whether it is in a suburban, exurban, or inner-city neighborhood, whether it is a split-level ranch house, a modern masterpiece of concrete and glass, or an old brick tenement, the house or apartment is almost invariably organized around the same set of spaces: kitchen, dining room, living room, bedrooms, garage or parking area. These spaces require someone to undertake *private* [emphasis added] cooking, cleaning, child care, and usually private transportation [...]. (1980, p. 174)

Hayden's critique of gendered, labor-divided space and her call for alternatives to it has prominent predecessors: the *Kommune 1* in West Berlin, which experimented with communal child rearing; the *Heimhof*, a service house in Red Vienna; and the politicization of the relationship between productive and reproductive labor pursued by the socialist feminist Alexandra Kollontai (1977). While liberalism and bourgeois family norms have a long joint history, socialists have a long history of claiming to have actually broken with this history, even if they have had limited success in doing so. To be sure, in East Germany women were integrated into the labor force, which brought them economic independence and resulted in the socialization of child care (Ghodsee 2018). Yet neither Red Vienna's nor East Germany's socialists broke with entrenched gender norms in the realm of built space. In practice, they did not fundamentally question gendered responsibilities in respect of reproductive labor, nor did they challenge the notion of the nuclear family. The socialists' focus on productive labor may account for the latter. Once society reorganizes '*production* on the basis of a free and equal association of the producers' [emphasis added], this will, Frederick Engels believed, 'put the whole machinery of state where it will then belong: into the museum of antiquity, by the side of the spinning-wheel and the bronze axe' (1884). Leaving aside the question of whether Engels was right with regard to the state, one may doubt whether an equal and free association of producers alone would have also put the gendered nature of reproductive labor into the museum. Engels, and more generally Marxists, tended to treat reproductive labor as a side contradiction of productive labor, which is hardly a solution to the 'care crisis' (Dowling 2021): the offloading of work (unpaid or less paid) onto the shoulders of women that has shaped the past and continues to mould the present – a present shaped by a pandemic that renders the home, the hearth, and the care for and the education of kids once again a female frontline. What a non-sexist city – and, more generally, a gender-equal everyday life – would look like continues to a be a question that is as topical today as when Dolores Hayden first asked it.

References

Bärnthaler, Richard, Andreas Novy, and Basil Stadelmann. 2020. 'A Polanyi-inspired perspective on social-ecological transformations of cities', *Journal of Urban Affairs* 1–25. DOI: 10.1080/07352166.2020.1834404.

Blühdorn, Ingolfur. 2022. 'Liberation and Limitation: Emancipatory Politics, Socio-Ecological Transformation and the Grammar of the Autocratic-Authoritarian Turn', *European Journal of Social Theory* 25(1): 26–52.

Dowling, Emma. 2021. *The Care Crisis: What Caused It and How Can We End It?* London/New York: Verso.

Engels, Frederick. 1884. *The Origin of the Family, Private Property, and the State.* https://www.marxists.org. Accessed 12 April 2021.

Foucault, Michel. 1980. 'Truth and Power'. In *Power/Knowledge*, ed. Michel Foucault, 109–133. New York: Pantheon Book.

———. 2008. *The Birth of Biopolitics: Lectures at the College de France, 1978–1979.* New York: Palgrave Macmillan.

Foundational Economy Collective. 2018. *Foundational Economy: The Infrastructure of Everyday Life.* Manchester: Manchester University Press.

Ghodsee, Kristen Rogheh. 2018. *Why Women Have Better Sex Under Socialism: And Other Arguments for Economic Independence.* New York: Nation Books.

Grinzinger, Elias, Justin Kadi, Florian Pühringer, and Antonia Schneider. 2021. Mietmonitor: Ist privates Wohnen in Wien noch leistbar?: Eine datenbasierte

Aufarbeitung des Instituts für Raumplanung der TU Wien. Interaktiver Forschungsbericht. https://mietmonitor.wien/. Accessed 12 April 2021.

Haderer, Margaret. 2018. '"Economic Policies Are the Best Social Policies": West German Neoliberalism and the Housing Question After 1945', *American Journal of Economics and Sociology* 77 (1): 149–167. DOI: 10.1111/ajes.12220.

Hayden, Dolores. 1980. 'What Would a Non-Sexist City Be Like? Speculations on Housing, Urban Design, and Human Work', *Signs* 5 (3): 170–187.

Hayek, Friedrich von. 1930/2001. 'Wirkungen der Mietzinsbeschränkungen'. In *Wirtschaft, Wissenschaft und Politik*, ed. Friedrich von Hayek, 208–223. Tübingen: Mohr Siebeck.

Holm, Andrej. 2014. 'Berlin's Gentrification Mainstream'. In *Doing Urban Space*, ed. Sandra Maria Geschke, 171–188. Bielefeld: transcript.

Honay, Karl (ed.). 1926. *The Housing Policy of the Municipality of Vienna.* Vienna: Deutsch-Österreichischer Städtebund.

Kallis, Giorgos. 2019. *Limits. Why Malthus Was Wrong and Why Environmentalists Should Care.* Stanford, CA: Stanford University Press.

Kadi, Justin. 2015. 'Recommodifying Housing in Formerly "Red" Vienna?', *Housing, Theory and Society* 32 (3): 247–265. DOI: 10.1080/14036096.2015.1024885.

Kollontai, Alexandra (ed.). 1977. *Selected Writings of Alexandra Kollontai.* London: Allison & Busby.

Lefebvre, Henri. 1991. *The Production of Space.* Oxford: Blackwell.

———. 2003. *The Urban Revolution.* Minneapolis: University of Minnesota.

Maderthaner, Wolfgang, and Lutz Musner. 2008. *Unruly Masses.* New York: Berghahn Books.

Marcuse, Peter, and Wolfgang Schumann. 1992. 'Housing in the Colours of the GDR'. In *The Reform of Housing in Eastern Europe and the Soviet Union*, eds. Bengt Turner, Joszef Hegedus, and Ivan Tosics, 74–144. London/New York: Routledge.

Marx, Karl. 1845/1978. 'Theses on Feuerbach'. In *The Marx-Engels Reader*, ed. Robert C. Tucker, 143–144. New York: Norten & Company.

———. 1852/1978. 'The Eighteenth Brumaire of Louis Bonaparte'. In *The Marx-Engels Reader*, ed. Robert Tucker, 594–617. New York, London: Norton & Company.

McCamant, Kathryn, and Charles Durrett. 2011. *Creating Cohousing: Building Sustainable Communities.* Gabriola Island: New Society Publishers.

Miraß, Tilman. Mietenwatch. https://www.mietenwatch.de. Accessed 12 April 2021.

Rancière, Jacques. 1991. *The Ignorant Schoolmaster.* Stanford, CA: Stanford University Press.

Ronald, Richard. 2008. *The Ideology of Home Ownership.* London: Palgrave Macmillan UK.

Ross, Kristin. 2016. *Communal Luxury: The Political Imaginary of the Paris Commune.* London/New York: Verso.

Smith, Susan J. 2015. 'Owner Occupation: at Home in a Spatial, Financial Paradox', *International Journal of Housing Policy* 15 (1): 61–83. DOI: 10.1080/14616718.2014.997432.

Tummers, Lidewij. 2016. 'The Re-Emergence of Self-Managed Co-Housing in Europe: A Critical Review of Co-Housing Research', *Urban Studies* 53 (10): 2023–2040. DOI: 10.1177/0042098015586696.

Van Dyk, Silke. 2018. 'Post-Wage Politics and the Rise of Community Capitalism', *Work, Employment and Society* 32 (3): 528–545. DOI: 10.1177/0950017018755663.

Vollmer, Lisa, and Justin Kadi. 2018. 'Wohnungspolitik in der Krise des Neoliberalismus in Berlin und Wien: Postneoliberaler Paradigmenwechsel oder punktuelle staatliche Beruhigungspolitik?', *Prokla* 48 (2): 247–264.

Zizek, Slavoj. 1998/2008. *The Sublime Object of Ideology.* London/New York: Verso.

References

Adler, Max. 1904/1978. 'Causality and Teleology [From: Kausalität und Teleologie im Streite um die Wissenschaft]'. In *Austro-Marxism*, eds. Tom Bottomore and Patrick Goode, 76–78. Oxford: Clarendon Press.

———. 1922. *Die Staatsauffassung des Marxismus: Ein Beitrag zur Unterscheidung von soziologischen und juristischen Methoden.* Vienna.

———. 1924. *Neue Menschen: Gedanken über sozialistische Erziehung.* Berlin: Laub.

———. 1928/1978. 'The Sociology of Revolution [From: Zur Soziologie der Revolution]'. In *Austro-Marxism*, eds. Tom Bottomore and Patrick Goode, 136–146. Oxford: Clarendon Press.

———. 1930/1978. 'Ideology as Appearance [From: Lehrbuch der materialistischen Geschichtsauffassung, Chapter 11]'. In *Austro-Marxism*, eds. Tom Bottomore and Patrick Goode. Oxford: Clarendon Press.

Adler, Victor. 1989. 'Zur Lage der Wienerberger Ziegelarbeiter'. In *Vision und Wirklichkeit: Ein Lesebuch zum Austromarxismus*, ed. Alfred Pfabigan, 18–24. Vienna: Löcker.

Adorno, Theodor. 1950. 'Spengler nach dem Untergang', *Der Monat* (20): 115–128.

———. 1965/1997. 'Functionalism Today'. In *Rethinking Architecture*, ed. Neil Leach, 6–19. Oxon, New York: Routledge.

Autorengruppe 'Märkische Viertel Zeitung' (ed.). 1974. *Stadtteilzeitung.* Reinbeck bei Hamburg: Rowohlt.

Bärnthaler, Richard, Andreas Novy, and Basil Stadelmann. 2020. 'A Polanyi-inspired perspective on social-ecological transformations of cities', *Journal of Urban Affairs* 1–25. DOI: 10.1080/07352166.2020.1834404.

Bauer, Otto. 1919/1978. 'Political and Social Revolution [From: Der Weg zum Sozialismus]'. In *Austro-Marxism*, eds. Tom Bottomore and Patrick Goode, 146–151. Oxford: Clarendon Press.

———. 1924/1978. 'Problems of the Austrian Revolution [From: Die österreichische Revolution]'. In *Austro-Marxism*, eds. Tom Bottomore and Patrick Goode, 156–167. Oxford: Clarendon Press.

———. 1927/1976. 'Sozialdemokratie, Religion und Kirche'. In *Otto Bauer. Werkausgabe, Vol. 3*, 449–531. Wien: Europaverlag.

———. 1927/1978. 'What is Austromarxism?'. In *Austro-Marxism*, eds. Tom Bottomore and Patrick Goode, 45–48. Oxford: Clarendon Press.

———. 1928. 'Klassenkampf und Ideologie'. In *Der Kampf. Sozialdemokratische Monatsschrift* 21 (7): 281–288.

———. 1936/1978. 'The Dictatorship of the Proletariat [From: Zwischen zwei Weltkriegen]'. In *Austro-Marxism*, ed. T. B. Bottomore and Patrick Goode, 201–203. Oxford: Clarendon Press.

———. 1938/1978. 'Fascism [From: 'Der Faschismus', Der Sozialistische Kampf]'. In *Austro-Marxism*, ed. Tom Bottomore and Patrick Goode, 167–186. Oxford: Clarendon Press.

———. 1976a. 'Der Kampf um die Macht'. In *Werkausgabe: 2*, ed. Otto Bauer, 947–967. Wien: Europaverlag.

———. 1976b. 'Der Weg zum Sozialismus'. In *Werkausgabe: 2*, ed. Otto Bauer, 89–131. Wien: Europaverlag.

———. 1976c. 'Die österreichische Revolution'. In *Werkausgabe: 2*, ed. Otto Bauer, 489–866. Wien: Europaverlag.

———. 1976d. 'Mieterschutz, Volkskultur und Alkoholismus'. In *Werkausgabe: 3*, ed. Otto Bauer, 593–608. Wien: Europaverlag.

——— (ed.). 1976e. *Werkausgabe: 2*. Wien: Europaverlag.

Bauman, Zygmunt. 2017. *Retrotopia*. Oxford: Polity Press.

Beck, Johannes, Heiner Böhncke, and Gerhard Vinnai (eds.). 1975. *Wohnste sozial, haste die Qual*. Reinbeck bei Hamburg: Rowohlt Taschenbuch Verlag.

Beer, Ingeborg. 1994. *Architektur für den Alltag*. Berlin: Schelzky & Jeep.

Beier, Gerhard, and Bruno Köbele. 1993. *Wir wollen freie Menschen sein: Der 17. Juni 1953: Bauleute gingen voran*. Köln: Bund Verlag.

Benjamin, Walter. 1968/2007. 'Theses on the Philosophy of History'. In *Illuminations*, ed. Walter Benjamin and Hannah Arendt, 253–264. Schocken Books: New York.

———. 2002. *The Arcades Project*. Cambridge, MA: Harvard University Press.

Berman, Marshall. 1988. *All that is Solid Melts into Air. The Experience of Modernity*. New York: Penguin Books.

Blau, Eve. 1999. *The Architecture of Red Vienna. 1919–1934*. Cambridge, MA: MIT Press.

———. 2001. 'Die Kodifizierung von Identität und Differenz'. In *Otto Wagners Großstadt als Form und Idee*, eds. Moritz Csakz and Peter Stachel, 209–243. Vienna: Passagen Verlag.

———. 2013. 'ISOTYPE and Modern Architecture in Red Vienna'. In *Use Matters: An Alternative History of Architecture*, ed. Kenny Cupers, 15–34. Hoboken: Taylor and Francis.

Bloch, Anna. 1928. Zur Rundfrage: Das Bild im proletarischen Heim. *Bildungsarbeit. Blätter für Sozialistisches Bildungswesen*) 1:50–51.

Blühdorn, Ingolfur. 2022. 'Liberation and limitation: Emancipatory politics, Socio-ecological Transformation and the Grammar of the Autocratic-authoritarian Turn', *European Journal of Social Theory* 25(1): 26–52.

Bodenschatz, Harald. 1987. *Platz frei für das neue Berlin*. Berlin: Transit Buchverlag.

Bolz, Lothar (ed.). 1951. *Von deutschem Bauen. Reden und Aufsätze.* Berlin (Ost): Verlag der Nation.

Bottomore, Tom, and Patrick Goode. 1978. *Austro-Marxism.* Oxford: Clarendon Press.

Braunthal, Julius. 1948. *Auf der Suche nach dem Millenium, Bd. 2.* Nürnberg.

Buck, Hannsjörg. 2004. *Mit hohem Anspruch gescheitert. Wohnungspolitik der DDR.* Münster: Lit Verlag.

Buck-Morss, Susan. 1992. 'Aesthetics and Anaesthetics', *October* 62 (8): 3–41.

———. 2002. *Dreamworld and Catastrophe.* Cambridge, MA: MIT Press.

Khrushchev, Nikita. 1955. *Besser, billiger und schneller bauen. Rede auf der Unionskonferenz der Baufachleute der UdSSR in Moskau am 7. Dezember 1954.* Berlin: Dietz Verlag.

Cole, G.D.H., and Richard Vernon. 1980. *Guild Socialism Restated.* Somerset: Taylor and Francis.

Danneberg, Robert. 1929. *Die Wohnungspolitik der Gemeinde Wien.* Vienna: Gesellschafts- und Wirtschaftsmuseum.

Debord, Guy. 1957/2004. 'Report on the Construction of Situations and on the Terms of Organization and Action of the International Situationist Tendency'. In *Guy Debord and the Situationist International*, 29–50. Cambridge, MA: MIT Press.

Deutsche Bauakademie, and Ministerium für Leichtindustrie. 1954. *Besser Leben – Schöner Wohnen: Raum und Möbel.* Leipzig: Graphische Werkstätten.

Deutscher Normenausschuss. 1953. *Pflichtnormen für den sozialen Wohnungsbau und das öffentliche Bauwesen. Erste, zweite und dritte Zusammenstellung.* Berlin West: Beuth-Vertrieb GmbH.

Deutscher Werkbund Berlin (ed.). 1958. *Wohnen in unserer Zeit. Wohnungsgestaltung der Interbau.* Darmstadt: Das Beispiel.

Dietrich, Isolde. 2003. *Hammer, Zirkel, Gartenzaun. Die Politik der SED gegenüber Kleingärtnern.* Norderstedt: BoD.

Dobson, Andrew. 2007. *Green Political Thought*, 4th ed. Hoboken: Taylor & Francis.

Dörhofer, Kerstin. 1999. 'Der "Männliche Blick" in der Bauentwurfslehre'. In *Ernst Neufert: Normierte Baukultur im 20. Jahrhundert*, ed. Walter Prigge, 159–167. Frankfurt am Main: Campus.

Dowling, Emma. 2021. *The Care Crisis: What Caused It and How Can We End It?* London/New York: Verso.

Durth, Werner. 1989. 'Utopia im Niemands-Land'. In *So viel Anfang war nie. Deutsche Städte 1945–1949*, ed. Hermann Glaser, 214–225. Berlin: Siedler Verlag.

Durth, Werner, and Niels Gutschow. 1993. *Träume in Trümmern.* Munich: Deutscher Taschenbuchverlag.

Eagleton, Terry. 1990. *The Ideology of Aesthetics.* Oxford: Blackwell.

Engels, Frederick. 1884. The Origin of the Family, Private Property, and the State. https://www.marxists.org. Accessed 12 April 2021.

Erhard, Ludwig. 1948/1981. Rede vor der 14. Vollversammlung des Wirtschaftsrates des Vereinigten Wirtschaftsgebietes am 21. April 1948, Frankfurt am Main. In *Grundtexte zur sozialen Marktwirtschaft. Zeugnisse aus zwei Jahren ordnungspolitischer Diskussion*, ed. W. Stützel, 39–42. Bonn, Stuttgart, New York: Ludwig-Erhard-Stiftung.

———. 1957. *Wohlstand für Alle.* Düsseldorf: Econ-Verlag.

Fainstein, Susan. 2010. *The Just City.* Ithaca/London: Cornell University Press.

Fehl, Gerhard. 1995. 'Welcher Fordismus eigentlich?'. In *Zukunft aus Amerika*, ed. Stiftung Bauhaus Dessau, 18–37. Dessau: Stiftung Bauhaus.

Flierl, Bruno. 1993. In *Den Himmel überlassen wir den Engeln und den Spatzen. Neun autobiographische Gespräche*, ed. Otto Fritz Hayner and Michael Peschke. Berlin: Volksbühne am Rosa Luxemburg-Platz.

Foucault, Michel. 1977/1995. *Discipline and Punish: The Birth of the Prison.* New York: Random House.

———. 1980. 'Truth and Power'. In *Power/Knowledge*, ed. Michel Foucault, 109–133. New York: Pantheon Book.

———. 2003. *Society Must be Defended: Lectures at the Collège de France, 1975–1976.* New York: Picador.

———. 2008. *The Birth of Biopolitics: Lectures at the College de France, 1978–1979.* New York: Palgrave Macmillan.

Foundational Economy Collective. 2018. *Foundational Economy: The Infrastructure of Everyday Life.* Manchester: Manchester University Press.

Francé, Raoul H. 1907. *Streifzüge im Wassertropfen.* Stuttgart: Kosmos.

Frank, Josef. 1927. 'Der Gschnas fürs G'muet und der Gschnas als Problem'. In *Bau und Wohnung*, ed. Deutscher Werkbund, 49–57. Stuttgart: Wedekind & Co.

Freeden, Michael. 2006. 'Ideology and political theory', *Journal of Political Ideologies* 11 (1): 3–22. DOI: 10.1080/13569310500395834.

———. 2008. *Ideologies and Political Theory: A Conceptual Approach.* Oxford: Clarendon Press.

———. 2015. *The Political Theory of Political Thinking: The Anatomy of a Practice.* Oxford: Oxford Univ. Press.

Freeden, Michael, Lyman Tower Sargent, and Marc Stears (eds.). 2015b. *The Oxford Handbook of Political Ideologies.* Oxford: Oxford University Press.

Frei, Alfred Georg. 1984. *Rotes Wien.* Berlin (West): DVK-Verlag.

Frisch, Max. 1965. *Tagebuch 1946–1949.* Munich/Zürich: Piper.

Garcelon, Marc. 1997. 'The Shadow of Leviathan: Public and Private in Communist and Post-Communist Society'. In *Public and Private in Thought and Practice. Perspectives on a Grand Dichotomy*, eds. Jeff Weintraub and Krishan Kumar, 303–332. Chicago: University of Chicago Press.

Geist, Johann Friedrich, and Klaus Kürvers. 1980. *Das Berliner Mietshaus.* Munich: Prestel.

Ghodsee, Kristen Rogheh. 2018. *Why Women Have Better Sex Under Socialism: And Other Arguments for Economic Independence.* New York: Nation Books.

Glaser, Hermann (ed.). 1989. *So viel Anfang war nie.* Berlin: Sieder Verlag.

Göderitz, Johannes, Roland Rainer, and Hubert Hoffmann. 1957. *Die gegliederte und aufgelockerte Stadt.* Tübingen: Wasmut.

Goonewardena, Kanishka. 2009. 'Urban studies, Critical Theory, Radical Politics. Eight Theses for Peter Marcuse', *City* 13 (2–3): 2008–2018.

Gramsci, Antonio. 2008. *Selections from the Prison Notebooks.* New York: International Publishers.

Gremler, Claudia. 2007. 'Country Escapes and Designs for Living: Christa Wolf, Sarah Kirsch and Judith Hermann'. In *Women's Writing in Western Europe: Gender, Generation and Legacy,* eds. Adalgisa Giorgio and Julia Waters, 119–131. Newcastle, UK: Cambridge Scholars Publications.

Grinzinger, Elias, Justin Kadi, Florian Pühringer, and Antonia Schneider. 2021. Mietmonitor: Ist privates Wohnen in Wien noch leistbar?: Eine datenbasierte Aufarbeitung des Instituts für Raumplanung der TU Wien. Interaktiver Forschungsbericht. https://mietmonitor.wien/. Accessed April 12th, 2021.

Grotewohl, Marlene. 1952. Über die Wohnung der werktätigen Frau. *Planen und Bauen* 6 (5): 98–101.

Gruber, Helmut. 1991. *Red Vienna.* New York: Oxford University Press.

Gulick, Charles Adams. 1948. *Austria from Habsburg to Hitler.* Berkeley, CA: University of California Press.

Gurney, Craig M. 1999. 'Pride and Prejudice: Discourses of Normalisation in Public and Private Accounts of Home Ownership', *Housing Studies* 14 (2): 163–183. DOI: 10.1080/02673039982902.

Habermas, Jürgen. 1962/1990. *Strukturwandel der Öffentlichkeit.* Frankfurt am Main: Suhrkamp.

Haderer, Margaret. 2018. '"Economic Policies Are the Best Social Policies": West German Neoliberalism and the Housing Question After 1945', *American Journal of Economics and Sociology* 77 (1): 149–167. DOI: 10.1111/ajes.12220.

Hafner, Thomas. 1993. *Vom Montagehaus zur Wohnscheibe: Entwicklungslinien im deutschen Wohnungsbau; 1945–1970.* Basel: Birkhäuser.

Hain, Simone. 1993. 'Reise nach Moskau. Erste Betrachtungen zur politischen Struktur des städtebaulichen Leitbildes des Jahres 1950 in der DDR'. Hochschule für Architektur und Bauwesen (Weimar): Wissenschaftliche Zeitschrift / A, 39(2), 5–14.

———. 1996a. *Archäologie und Aneignung. Ideen, Pläne und Stadtfigurationen. Aufsätze zur Ostberliner Stadtentwicklung nach 1945.* Erkner (bei Berlin): Institut für Regionalentwicklung und Strukturplanung, IRS.

———. 1996b. 'Kolonialarchitektur'. In *Karl-Marx-Allee. Magistrale in Berlin,* eds. Helmut Engel and Wolfgang Ribbe, 75–101. Berlin: Akademie-Verlag.

Hanauske, Dieter. 1995. *'Bauen, bauen, bauen…!' Die Wohnungspolitik in Berlin (West), 1945–1961.* Berlin: Akademie Verlag.

Hannemann, Christine. 1996. *Die Platte. Industrialisierter Wohnungsbau in der DDR.* Braunschweig/Wiesbaden: Vieweg.

———. 1999. 'Normiertes Glück Ost und West'. In *Ernst Neufert: normierte Baukultur im 20. Jahrhundert 1999*, ed. Walter Prigge, 405–429. Frankfurt: Campus.

———. 2005. *Die Platte. Industrialisierter Wohnungsbau in der DDR.* Berlin: Verlag Hans Schiler.

Harlander, Tilman. 1992. 'Kleinsiedlung und Selbsthilfe im Wiederaufbau'. In *Siedeln tut not: Wohnungsbau und Selbsthilfe im Wiederaufbau. Aachen*, eds. Hermann Gödde, Tilman Harlander, and Katrin Hater, 19–37. Aachen: Einhard.

Harth, Annette. 2010. Frauen, Wende(n), Wohnen. 'Zur Wohnweise ostdeutscher Frauen im Transformationsprozess'. In *Wohnen und Gender. Theoretische, politische, soziale und räumliche Aspekte*, ed. Darja Reuschke, 132–149. Wiesbaden: Verlag für Sozialwissenschaften.

Harvey, David. 1989. *The Condition of Postmodernity. An Enquiry into the Origins of Cultural Change.* Oxford: Blackwell.

———. 2000. *Spaces of Hope.* Berkeley, CA: University of Berkeley Press.

Häußermann, Hartmut, and Walter Siebel. 1996. *Soziologie des Wohnens.* Weinheim/Munich: Juventa.

Hayden, Dolores. 1980. 'What Would a Non-Sexist City Be Like? Speculations on Housing, Urban Design, and Human Work', *Signs* 5 (3): 170–187.

Hayek, Friedrich von. 1930/2001. 'Wirkungen der Mietzinsbeschränkungen'. In *Wirtschaft, Wissenschaft und Politik*, ed. Friedrich von Hayek, 208–223. Tübingen: Mohr Siebeck.

Henselmann, Hermann. 1991. 'Aus der Werkstatt des Architekten'. In *Zwischen Bauhaus und Stalinallee*, ed. Andreas Schätzke, 156–165. Braunschweig/Wiesbaden: Vieweg & Sohn.

Herf, Jeffrey. 1984. *Reactionary Modernism: Technology, Culture, and Politics in Weimar and the Third Reich.* Cambridge: Cambridge University Press.

Hochhäusl, Sophie. 2011. *Otto Neurath – City Planning.* Innsbruck: Innsbruck University Press.

———. 2013. 'From Vienna to Frankfurt Inside Core-House Type 7: A History of Scarcity through the Modern Kitchen', *Architectural Histories* 1 (1): 24. DOI: 10.5334/ah.aq.

———. 2019. 'Traveling Exhibitions in the Field: Settlements, War-Economy, and the Collaborative Practice of Seeing, 1919–1925'. In *Neurath Reconsidered: New Sources and Perspectives*, eds. Jordi Cat and Adam Tamas Tuboly, 141–176. Cham: Springer International Publishing.

Holm, Andrej. 2014. 'Berlin's Gentrification Mainstream'. In *Doing Urban Space*, ed. Sandra Maria Geschke, 171–188. Bielefeld: transcript.

Holtmann, Everhard. 1996. 'Die Organisation der Sozialdemokratie in der Ersten Republik, 1918–1934'. In *Die Organisation der österreichischen Sozialdemokratie 1889–1995*, eds. Wolfgang Maderthaner and Wolfgang C. Müller, 93–167. Vienna: Löcker.

Honay, Karl (ed.). 1926. *The Housing Policy of the Municipality of Vienna*. Vienna: Deutsch-Österreichischer Städtebund.

Horkheimer, Max, and Theodor Adorno. 1947/2002. *Dialectic of Enlightenment*. Stanford, CA: Stanford University Press.

Hoscislawski, Thomas. 1991. *Bauen zwischen Macht und Ohnmacht: Architektur und Städtebau in der DDR*. Berlin: Verlag für Bauwesen.

Hösl, Wolfgang, and Gottfried Pirhofer. 1982. 'Otto Neurath und der Städtebau'. In *Arbeiterbildung in der Zwischenkriegszeit. Otto Neurath – Gerd Antz*, ed. Friedrich Stadler, 157–161. Vienna: Löcker.

Hughes, Thomas P. 1989. *American Genesis: A Century of Invention and Technological Enthusiasm, 1870–1970*. New York: Viking.

Hund, Johanna. 1987. 'Das Recht auf Arbeit und gleichen Lohn'. In *Geschichte der Deutschen Frauenbewegung. Zur gewerkschaftlichen Frauenarbeit in der Bundesrepublik*, ed. Florence Herve, 235–254. Cologne: Pahl-Rugenstein Verlag.

Interbau GmbH (ed.). 1957. *Die Stadt von Morgen*. Berlin: Interbau GmbH.

John, Michael. 1996. 'Straßenwalle und Exzesse'. In *Wien – Prag – Budapest*, eds. Gerhard Melinz and Susan Zimmermann, 230–244. Vienna: Promedia.

Kadi, Justin. 2015. 'Recommodifying Housing in Formerly "Red" Vienna?', *Housing, Theory and Society* 32 (3): 247–265. DOI: 10.1080/14036096.2015.1024885.

Kahl, Alice. 2003. *Erlebnis Plattenbau. Eine Langzeitstudie*. Opladen: Leske + Budrich.

Kähler, Gert. 1988. 'Von der "Raumzelle" zum "Freien Grundriss" – und zurück'. In *Massenwohnung und Eigenheim*, eds. Axel Schildt and Arnold Sywottek, 537–568. Frankfurt am Main/New York: Campus Verlag.

Kallis, Giorgos. 2019. *Limits. Why Malthus was Wrong and Why Environmentalists Should Care*. Stanford, CA: Stanford University Press.

Katholischer Siedlungsdienst e.V. 1956. *Heim und Familie. Zehn Jahre katholische Siedlungsarbeit*. Cologne: Katholischer Siedlungsdienst e.V.

Kirschenmann, Jörg C., and Eberhard Syring (eds.). 1993. *Hans Scharoun: die Forderung des Unvollendeten*. Stuttgart: Deutsche Verlags-Anstalt.

Kleinschmidt, Christian. 2008. *Konsumgesellschaft*. Göttingen: Vandenhoeck & Ruprecht.

Kohl, Sebastian. 2018. 'Why Housing Studies Still Lack Social Theory and What to Do About It', *Housing, Theory and Society*, 35:2, 231–234. DOI: 10.1080/14036096.2017.1366943.

———. 2019. *Homeownership, Renting and Society: Historical and Comparative Perspectives*. London/New York: Routledge.

Kohn, Margaret. 2003. *Radical Space. Building the House of the People*. Ithaca, NY: Cornell University Press.

Kollontai, Alexandra (ed.). 1977. *Selected Writings of Alexandra Kollontai*. London: Allison & Busby.

Kopp, Anatole. 1978. *L'Architecture de la Periode Stalinienne*. Grenoble: Presses Universitaires de Grenoble.

Kopstein, Jeffrey. 1997. *Politics of Economic Decline in East Germany. 1945–1989*. Chapel Hill/London: The University of North Carolina Press.

Korthals Altes, Willem, and Andreas Faludi. 1995. 'Why the Greening of Red Vienna Did Not Come to Pass: An Unknown Chapter of the Garden City Movement 1919–1934', *European Planning Studies*, 1995.

Kosel, Gerhard. 1957. *Produktivkraft Wissenschaft*. Berlin: Verlag der Wirtschaft.

Kropp, Cordula. 2011. 'Gärtner(n) ohne Grenzen: Eine neue Politik des 'Sowohl-als-auch' urbaner Gärten?', In *Urban Gardening*, ed. Christa Müller, 76–87. Munich: oekom Verlag.

Kunzelmann, Dieter. 1968/1977. 'Notizen zur Gründung revolutionärer Kommunen in den Metropolen'. In *Klau mich*, eds. Rainer Langhans and Fritz Teufel. Munich: Trikont.

Ladd, Brian. 2008. *The Ghosts of Berlin: Confronting German History in the Urban Landscape*. Chicago: University of Chicago Press.

Langhans, Rainer, and Christa Ritter. 2008. *K1. Das Bilderbuch der Kommune*. Munich: Blumenbar Verlag.

Langhans, Rainer, and Fritz Teufel (eds.). 1968/1977. *Klau mich*. Munich: Trikont.

Le Corbusier. 1973. *Athens Charter*. New York: Grossman Publishers.

Lefebvre, Henri. 1991. *The Production of Space*. Oxford: Blackwell.

———. 2003. *The Urban Revolution*. Minneapolis: University of Minnesota.

Lichtenberger, Elisabeth. 1993. *Wien, Prag: Metropolenforschung*. Vienna: Böhlau Verlag.

Liebknecht, Kurt. 1954. 'Die Architektur der Wohnung für die Werktätigen unter besonderer Berücksichtigung des Möbels'. In *Besser Leben – Schöner Wohnen: Raum und Möbel*, ed. Deutsche Bauakademie and Ministerium für Leichtindustrie, 7–74. Leipzig: Graphische Werkstätten.

Liebscher, Robert. 2009. *Wohnen für alle. Eine Kulturgeschichte des Plattenbaus*. Berlin: Vergangenheitsverlag.

Maaß, Anita. 2006. *Wohnen in der DDR: Dresden-Prohlis: Wohnungspolitik und Wohnungsbau 1975 bis 1981*. Munich: m press Martin Meidenbauer Verlag.

Madden, David J., and Peter Marcuse. 2016. *In Defense of Housing: The Politics of Crisis*. London/New York: Verso.

Maderthaner, Wolfgang. 2006. 'Von der Zeit um 1860 bis zum Jahr 1945'. In *Wien. Geschichte einer Stadt*, eds. Peter Csendes and Ferdinand Opll, 175–544. Vienna: Böhlau Verlag.

Maderthaner, Wolfgang, and Lutz Musner. 2008. *Unruly Masses.* New York: Berghahn Books.

Maimann, Helene (ed.). 1981. *'Mit uns zieht die neue Zeit. Arbeiterkultur in Österreich 1918–1934'.* Vienna: Habarta & Habarta.

Marcuse, Peter, and Wolfgang Schumann. 1992. 'Housing in the Colours of the GDR'. In *The Reform of Housing in Eastern Europe and the Soviet Union*, eds. Bengt Turner, Joszef Hegedus, and Ivan Tosics, 74–144. London/New York: Routledge.

Marx, Karl. 1843/1978. 'On the Jewish Question'. In *The Marx-Engels Reader*, ed. Robert C. Tucker, 26–52. New York: Norton.

———. 1844/1978a. 'Economic and Philosophic Manuscripts of 1844'. In *The Marx-Engels Reader*, ed. Robert C. Tucker, 66–125. New York: Norton.

———. 1844/1978b. 'For a Ruthless Criticism of Everything Existing'. In *The Marx-Engels Reader*, ed. Robert C. Tucker, 12–15. New York/London: Norton & Company.

———, 1845/1978. 'Theses on Feuerbach'. In *The Marx-Engels Reader*, ed. Robert C. Tucker, 143–144. New York: Norton & Company.

———. 1852/1978. 'The Eighteenth Brumaire of Louis Bonaparte'. In *The Marx-Engels Reader*, ed. Robert Tucker, 594–617. New York/London: Norton & Company.

———. 1875/1978. 'Critique of the Gotha Program'. In *The Marx-Engels Reader*, ed. Robert C. Tucker, 525–541. New York: Norton.

———. 1887. *Capital.* Moscow: Progress Publishers.

———. 1938. 'A Workers' Inquiry', *The New International* 4 (12): 379–381.

———. 1969. 'The Class Struggle in France: 1848–1850'. In *Selected Works*, ed. Karl Marx. Moscow: Progress Publishers.

McCamant, Kathryn, and Charles Durrett. 2011. *Creating Cohousing: Building Sustainable Communities.* Gabriola Island: New Society Publishers.

Meinhof, Ulrike. 1990. 'Vorläufiges Strategiepapier MV'. In *Das Märkische Viertel*, ed. Alexander Wilde, 120–121. Berlin: Nicolaische Verlagsbuchhandlung.

Merkel, Ina. 1996. 'Der aufhaltsame Aufbruch in die Konsumgesellschaft'. In *Wunderwirtschaft. DDR-Konsumkultur in den 60er Jahren*, eds. Ina Merkel and Felix Mühlberg, 8–20. Cologne: Böhlau Verlag.

Merrifield, Andrew. 1993. 'Place and Space: A Lefebvrian Reconciliation', *Transactions of the Institute of British Geographers* 18 (4): 516. DOI: 10.2307/622564.

Miraß, Tilman. Mietenwatch. https://www.mietenwatch.de. Accessed 12 April 2021.

Mumford, Eric. 2000. *The CIAM Discourse on Urbanism: 1928–1960.* Cambridge, MA: MIT Press.

Neues Deutschland. 1951. 'Wäre es schön? Es wäre schön!', November 25.

Neurath, Otto. 1921. Erziehungsaufgaben des Sozialismus. *Bildungsarbeit. Blätter für sozialistisches Bildungswesen,* 1921.

———. 1923. Neu-Wiens Gesamtarchitektur – eine Aufgabe des Proletariats. *Arbeiter Zeitung,* October 28.

———. 1926a. Bauformen und Klassenkampf. *Bildungsarbeit. Blätter für sozialistisches Bildungswesen* XIII (4): 61–64.

———. 1926b. 'Rationalismus, Arbeiterschaft und Baugestaltung', *Der Aufbau* (May): 49–52.

———. 1928. Proletarische Lebensgestaltung. *Der Kampf,* 1928.

———. 1933. Museums of the Future. *Survey Graphic,* 1933.

———. 1937. Visual Education: A New Language. *Survey Graphic,* 1937.

———. 1979. Statistik und Sozialismus. In *Otto Neurath – Wissenschaftliche Weltauffassung, Sozialismus und logischer Empirismus,* eds. Otto Neurath and Rainer Hegelsmann, 288–294. Frankfurt: Suhrkamp.

Nicolaus, Herbert, and Alexander Obeth. 1997. *Die Stalinallee: Geschichte einer deutschen Straße.* Berlin: Verlag für Bauwesen.

Nussbaum, Andrea. 2007. 'Kleiner roter Ziegelstein, baut die neue Welt'. In *Karl-Marx Hof. Versailles der Arbeiter,* eds. Gerold Kriechbaum and Genoveva Kriechbaum, 50–79. Vienna: Holzhausen Verlag.

Oldenziel, Ruth, and Karin Zachmann (eds.). 2009. *Cold War Kitchen: Americanization, Technology, and European Users.* Cambridge, MA: MIT Press.

Otto, Karl (ed.). 1959. *die stadt von morgen: gegenwartsprobleme für alle.* Berlin: Mann.

Palmowski, Jan. 2009. *Inventing a Socialist Nation: Heimat and the Politics of Everyday Life in the GDR, 1945 – 1990.* Cambridge: Cambridge University Press.

Pfoser, Alfred. 1982. 'Das Glück in der Vernunft – Überlegungen zu Otto Neuraths Kulturtheorie und zur austromarxistischen Lebensreform'. In *Arbeiterbildung in der Zwischenkriegszeit. Otto Neurath – Gerd Antz,* ed. Friedrich Stadler, 168–172. Vienna: Löcker.

Philippovich, Eugen. 1894. Wiener Wohnungsverhältnisse. *Archiv für soziale Gesetzgebung und Statistik* 7: 215–277.

Pircher, Wolfgang. 1982. 'Bemerkungen zu "Statstik und Sozialismus"'. In *Arbeiterbildung in der Zwischenkriegszeit. Otto Neurath – Gerd Antz,* ed. Friedrich Stadler, 162–167. Vienna: Löcker.

Pirhofer, Gottfried, and Reinhard Sieder. 1982. 'Zur Konstitution der Arbeiterfamilie im Roten Wien: Familienpolitik, Kulturreform, Alltag und Ästhetik'. In *Historische Familienforschung,* eds. Michael Mitterauer and Reinhard Sieder, 326–368. Frankfurt am Main: Suhrkamp.

Ptak, Ralf (2009). "3. Neoliberalism in Germany: Revisiting the Ordoliberal Foundations of the Social Market Economy". In The Road from Mont Pèlerin: The Making of the Neoliberal Thought Collective, eds.Philip Mirowski and Dieter Plehwe, 98-138. Cambridge, MA and London, England: Harvard University Press. DOI: 10.4159/9780674054264-004

Rabinbach, Anson. 1989. *Vom Roten Wien zum Bürgerkrieg.* Vienna: Löcker Verlag.

Rancière, Jacques. 1991. *The Ignorant Schoolmaster.* Stanford, CA: Stanford University Press.

Reiche, Jürgen. 1989. 'Zukunft nach dem Ende'. In *So viel Anfang war nie*, ed. Hermann Glaser, 36–49. Berlin: Sieder Verlag.

Richie, Alexandra. 1999. *Faust's Metropolis: A History of Berlin.* New York: Carroll & Graf.

Roberts, John. 2006. *Philosophizing the Everyday. Revolutionary Praxis and the Fate of Cultural Theory.* London: Pluto Press.

Ronald, Richard. 2008. *The Ideology of Home Ownership.* London: Palgrave Macmillan UK.

Ronneberger, Klaus. 1999. 'Bio-Macht und Hygiene. Disziplinierung und Normalisierung im Fordistischen Wohnungsbau'. In *Ernst Neufert: normierte Baukultur im 20. Jahrhundert 1999*, ed. Walter Prigge, 432–464. Frankfurt: Campus.

Ross, Kristin. 2016. *Communal Luxury: The Political Imaginary of the Paris Commune.* London/New York: Verso.

Rubin, Eli. *Amnesiopolis: Modernity, Space and Memory in East Germany.* Oxford: Oxford University Press, 2016.

Scharoun, Hans. 1946/1974. Vortrag anlässlich der Ausstellung ,Berlin plant-erster Bericht', September 5. In *Hans Scharoun. Bauten, Entwürfe, Texte*, ed. Peter Pfankuch, 156–168. Berlin: Gebr. Mann Verlag.

Scharoun, Hans. 1946. Vortrag Scharoun, April 4: Protokoll der 9. Sitzung des BWA. Berlin: Archiv der Akademie der Künste/ SB Nachlass Scharoun (Mag I/2).

———. 1949/1974. 'Zur Wohnzelle Friedrichshain'. In *Bauten, Entwürfe, Texte*, ed. Peter Pfankuch, 184–188. Berlin: Gebr. Mann Verlag.

———. 1954/1974. 'Vom Stadt-Wesen und Architekt-Sein'. In *Hans Scharoun. Bauten, Entwürfe, Texte*, ed. Peter Pfankuch, 228–232. Berlin: Gebr. Mann Verlag.

Schretzenmayr, Martina. 1998. 'Wohnungsbau in der ehemaligen DDR', disP -The Planning Review, 34: 133, 40–48, DOI: 10.1080/02513625.1998.10556676.

Scheffler, Karl. 1947. Phantom Großstadt. *Baumeister,* Vol. 44., Issue 1–12 Munich: Verlag Herrmann Rinn. Schmidt, Heike. 2007. *Frauenpolitik in der DDR. Gestaltungsräume und -grenzen in der Diktatur.* Berlin: Wissenschaftlicher Verlag Berlin.

Schorske, Carl E. 1981. *Fin-de-Siecle Vienna. Politics and Culture.* New York: Vintage Books.

Schuster, Franz. 1984. 'Die neue Wohnung und der Hausrat'. In *Neues Bauen, Neues Gestalten: Das Neue Frankfurt/die neue Stadt – Eine Zeitschrift zwischen 1926 und 1933*, ed. Heinz Hirdina, 174–178. Dresden: VEB Verlag der Kunst Dresden.

Schuster, Franz, and Franz Schacherl. 1926. Proletarische Architektur. *Der Kampf* XIX:34ff.

Scott, James. 1998. *Seeing Like a State*. New Haven: Yale University Press.

Sedlmayr, Hans. 1951. *Verlust der Mitte: die bildende Kunst des 19. und 20. Jahrhunderts als Symptom und Symbol der Zeit.* Salzburg: Otto Müller.

Sennett, Richard. 2008. *The Craftsman*. New Haven: Yale University Press.

Sieder, Reinhard. 1988. Zur alltäglichen Praxis der Wiener Arbeiterschaft im ersten Drittel des 20. Jahrhunderts. Habilitation, Universität Wien, Wien.

Slobodian, Quinn. 2018. *The Globalists. The End of Empire and the Birth of Neoliberalism.* Cambridge, MA: Harvard University Press.

Smith, Susan J. 2015. 'Owner Occupation: At Home in a Spatial, Financial Paradox', *International Journal of Housing Policy* 15 (1): 61–83. DOI: 10.1080/14616718.2014.997432.

Sohn, Elke. 2007. 'Organicist Concepts of the City Landscape in German Planning after the Second World War', *Landscape Research* 32 (4): 499–523.

Spengler, Oswald. 1928. *The Decline of the West. Perspectives on World History.* New York: Alfred A. Knopf Incorporated.

Stadt und Land Wohnbauten-Gesellschaft mbH. Museumswohnung WBS 70. https://www.stadtundland.de/Unternehmen/Museumswohnung.php. Accessed 25 March 2021.

Stalin, Joseph V. 1954. 'Concerning Questions of Leninism'. In *Stalin Works: Vol. VIII*, ed. Joseph V. Stalin, 13–96. Moscow: Foreign Languages Publishing House.

Stam, Mart. 1984. 'Das Mass, das richtige Mass, das Minimum Mass'. In *Neues Bauen, Neues Gestalten: Das Neue Frankfurt/die neue Stadt – Eine Zeitschrift zwischen 1926 und 1933*, ed. Heinz Hirdina, 215–217. Dresden: VEB Verlag der Kunst Dresden.

Stangl, Paul. 2018. *Risen from Ruins: The Cultural Politics of Rebuilding East Berlin.* Stanford, CA: Stanford University Press.

Tandler, Julius. 1928. 'Gefahren der Minderwertigkeit'. In *Das Wiener Jugendhilfswerk*, ed. Franz Breunlich, 1–22. Vienna: Verlag des Jugendamtes der Stadt Wien.

Taut, Bruno. 1926. 'Die Frau als Schöpferin der Wohnung'. *Der Aufbau. Österreichische Monatshefte für Siedlung und Städtebau* (2).

Topfstedt, Thomas. 1988. *Städtebau in der DDR.* Leipzig: Seemann Verlag.

Tummers, Lidewij. 2016. 'The Re-Emergence of Self-Managed Co-Housing in Europe: A Critical Review of Co-Housing Research', *Urban Studies* 53 (10): 2023–2040. DOI: 10.1177/0042098015586696.

Ulbricht, Walter. 1951. 'Das nationale Aufbauwerk und die Aufgaben der deutschen Architektur'. Speech on December 8. Berlin: Amt für Information der Regierung der Deutschen Demokratischen Republik.

Ulbricht, Walter. 1991. 'Kunst und Wissenschaft im Plan. Rede vor der Volkskammer'. 31.10.1951. In *Zwischen Bauhaus und Stalinallee. Architekturdiskussionen im östlichen Deutschland. 1945–1949*, ed. Andreas Schätzke, 143–145. Braunschweig/Wiesbaden: Vieweg & Sohn.

Urban, Florian. 2012. *Tower and Slab: Histories of Global Mass Housing.* Abingdon/New York: Routledge.

Van Dyk, Silke. 2018. 'Post-Wage Politics and the Rise of Community Capitalism', *Work, Employment and Society* 32 (3): 528–545. DOI: 10.1177/0950017018755663.

Voigt, Wolfgang. 1999. 'Vitruv der Moderne: Ernst Neufert'. In *Ernst Neufert: Normierte Baukultur im 20. Jahrhundert*, ed. Walter Prigge, 20–34. Frankfurt am Main: Campus.

Vollmer, Lisa, and Justin Kadi. 2018. 'Wohnungspolitik in der Krise des Neoliberalismus in Berlin und Wien: Postneoliberaler Paradigmenwechsel oder punktuelle staatliche Beruhigungspolitik?', *Prokla* 48 (2): 247–264.

Anonymous. 1966/1976. 'Vorbereitende Probleme zur Konstruktion einer Situation'. In *Situationistische Internationale 1958–1969. Gesammelte Ausgaben des Organs der Situationistischen Internationale*, eds. P. Gallissaires and H. Mittelstädt, 16–18. Hamburg: MAD Verlag.

Wagner, Otto. 1911. *Die Groszstadt: Eine Studie über diese.* Vienna: Schroll.

———. 1988. *Modern Architecture: A Guidebook for his Students to this Field of Art.* Santa Monica, CA: Getty Center for the History of Art and the Humanities

Wagner-Conzelmann, Sandra. 2007. *Die Interbau 1957 in Berlin.* Petersberg: Michael Imhof Verlag.

Wasserman, Janek. 2014. *Black Vienna: The Radical Right in the Red City, 1918–1938.* Ithaca: Cornell University Press.

Weihsmann, Helmut. 1985. *Das rote Wien: sozialdemokratische Architektur und Kommunalpolitik, 1919–1934.* Vienna: Promedia.

Wilde, Alexander (ed.). 1990a. *Das Märkische Viertel.* Berlin: Nicolaische Verlagsbuchhandlung.

———. 1990b. *Das Märkische Viertel.* Berlin: Nicolaische Verlagsbuchhandlung Beuermann GMBH.

Winter, Max. 1901. Rund um Favoriten: Eine Skizze aus dem Leben der Enterbten. *Arbeiter Zeitung,* December 14.

———. 1982. 'Zinsburgen und Chaluppen'. In *Max Winter. Das schwarze Wienerherz: Sozialreportagen aus dem frühen 20. Jahrhundert*, ed. Helmut Strutzmann, 94–108. Vienna: Österreichischer Bundesverlag.

Zieleniec, Andrzej. 2018. 'Lefebvre's Politics of Space: Planning the Urban as Oeuvre', *Urban Planning* 3 (3): 5–15. DOI: 10.17645/up.v3i3.1343.

Zizek, Slavoj. 1998/2008. *The Sublime Object of Ideology.* London/New York: Verso.

Index